DAILY RITUALS

Women at Work

DAILY RITUALS
Women at Work

. . . .

Mason Currey

PICADOR

First published 2019 as a Borzoi Book by Alfred A. Knopf,
a division of Random House, Inc., New York,
and in Canada by Random House of Canada Limited, Toronto

First published in the UK 2019 by Picador
an imprint of Pan Macmillan
20 New Wharf Road, London N1 9RR
Associated companies throughout the world
www.panmacmillan.com

ISBN 978-1-5098-5283-3

1 3 5 7 9 8 6 4 2

A CIP catalogue record for this book is available from the British Library.

Printed and bound by CPI Group (UK) Ltd, Croydon, CR0 4YY

Visit **www.picador.com** to read more about all our books
and to buy them. You will also find features, author interviews and
news of any author events, and you can sign up for e-newsletters
so that you're always first to hear about our new releases.

For Rebecca

Habits gradually change the face of one's life as time changes one's physical face; & one does not know it.

—VIRGINIA WOOLF, diary entry, April 13, 1929

CONTENTS

BOREDOM AND SUFFERING

PURE NEGLECT

A BALLOON, A SPACESHIP, A SUBMARINE, A CLOSET

RESIGNATION AND RELIEF

AN ABNORMAL LIFE

A SUBTLE AND DEEP-LAID PLAN

DEADLY DETERMINATION

VIBRATIONS OF CHANCE

A PRIVILEGED SPACE

FROM RAGE TO DESPAIR AND BACK AGAIN

INTRODUCTION

This is a sequel, and a corrective. In 2013, I published *Daily Rituals: How Great Minds Make Time, Find Inspiration, and Get to Work*, a collection of brief profiles of the day-to-day working lives of novelists, poets, painters, composers, philosophers, and other inspired minds. I'm proud of that book, and delighted that it has found an audience of fellow creative-process voyeurs interested to know that Beethoven counted out precisely sixty coffee beans for his morning cup, or that George Balanchine did his best work while ironing, or that Maya Angelou wrote in a "tiny, mean" hotel room, surrounded by a dictionary, a Bible, a deck of cards, and a bottle of sherry. But the book had, I now admit, a major flaw: Of the 161 figures I included, only 27 were women. Less than 17 percent.

How could I have let the book go to press with such a glaring gender imbalance? I don't have a great answer. My idea for the book had been to profile the "great minds" of Western culture from the last few hundred years, and I thought that its success depended on the high-low juxtaposition of famous names and their mundane daily habits. Unfortunately, the side effect of focusing on the most well-known figures in Western literature, painting, and classical music is that they are overwhelmingly men. That I didn't work harder to find more women's stories to tell shows a dismal lack of imagination on my part, and is something I sincerely regret.

So this volume is a belated effort to correct that gender

imbalance, but also to better fulfill my ambition for the original book. With it, I had hoped to achieve something more than just a collection of highbrow trivia; I wanted the book to be genuinely useful to readers who were trying to do their own creative projects and struggling to make the time or get into the right state of mind on a regular basis. That has often been my situation as a writer, and as a result I have always been hungry for stories of how others pulled it off, at the most basic level. Did they write or paint or compose every day, and if so, for how long, and starting at what time? Did that include weekends, too? How did they do that and also earn a living, and get enough sleep, and attend to the other people in their lives? And even if they could manage the logistical side of things—the when and where and for how long—how did they cope with more slippery crises of self-confidence and self-discipline?

Those are all questions I tried to address, at least obliquely, through the profiles in the first *Daily Rituals*. But the problem with disproportionately focusing on famous and successful men is that the obstacles they faced were frequently mitigated by devoted wives, paid servants, sizable inheritances, and, oh yes, centuries of accrued privilege. For the contemporary reader, this blunts their usefulness as models. Too often, the Great Mind's daily routine seems quaintly fantastical, with neatly apportioned rounds of work, walks, and naps unsullied by such pedestrian concerns as earning money, preparing meals, or spending time with loved ones.

Switching the focus to women, by contrast, opens up dramatic new vistas of frustration and compromise. Granted, plenty of the women in this book came from privileged backgrounds, and not all of them were constantly hurdling obstacles in their daily lives—but a lot of them were. Most grew up in societies that ignored or rejected women's creative work, and many had parents or spouses who vigorously opposed their attempts to prioritize self-expression over the traditional roles of wife, mother, and homemaker. A number of them had children and faced excruciating choices in balancing the needs of their dependents with their own ambitions. Virtually all of them confronted sexism among their audiences and among the gatekeepers to professional success—the editors, publishers, curators, critics, patrons, and other tastemakers who, over and over, just happened to find men's work superior. And this does not even take into account the woman artist's internal obstacles, the various species of anger, guilt, and resentment that come with forcing the world to make space for you and your achievements.

Of course, I'm aware of the danger of separating "women artists" from just *artists* (and in a book by a man, no less!). Many of the women profiled here were used to seeing their accomplishments tied to their gender, and none of them liked it. As the painter Grace Hartigan told an interviewer, "I was never conscious of being a female artist and I resent being called a woman artist. I'm an artist." For what it's worth, I have endeavored to treat the artists in this collection in the same manner as I did the men (and women) in the original volume, with entries that draw on letters, diaries, interviews, and secondhand accounts to assemble capsule portraits of how they got their work done on a daily basis.

That said, there are a few key differences between this book and its predecessor. Whereas in the previous volume I included only figures for whom I could provide a reasonably complete summary of their typical workday, here I have given myself more latitude to write about artists who didn't really follow a regular schedule, either because they could not afford that luxury or because they didn't care to do so. In addition, because I'm assuming that readers may not be

familiar with many of these women—they were all major figures in their fields but are not necessarily well known to a
general audience—I have devoted more space to sketching
their biographies and putting their workdays in the context
of their careers.

This volume also pays more attention to its subjects' family dynamics. For so many of these artists, children were *the*
major competing demand on their time (needy or obstreper-
ous spouses were a close second), and explaining how they
managed to juggle their creative work with their domestic
worries and obligations—whether through a fanatical work
ethic, the clever parceling out of their time, strategic neglect
of certain duties, or some combination of these—was crucial to portraying the day-to-day realities of their practice. It
was also part of my aforementioned effort to make this book
more relevant to contemporary readers trying to untie their
own creative-logistical knots. As much as possible, I wanted
to accurately capture the daily obstacles these women faced,
and explain how they actually surmounted them, if indeed
they were able to.

I don't mean to suggest that being an artist is some kind
of joyless slog. Even as making space for creative work may
require reserves of cunning and sacrifice, the work itself is
often deeply absorbing and restorative. In these pages, I
have tried to do justice to that duality—to the impossibility
of reconciling "the Life and the Project," as Susan Sontag
put it, and to the equal impossibility of giving up the effort.
Compiling this material, the question I kept asking myself
was the same one Colette once asked about George Sand:
How the devil did she manage? Here are 143 attempts at an
answer.

A NOTE ABOUT THE SEQUENCE

I wrote these profiles separately, then puzzled over how to best arrange them for publication. The obvious organizational schemes—chronological, alphabetical, thematic—all proved defective in one way or another. In the end, I decided to gather the entries into thirteen loose sections, which allowed me to group together entries that I thought spoke to one another in some way, but without (I hope) being too obvious or literal. I also tried to distribute the entries in a way that will make for a pleasurable front-to-back read—but I expect that many readers will prefer to flip around and take things more or less at random, an approach that I condone and even encourage.

SOME WEIRDNESS

Octavia Butler (1947–2006)

Butler started writing science fiction at age twelve, after seeing the 1954 movie *Devil Girl from Mars* on television. "As I was watching this film, I had a series of revelations," the California-born author recalled years later. "The first was that 'Geez, I can write a better story than that.' And then I thought, 'Gee, anybody can write a better story than that.' And my third thought was the clincher: 'Somebody got paid for writing that awful story.' So I was off and writing, and a year later I was busy submitting terrible pieces of fiction to innocent magazines." After college, Butler worked a series of "horrible little jobs"—including as a dishwasher, a telemarketer, a warehouse worker, and a potato-chip inspector—while continuing to write in the early mornings. "I felt like an animal, just living in order to live, just surviving," she said. "But as long as I wrote, I felt that I was living in order to do something more, something I actually cared about." She finally published her first novel, *Patternmaster,* in 1976, and went on to publish a novel a year for the next four years, including one of her best-known works, 1979's *Kindred,* after which she was able to support herself by her writing alone.

As she became an internationally acclaimed author, Butler was often asked for her advice to young writers. She always said that the most important thing was to write every day, whether you feel like it or not. "Screw inspiration," she said. Butler also suggested that aspiring writers might "look at the lives of a half dozen writers to see what they do."

That doesn't mean that you'll do what any of them do, but what you'll learn from what they do is that they have felt their ways. They have found out what works for them. For instance, I get up between three or four o'clock in the morning, because that's my best writing time. I found this out by accident, because back when I used to work for other people I didn't have time to write during the day. I did physical work, mostly hard physical work, so I was too tired when I came in at night. I was also too full of other people. I found that I couldn't work very well after spending a lot of time with other people. I had to have some sleep between the time that I spent with other people and the time that I did the writing, so I would get up early in the morning. I generally would get up around two o'clock in the morning, which was really very much too early. But I was ambitious, and I would write until I had to get ready to go to work.

As she got older, Butler's schedule loosened somewhat. According to a 2000 profile in *The Seattle Times,* her routine was "waking between 5:30 and 6:30 a.m., taking care of things around the house, and sitting down at her computer to write at 9 a.m." She considered herself a slow writer, and spent much of her working day "reading books or sitting and staring or listening to book tapes or music or something and then all of a sudden I'm writing furiously." This meant lots of time on her own, which suited the "comfortably asocial" author just fine. "I enjoy people best if I can be alone much of the time," Butler said in 1998. "I used to worry about it because my family worried about it. And I finally realized: This is the way I am. That's that. We all have some weirdness, and this is mine."

Yayoi Kusama (b. 1929)

"I fight pain, anxiety, and fear every day, and the only method I have found that relieves my illness is to keep creating art," the Japanese conceptual artist wrote in her 2011 autobiography, *Infinity Net*. Kusama has suffered from visual and aural hallucinations since she was a child, and in 1977 she checked herself into the Tokyo mental hospital where she still lives. Across the street, she built a studio where she works every day. In her autobiography, Kusama described her routine:

> Life in the hospital follows a fixed schedule. I retire at nine o'clock at night and wake up the next morning in time for a blood test at seven. At ten o'clock each morning I go to my studio and work until six or seven in the evening. In the evening, I write. These days I am able to concentrate fully on my work, with the result that since moving to Tokyo I have been extremely prolific.

Indeed, as the international art world has rediscovered Kusama over the last two decades, she has had to hire a small army of assistants to help her keep up with the demand for her work—and nowadays the artist works harder than ever. "Every day I am creating a new world by making artworks," Kusama said in 2014. "I wake up early in the morning and stay up late at night, sometimes until 3 a.m., just to make art. I am fighting for my life and don't take any rest."

Elizabeth Bishop (1911–1979)

"Some days all I do is write and then for months I don't write a thing," the American poet said in 1978. Bishop's friend and fellow poet Frank Bidart confirmed that "she didn't (so far as I know) write every day, or in any kind of regular pattern. . . . When an idea for a poem possessed her, she carried it as far as she could, and then might let the fragments lie waiting to be finished for immense lengths of time." Between starting and finishing her poem "The Moose," for instance, twenty years elapsed.

Bishop often felt guilty about her modest output—she published only about a hundred poems in her lifetime—and wished that she had written more. Briefly, in the early 1950s, she tried to speed along the process with stimulants. Bishop had recently moved from the United States to Brazil to be with her lover, the architect Lota de Macedo Soares. But upon settling in her new home, she discovered that her chronic asthma had grown much worse. To control it, Bishop began taking cortisone, and she found that the drug's side effects were potentially useful for a writer—it produced sleeplessness combined with a kind of creative euphoria, which she thought could be beneficial for her poetry and for the short stories she was trying to write at the time. "To begin with it is absolutely marvelous," Bishop reported to the poet Robert Lowell, her close friend and confidant.

You can sit up typing all night long and feel wonderful the next day. I wrote two stories in a week. The letdown isn't bad if you do all the proper things, but once I didn't and found myself shedding tears all day long for no reason at all. This time I'm hoping it will help me get that last impossible poem off to H. Mifflin [her publisher]. . . . Try it sometime. It seems to apply to just about anything.

The euphoria was short-lived—Bishop soon grew afraid of the drug's effect on her emotions and stopped taking it. Over time, she seemed to reconcile herself to her halting, gradual work style. She liked to quote Paul Valéry: "A poem is never finished, only abandoned."

Pina Bausch (1940–2009)

The German choreographer expanded the possibilities of modern dance by incorporating dreamlike sequences, elaborate stage sets, dramatic speeches, and snatches of dialogue into her hugely influential "dance theater." Famously, from the late 1970s on, she developed her pieces through a question-and-answer process, drawing on her dancers' memories and everyday lives as the basis for a new performance. "Pina asks questions," one of her longtime dancers explained. "Sometimes it's just a word or a sentence. Each of the dancers has time to think, then gets up and shows Pina his or her answer, either danced, spoken, alone, with partner, with props with everyone, whatever. Pina looks at it all, takes notes, thinks about it." For Bausch, the questions were a way to get at ideas that she couldn't access on her own. "The 'questions' are there for approaching a topic quite carefully," she once said. "It's a very open way of working but again a very precise one. It leads me to many things, which alone, I wouldn't have thought about." She was always searching for something she couldn't easily define, "not something I know with my head exactly," she said, "but to find the right images. And I have no words for that. But I know right away when I've got it."

To people on the outside of this process, it could be daunting to watch her at work. "The anguish that she goes through is enormous," Bausch's partner, Ronald Kay, told *The Guardian* in 2002. "She comes home like a heap of ashes. I have learned to look at it from a distance. To be absolutely outside of it is the only way I can help." Kay went on to describe Bausch's work schedule during the rehearsals for a new performance:

> She works in the rehearsal room from 10 in the morning, and rehearsals don't end till late in the evening. She comes home at about 10 at night, we eat, and then she sits there till two or three o'clock getting an idea of what it was all about, what can be kept, what are the little jewels of the piece. And then she gets up at seven, sometimes even earlier, to prepare. She always manages to keep the same intensity.

Bausch herself struggled to explain the source of this intensity. When faced with the prospect of developing a new piece, her immediate response was closer to despair than enthusiasm. "There is no plan, no script, no music, and no set," she said.

> But there is a date for the premiere and little time. Then I think: it is no pleasure to do a piece at all. I never want to do one again. Each time it is a torture. Why am I doing it? After so many years I still haven't learnt. With every piece I have to start from the beginning again.

That's difficult. I always have the feeling that I never achieve what I want to achieve. But no sooner has a premiere passed than I am already making new plans. Where does this power come from? Yes, discipline is important. You simply have to keep working and suddenly something emerges—something very small. I don't know where that will lead, but it is as if someone is switching on a light. You have renewed courage to keep on working and you are excited again. Or someone does something very beautiful. And that gives you the power to keep on working so hard—but with desire. It comes from inside.

Marisol (1930–2016)

María Sol Escobar was born to a wealthy Venezuelan family, grew up in Paris and Caracas, went to high school in Los Angeles, and studied art in Paris and New York. She initially pursued painting but, in 1953, began making sculptural figurines "as a kind of rebellion," she said. "Everything was so serious. I was very sad myself and the people I met were so depressing. I started doing something funny so that I would become happier—and it worked. I was also convinced that everyone would like my work because I had so much fun doing it. They did." She soon adopted the name Marisol and, by the mid-1960s, was a New York art-world star, known for her witty melding of Pop and folk art, and for her enigmatic public persona. "The first girl artist with *glamour*," declared Andy Warhol, who cast her in his films *The Kiss* and *13 Most Beautiful Women*. Like Warhol, Marisol had a

Marisol, New York, 1964

knack for terse pronouncements that walked a line between naïveté and profundity. "I don't think much myself," she said in a 1964 interview. "When I don't think, all sorts of things come to me."

In 1965, a *New York Times* reporter sketched the artist's daily routine. It began at about noon, when Marisol woke up and ate her standard breakfast of ham and eggs. Then she headed from her Murray Hill apartment to her loft on lower Broadway, stopping along the way to purchase materials—"nails, glue, chair legs, barrel staves, pine planks from a lumber yard"—while also keeping an eye out for new additions to her cherished collection of "props," which ranged from tiny parasols to a stuffed dog's head from a taxidermist's.

"I do my research in the Yellow Pages," she said. Once inside her ninety-by-twenty-five-foot studio, Marisol began working with a mix of carpentry, carving, and power tools, sawing, hammering, chiseling, and sanding her sculptures into existence. She continued until the evening, when, most nights, she headed uptown for gallery openings or parties, often escorted by Warhol. She ate a late dinner and frequently returned to work afterward. "Her discipline is iron," the painter Ruth Kligman said. "Sometimes I've passed her studio at 2 a.m. and seen her there still plugging away."

At openings and parties, Marisol was notorious for her silences; many friends and acquaintances recalled spending hours with the artist without her uttering a word. According to the critic John Gruen, "When Marisol was quiet she could sit in a chair for hours without moving a muscle." In his memoir of the New York art world in the 1950s, Gruen describes an outdoor lunch on Long Island that Marisol attended along with a number of other artists and musicians:

> Marisol was listening to the lively conversation around the table. Silent as a statue, she sat totally still for at least two hours. At one point I turned toward her and noticed, to my astonishment, that a spider had spun a complete web, filling in the triangle formed by her bare upper arm, her torso, and her armpit. When I pointed this out to her—and to the rest of the company— Marisol calmly glanced at the spider and its work, saying, "The same thing happened to me once in Venezuela. It's nothing new to me. I'm used to it."

Although this extreme reticence could seem like an act, Marisol's friends swore that it was genuine. In 1965, a friend defended her behavior to *The New York Times:* "A, she's genuinely shy. B, she realizes that most people have nothing much to say. So why should she put out more energy than she has to? She saves it for work. When she does say something, it's direct and to the point. She puts things in their place."

For her part, Marisol claimed not to understand—or care about—all the attention devoted to her public persona. "I don't feel like a myth," she said in the 1970s. "I spend most of my time in my studio." As for her years of relentlessly making the rounds of parties—she went to those things "to relax," she said. "Because it's very depressing to be so profound all day."

Nina Simone (1933–2003)

In her autobiography, *I Put a Spell on You,* Simone compared her best performances to a bullfight she once witnessed in Barcelona, a shocking display of violence that touched something deep in the audience and left them feeling transformed. Onstage, Simone felt that she occupied a role similar to that of the toreador—and, she wrote, "people came to see me because they knew I was playing close to the edge and one day I might fail."

But getting audiences to experience something profound was also a matter of technique, and Simone honed her methods over years of touring:

> To cast the spell over an audience I would start with a song to create a certain mood which I carried into the next song and then on through into the third, until I cre-

Nina Simone, Pittsburgh, 1965

ated a certain climax of feeling and by then they would be hypnotized. To check, I'd stop and do nothing for a moment and I'd hear absolute silence: I'd got them. It was always an uncanny moment. It was as if there was a power source somewhere that we all plugged into, and the bigger the audience the easier it was—as if each person supplied a certain amount of the power. As I moved on from clubs into bigger halls I learned to prepare myself thoroughly: I'd go to the empty hall in the afternoon and walk around to see where the people were sitting, how close they'd be to me at the front and how far away at the back, whether the seats got closer together or further apart, how big the stage was, how the lights were positioned, where the microphones were going to hit—everything. . . . So by the time I got on stage I knew exactly what I was doing.

Before important concerts, Simone would practice alone for hours at a time, sometimes playing the piano for so long that her arms "would seize up completely." She made sure her band was just as rigorously prepared; she rehearsed every detail of the show with them, and she made an effort to gather musicians around her who understood and empathized with the particular experience she was trying to create. On concert nights, Simone didn't give the band a set list until the very last minute, sometimes right as they were walking out onstage; before she chose the songs, she wanted to soak up the mood of the audience and the venue for as long as possible. When she walked out, she was "super-sensitive" to the crowd, and yet at the same time she tried to play for herself alone and draw the audience into what she was feeling. Even with all this preparation, however, Simone could never predict when a given show would make the leap from a solid professional performance to something strange and sublime. "Whatever it was that happened out there under the lights," she wrote, "it mostly came from God, and I was just a place along the line He was moving on."

Diane Arbus (1923–1971)

A photograph, Arbus said, "is a secret about a secret." And Arbus loved secrets. "I can find out anything," she once said. She took up photography, in part, because she thought of it as "a sort of naughty thing to do" and "very perverse." Throughout her career, Arbus almost exclusively shot portraits, on commission for magazines like *Harper's Bazaar, Esquire,* and *New York,* and on her own time, cruising parks, circuses, freak shows, nudist colonies, society balls, swinger parties, and psychiatric institutions for new subjects. Her favorite people to shoot were outsiders and misfits, especially the more subtle varieties. Beatniks and hippies bored her; she preferred people who couldn't help being a little off-center, and the thrill was getting them to reveal something of their inner self to the camera.

To make this happen, Arbus played a waiting game. Arriving for a shoot, often inside the subject's home, Arbus would be reserved and soft-spoken but friendly, not at all bossy or demanding. Gently, she would ask her subjects to move about until they arrived at a pose that she liked; then, Arbus would ask them to hold the pose for fifteen or twenty minutes—a long time for anyone to hold a single pose, especially the non-professional models who were Arbus's usual subjects. Finally, Arbus would allow them a short break, only to ask them to resume the same pose for another fifteen minutes. She would keep this up for hours, far longer than her subjects expected, and far beyond most people's ability to remain poised in front of the camera. "She would try to wear people down," said the photographer Deborah Turbeville, who worked with Arbus on *Harper's Bazaar* assignments in the mid-1960s. "They just stood there looking wilted." (Turbeville and her assistant would sometimes covertly remove rolls of film from Arbus's camera bag to bring the shoot to an end sooner.) But Arbus needed the shoots to drag on, both because she wanted her subjects to drop their guard and because she sought a particular kind of connection with them. As Turbeville explained, "It was an endurance process, while she tried to get herself excited and then to get a response from [the subjects]. She would ask them questions. She would reveal something about herself and hope these people would react and then she would go from there and get more and more intimate until she'd slam a home run."

It was similar to the kind of charge that Arbus sought out in her sex life, which was unusually vigorous, even by the standards of the sexual revolution. Arbus frequently slept with her photographic subjects, and she told one confidant that she had never in her life turned down anyone who asked her to bed. According to the biographer Arthur Lubow, when Arbus started seeing a psychiatrist in the late 1960s, she "described going up to strangers on the street and propositioning them for sex. She spoke of answering ads in swinger magazines and bedding physically unattractive couples. She recounted sexual escapades on Greyhound buses and at orgies. She detailed episodes of sexual intercourse with sailors, women, nudists. . . . Most startling of all, she said in an offhand way that she slept with her brother, Howard, whenever he came to New York."

The therapist was perturbed, but Arbus could never explain her own impulses, in art or in life, and she wasn't very interested in trying. "I photograph, I can't even really figure out what the reason is," she once said. "I don't know what else to do. It became a thing, really, that the more I did it the more I could do it." The closest she came to clarifying her artistic motivations was in answer to a question about how she chose her subjects. Arbus said, "I do what gnaws at me."

OYSTERS AND CHAMPAGNE

Louise Nevelson (1899–1988)

The Russian-born American sculptor possessed all the usual traits of the prolific: intense drive, large stores of physical energy, and a powerful need to prove her worth to the world. But, she said, "I'm also prolific because I know how to use time." In her autobiography, Nevelson described her daily routine:

I get up, six in the morning. And I wear cotton clothes so that I can sleep in them or I can work in them—I don't want to waste time. I go to the studio, and usually I put in pretty much of a big day. And very often, almost all the time (I think I have a strong body), it wears me out. The physical body is worn out before the creative. When I finish, I come in and go to sleep if I'm tired, have something to eat. . . .

Sometimes I could work two, three days and not sleep and I didn't pay any attention to food, because . . . a can of sardines and a cup of tea and a piece of stale bread seemed awfully good to me. You know, I don't care about food and my diet has very little variety. I read once that in her old age Isak Dinesen only ate oysters and drank champagne, and I thought what an intelligent solution to ridding oneself of meaningless decision-making.

Louise Nevelson's bathtub, 1958

Nevelson gave this account in 1976, when she was seventy-seven years old and one of the world's most famous living artists. But before reaching this pinnacle she had toiled in near obscurity for decades. A bad marriage at eighteen, and an unplanned pregnancy the next year, derailed her early ambitions, and it took Nevelson more than a decade to escape her marriage and establish herself as an independent artist in New York. Even after that, she exhibited her work for twenty-five years without making a sale, didn't have her first solo exhibition until she was forty-two years old, and didn't get her big break until her work was included in a 1958 exhibition at the Museum of Modern Art, when Nevelson was almost sixty.

Until then, the artist got by thanks to regular infusions of money from her family and occasional gifts from her many lovers. (She never had a day job.) Her brother, who owned a successful hotel in Maine, was especially supportive—for years he gave Nevelson a monthly allowance, and in 1945 he bought her a four-story town house on Manhattan's East 30th Street. By then, Nevelson's son had left home to join the merchant marine (and had also started sending his mother regular checks), and it was over the subsequent decade that Nevelson, through much experimentation, arrived at her mature style. After years of making small and medium-size sculptures from salvaged pieces of wood, she started to build massive monochrome carved-wood walls, essentially inventing the field of environmental sculpture. She later told her friend Edward Albee that she found her true identity as a sculptor when she "stood up the wood."

As she gained confidence in her new work, Nevelson became increasingly prolific, producing about sixty sculptures a year; by the late 1950s she had filled her home with approximately nine hundred sculptures. Decades later, the *New York Times* art critic Hilton Kramer recalled visiting Nevelson's town house around this time:

Nothing that one had seen in the galleries or museums or, indeed, in other artists' studios could have prepared one for the experience that awaited a visitor to this strange house. It was certainly unlike anything one had ever seen or imagined. Its interior seemed to have been stripped of everything—not only furniture and the common comforts of daily living, but of many mundane necessities—that might divert attention from the sculptures that crowded every space, occupied every wall, and at once filled and bewildered the eye wherever it turned. Divisions between the rooms seemed to dissolve in an endless sculptural environment. When one ascended the stairs, the walls of the stairwell enclosed the visitor in this same unremitting spectacle. Not even the bathrooms were exempted from its reach. Where, I wondered, did one take a bath in this house? For the bathtubs, too, were filled with sculpture.

By all accounts, Nevelson enjoyed her late-life renown, and it was around the time of her 1958 MoMA exhibition that she began to don the outrageous wardrobe that became her signature, wearing thick eyelashes made from mink, elaborate headscarves, flowing dresses, and flamboyant jewelry. But she still spent the vast majority of her time alone in the studio. After her disastrous first marriage, Nevelson swore off that institution forever—"It's a lot of work and it's not that interesting," she said of marriage—and although she had many lovers and a wide circle of friends and admirers, she kept most of them at arm's length. As Edward Albee put it: "I imagine I was kept in my compartment like everyone else was—in my Nevelson box."

As she grew older, Nevelson only became more devoted to her work, which after all had been the one sustaining force in her life. "I like to work," she said. "I always did. I think there is such a thing as energy—creation overflowing. . . . In my studio I'm as happy as a cow in her stall. My studio is the only place where everything is all right."

Isak Dinesen (1885–1962)

Born Karen Dinesen in Copenhagen, she became Baroness Blixen upon marrying her cousin, a Swedish nobleman, in 1914. Shortly after their engagement, the couple settled in Kenya, where they intended to run a coffee plantation. Both ventures—the marriage and the plantation—eventually failed, and in 1931 Dinesen returned to Denmark, rudderless and broke, to live with her mother. Her story might have ended there, but Dinesen had a new venture in mind. "During my last months in Africa, as it became clear to me that I could not keep the farm, I had started writing at night, to get my mind off the things which in the daytime it had gone over a hundred times, and on to a new track," she later recalled. While still in Kenya, Dinesen had penned the first two stories of what would become her first book, *Seven Gothic Tales*, an unlikely best seller when it was published in 1934 under the pseudonym Isak Dinesen. She followed it with *Out of Africa*, the classic memoir of her seventeen years in Kenya, completing her transformation into an international literary celebrity.

Unfortunately, as her writing career was taking off, Dinesen's health was flagging. During her marriage, Dinesen's philandering husband had given her syphilis, and the disease would cause her considerable anguish throughout her life; the effects included impaired balance, difficulty walking, anorexia complicated by ulcers, and attacks of abdominal pain so severe that they sometimes left her lying on the floor "howling like an animal." (Dinesen's secretary Clara Svendsen said it was "like one human being trying to stem an avalanche.") Dinesen's writing habits shifted with her health. "In her late forties and early fifties," the biographer Judith Thurman writes, "the bad days alternated with relatively long periods of good health and vigor, when she could visit her

Isak Dinesen, 1950s

neighbors on an old bicycle and swim in the Sound before sitting down to write in the morning. But as she aged, it sapped her ability to work, to eat, to concentrate, even to sit upright, and she would dictate much of her later work to Clara Svendsen lying on the floor or confined to bed."

In her later years, Dinesen famously claimed that she subsisted on a diet of oysters and champagne—but, as Thurman writes, it was actually amphetamines that "would give her the overdrive she required, and late in her life she took them recklessly, whenever strength was needed at an important moment." Doing so hastened her death, but Dinesen was determined to live as fully as possible—and to transform her experiences into writing—until the end. She told a friend, "I promised the Devil my soul, and in return he promised me that everything I was going to experience would be turned into tales."

Josephine Baker (1906–1975)

"I *had* to succeed," the American-born French dancer and singer once wrote. "I would never stop trying, never. A violinist had his violin, a painter his palette. All I had was myself. *I* was the instrument that I must care for, just as Sidney [Bechet] fussed over his clarinet." Baker spent thirty minutes every morning rubbing herself with half a lemon in an attempt to lighten her skin—a lifelong obsession—and the same amount of time preparing a special mixture to apply to her hair. But she didn't worry about her diet and didn't follow any special exercise regimen, at least not in the early days of her career, when she was dancing ten hours a day or more. In Paris in the 1920s, Baker would start her evening dancing at the Folies Bergère and then make subsequent appearances at other cabarets until finally heading home at dawn "through a murky Paris preparing for work—the Paris of the poor," she wrote. "Collapsing into bed, I would snuggle against my puppies and sleep until the maid awakened me at four."

Baker wasn't always able to sleep this late; for most of her life she was plagued by nightmares and insomnia, and was known to telephone friends as early as 5:30 in the morning, alert and ready to chat even after staying up most of the night.

Josephine Baker, circa 1925

"Her secret was little catnaps," one friend recalled. "Many times [in person] she would be talking to me and suddenly drop off to sleep in the middle of the conversation. Then, a half hour later, she would awaken abruptly, as if she had never napped, and continue on the same subject."

Baker's chronic lack of sleep, frenetic lifestyle, and outsize ambitions did seem to take their toll, however, as the dancer became prone to sudden outbursts of anger and irritation. "She was always in a crisis," one of her employees recalled. "I never knew what started them. Sometimes there would be one per day; other times two per day or only one per week. Sometimes a crisis would last a week. They were like seizures that took hold of her." Baker's first husband confirmed that she fundamentally did not know how to unwind. "Friends often asked us to spend a quiet day at their hacienda," he wrote. "Josephine would accept politely, but at the last minute would find a reason to break the engagement. There was always something else she wanted to do or see. 'Turn off your motor, Josephine,' I'd tease. Impossible. She simply couldn't slow down."

Lillian Hellman (1905–1984)

Hellman started writing drama in her late twenties and quickly vaulted into the first rank of American playwrights, a position she would occupy for the next twenty-five years. Her first play, a comedy, was never performed—but her second, *The Children's Hour,* opened in 1934 and was an immediate sensation, earning its twenty-nine-year-old author $125,000 from its first run and a $50,000 contract from Hollywood to write the film version. From then until the early 1960s, Hellman produced a new play almost every other year; in between, she wrote screenplays. But the New Orleans–born writer was never comfortable with success, and after her second hit play, 1939's *The Little Foxes,* she fled New York for

Hardscrabble Farm, a 130-acre property about an hour and a half drive north of the city. There Hellman quit drinking (mostly), and her relationship with the writer Dashiell Hammett eased from a combative love affair to a comfortable friendship (mostly), with the two writers sharing a home base but occupying separate bedrooms and independently entertaining their own friends and lovers.

It was not always an easy arrangement, but it proved durable. Hammett had by then ceased writing—after the success of his 1934 novel *The Thin Man,* he never published another book—but Hellman threw herself into her work. At Hardscrabble she seemed to tap into an unlimited reservoir of energy, writing several hours a day while pursuing all manner of projects on the farm. She hired two maids, a cook, a full-time farmer, and seasonal farm helpers. She planted vegetable gardens, raised chickens and sold their eggs, swam and fished in the eight-acre lake, bred standard poodles, and hosted friends for long visits—although she expected her guests to entertain themselves most of the time. "My friends come to stay and amuse themselves any way they want to—most of them read," Hellman told a reporter in 1941. "We meet at meals. When I write I still leave plenty of time around the meal hours; work three hours or so in the morning, two or three hours in the afternoon, and start again at 10 and work until 1 or 2 in the morning."

Her morning routine, she said in another interview, was to get up at 6:00, make coffee, and help the farmer milk the cows or clean the barn until 8:00, then eat breakfast before settling down to write. She worked at the typewriter, chain-smoking and drinking coffee while she wrote; according to a 1946 profile, she drank twenty cups of strong coffee and smoked three packs of cigarettes a day. To prevent interruptions from her houseguests, Hellman posted a warning on the door of her study:

> THIS ROOM IS USED FOR WORK
> DO NOT ENTER WITHOUT KNOCKING
> AFTER YOU KNOCK, WAIT FOR AN ANSWER
> IF YOU GET NO ANSWER, GO AWAY AND
> DON'T COME BACK
> THIS MEANS EVERYBODY
> THIS MEANS YOU
> THIS MEANS NIGHT OR DAY
>
> By order of the Hellman-Military-Commission-for-Playwrights.
> Court-martialling will take place in the barn,
> and your trial will not be a fair one.

Although she worked steadily each day, Hellman's writing progressed slowly; generally it took her a year or longer to complete a new play. In part, this was because she did extensive research before she began writing; for her 1941 play *Watch on the Rhine,* Hellman made digests of twenty-five books and filled her notebooks with "well over 100,000 words," almost none of which made it into the finished work. In addition, she went through numerous drafts of each play: *Watch on the Rhine* required eleven rough versions and four complete drafts. As she worked, Hellman paid fanatical attention to the dialogue, reading it out loud to herself every night and again every morning before she resumed writing. She carried the projects forward on successive currents of "elation, depression, hope," she said. "That is the exact order. Hope sets in toward nightfall. That's when you tell yourself that you're going to be better the next time, so help you God."

Coco Chanel (1883–1971)

Chanel was born in poverty, spent her adolescence in an orphanage, and received little formal education. Despite this disadvantaged start, she was a household name by age thirty and a multimillionaire by forty. Not surprisingly, work was her life, and the only truly reliable partner she ever found. Her unceasing dedication to the Chanel brand made her a formidable businesswoman—and, for her workers, a demanding and even tormenting employer. As the biographer Rhonda K. Garelick has written, Chanel's staff at her Paris headquarters was kept in a constant state of "watchful anxiety." Here, Garelick describes Chanel's work routine in Paris:

> While much of the staff reported to work at about eight thirty in the morning, Coco had never been an early riser and tended to show up hours later. When she did arrive, usually around one p.m., she was attended by a degree of fanfare befitting a five-star general or royal monarch. The moment Coco left her apartment across the street at the Ritz, hotel staff members would immediately telephone the operator at rue Cambon to alert her. A buzzer would sound throughout the studio to spread the word: Mademoiselle was on her way. Someone downstairs would spray a mist of Chanel No. 5 near the entrance, so that Coco could walk through a cloud of her own signature scent. . . . "When she entered the studio, everyone stood up," recalled the photographer Willy Rizzo, "like children at school." Then, the staff would form a line, hands at their sides, "as in the army," employee Marie-Hélène Marouzé put it.

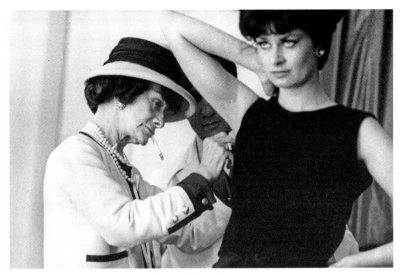

Coco Chanel, 1962

Once upstairs in her office, Chanel would set immediately to work on her designs. She refused to use patterns or wooden mannequins, and so would spend long hours draping and pinning fabrics on models, smoking one cigarette after another, rarely or never sitting down. According to Garelick, "She could remain standing for nine hours at a time, without pausing for a meal or a glass of water—without even a bathroom break, apparently." She stayed until late in the evening, compelling her employees to hang around with her even after work had ceased, pouring wine and talking nonstop, avoiding for as long as possible the return to her room at the Ritz and to the boredom and loneliness that awaited her there. She worked six days a week, and dreaded Sundays and holidays. As she told one confidant, "That word, 'vacation,' makes me sweat."

Elsa Schiaparelli (1890–1973)

In between the two world wars, Schiaparelli rose from obscurity to the top of the Paris fashion world, making dresses for Katharine Hepburn and Marlene Dietrich; collaborating with Salvador Dalí and Jean Cocteau; creating her own signature shade of pink, called Shocking—as well as her own signature perfume of the same name—and bringing dashes of surrealism to haute couture with hats in the form of lamb cutlets, pockets made to look like drawers, handbags shaped like balloons, and other playful unorthodoxies. Like so many self-made women, she was a workaholic. In his 1986 biography, Palmer White summarizes Schiaparelli's daily routine:

> Every morning Elsa rose at eight, no matter when she had gone to bed, sipped lemon-juice-and-water and a cup of tea for breakfast as she read the papers, handled private correspondence, made telephone calls and gave the menus of the day to the cook. Weather permitting, she often walked to work. "Always on time, five minutes early" was a motto with her. Punctual to the second everywhere in the world and livid if anyone else was one minute late, winter and summer she arrived at her office on the dot of ten. There she slipped a double-breasted white tailored cotton smock over her skirt and blouse or simple frock and outworked everyone until seven in the evening with power-house energy.

Although she spent long hours at the studio, Schiaparelli actually conceived her designs elsewhere. According to White, "Most of her designing Elsa did in her head, often while walking to work, alone in the countryside, driving or,

Elsa Schiaparelli, 1938

later, riding in her chauffeur-driven Delage, lined in white pine and fitted with a bar. By nature a rebel who hated restrictions of any kind, she did not think well between walls."

Martha Graham (1894–1991)

Graham established her own dance company in 1926 with a studio in New York's Greenwich Village, then a hotbed of intellectual and artistic activity. But Graham was not particularly interested in what her neighbors were doing. "Most of my time was spent in the studio," she wrote in her autobiography, *Blood Memory*.

> Around this time, things in the Village were very intellectual. People would sit around and talk about things constantly. I never really went in for that. If you talk something out, you will never do it. You can spend every evening talking with your friends and colleagues about your dreams, but they will remain just that—dreams. They will never be made manifest—whether in a play, a piece of music, a poem, or a dance. Talk is a privilege and one must deny oneself that privilege.

Over her long and restlessly innovative career, Graham grew to be an expert in this kind of self-denial; dance was her life, and little else mattered, or was permitted to matter. Her longest-running personal relationships were with her music director and with the first male dancer in her company, to whom she was briefly married. After her divorce she considered adopting a child but decided against it. "I chose not to have children for the simple reason that I felt I could never give a child the caring upbringing which I had as a child," she wrote. "I couldn't control being a dancer. I knew I had to choose between a child and dance, and I chose dance."

This is not to say she found the work enjoyable or easy. Dance was, she said, "permitting life to use you in a very intense way"—and the beginning of a new dance was "a time of great misery." She came to her dances through long hours in the studio alone, testing her body, searching for physical movements that embodied emotions, especially those emotions that could not be expressed through language. She said,

"Movement in modern dance is the product not of invention but of discovery—discovery of what the body will do." But Graham also found inspiration outside the studio, in nature, in the people she met, and especially in the books she read. "I owe all that I am to the study of Nietzsche and Schopenhauer," she once said. At night, she read voraciously, jotting down notes and copying passages that got her ideas flowing. Over time, the notes would begin to reveal a pattern, and Graham would next write out a scenario or script for her dance: "I would put a typewriter on a little table by my bed, bolster myself with pillows and write all night."

Once Graham had a script, she would begin to work with a composer, gradually bringing together her scenario, the music, and the movements she had developed in the studio. When it came time to get her dancers involved, she allowed them to help her realize and refine her ideas—but, one member of her company recalled, "she was there every second of the time, shaping, molding, modeling." When Graham ran into a "choreographic block," she would stare out the window, thinking, while her dancers sat on the floor and waited. And when the work didn't meet her high standards, she could become furious. "We used to watch her with alarm," another of Graham's dancers recalled. "She had her tantrums because she couldn't draw out of herself all of the devils she kept inside her. When she couldn't rid herself, cleanse herself, it was just frightful." After "the purge," however, would come a surge of "wonderful creativity."

Graham continued to dance onstage until she was seventy-five, and was devastated when she finally had to retire. But she kept working as a choreographer up until a few weeks before her death at ninety-six. A dance critic who profiled Graham on the eve of her ninetieth birthday found her

Martha Graham in rehearsal, 1965

working as many as six hours a day, from 2:00 to 5:00 in the afternoon and again from 8:00 to 10:00 or 11:00 at night, with a break in between to rest and eat a light meal. Returning home at the end of the night, Graham dealt with paperwork and had a late supper of scrambled eggs, cottage cheese, peaches, and Sanka. Afterward she would watch old movies on television until 1:00 a.m., and then be up again at 6:30 in the morning (although she might go back to bed if she didn't have any morning appointments). Even after a lifetime of dance, and the universal recognition of her genius, Graham was driven by chronic dissatisfaction. "Somewhere very long ago," she wrote in *Blood Memory,* "I remember hearing that in El Greco's studio, after he died, they found an empty canvas on which he had written only three words: 'Nothing pleases me.' This I can understand."

Elizabeth Bowen (1899–1973)

Bowen was an Anglo-Irish novelist and short-story writer whose books include *The Death of the Heart, The Heat of the Day,* and *The House in Paris.* In the late 1930s, the American poet May Sarton got to know Bowen in London, and observed how she divided her time between writing and entertaining. "I had never run a house, nor entertained, nor been responsible for ordering meals, and I had no idea what energy it all requires—the devouring machine that someone has to keep running smoothly," Sarton wrote.

In Elizabeth's life that machine had to be relegated to the periphery; central, of course, was her work. She worked extremely hard. No one saw her before one, and by then she had been at her desk for four hours. At one there was a break, lunch, and perhaps a short walk in Regent's Park just outside her front door. After that break she went back to her study for two more hours. At four or half past tea was brought up to the drawing room and intimate friends often dropped in for a tête-a-tête.

When Alan [Cameron, her husband] came home at half past five, the tensions subsided and everything became cozy and relaxed. He embraced Elizabeth, asked at once where the devil the cat was—a large fluffy orange cat—and when he had found her, settled down for a cocktail and an exchange about "the day." As in many successful marriages they played various games; Alan in his squeaky voice complained bitterly about some practical matter Elizabeth should have attended to, and she looked flustered, laughed, and pretended to be helpless. Alan's tenderness for her took the form of teasing and she obviously enjoyed it. I never saw real strain or needling between them, never for a second.

Bowen and Cameron's relationship has been described as "a sexless but contented union"; they were married for almost three decades, from 1923 until his death in 1952, but apparently the marriage was never consummated, and Bowen may have been a virgin until she started having extramarital affairs about ten years into the marriage. From then on, she had several affairs with men and women, including a thirty-year relationship with Charles Ritchie, a Canadian diplomat seven years her junior (who was also married for the latter twenty-five years of their affair). Despite the importance of these relationships to Bowen's happiness, and to her fiction, she managed to keep them carefully compartmentalized: Apparently, Cameron never learned of her long-term relationship with Ritchie or any of her other lovers.

Bowen's letters to Ritchie—and Ritchie's diary entries during their affair—were published in 2008, and they provide valuable glimpses of Bowen's creative process. "E was discussing her method of writing the other night," Ritchie noted in March 1942.

She says that when she is writing a scene the first time, she always throws in all the descriptive words that come to her mind. . . . Like, as she said, someone doing clay-modelling who will smack on handfuls of clay before beginning to cut away and do the fine modelling. Then afterwards she cuts down and discards and whittles away. The neurotic part of writing, she says, is the temptation to stop for the exact words or the most deliberate analysis of a situation.

For her part, Bowen said that novel-writing was "agitating but makes me very absorbed, and in one kind of way happy." Working on *The Heat of the Day* in 1946, she wrote, "I discard every page, rewrite it and throw discarded sheets of conversation about the floor. . . . From rubbing my forehead I have worn an enormous hole in it, which bleeds."

Frida Kahlo (1907–1954)

"I have suffered two serious accidents in my life," Kahlo once told a friend, "one in which a streetcar ran over me. . . . The other accident is Diego." Kahlo married Diego Rivera in 1929 when she was twenty-two and the celebrated muralist was forty-two. She had started painting four years earlier, while convalescing from the gruesome streetcar accident that had fractured her spine and crushed her pelvis and one foot. (During her recovery, she taught herself to paint using a specially built easel that allowed her to work in bed.) Over the next several years, Kahlo followed Rivera to San Francisco, Detroit, and New York, where he had landed a series of prominent mural commissions; meanwhile, Kahlo continued to develop as a painter while yearning to return home. In 1934, Rivera reluctantly agreed and the married artists returned to Mexico City, where they had commissioned the architect Juan O'Gorman to build them a modernist house in the wealthy neighborhood of San Ángel. The dwelling was actually two houses, one for each artist, connected by a

Frida Kahlo and Diego Rivera at lunch, 1941

rooftop bridge and enclosed by a fence of tall cactuses. In her biography of Kahlo, Hayden Herrera summarizes the artists' routine in San Ángel:

> When all was well between Frida and Diego, the day usually began with a long, late breakfast in Frida's house, during which they read the mail and sorted out their plans—who would need the chauffeur, which meals they would eat together, who was expected for lunch. After breakfast, Diego would go to his studio; occasionally he would disappear on sketching trips to the countryside, from which he would not return until late at night. . . .
>
> Occasionally after breakfast, Frida would go upstairs

to her studio, but she did not paint consistently, and weeks went by when she did not work at all. . . . More often, once the affairs of the household had been settled, the chauffeur would drive her into the center of Mexico City to spend the day with a friend.

One of Kahlo's friends, the Swiss-born artist Lucienne Bloch, wrote in her diary that "Frieda [sic] has great difficulty doing things regularly. She wants schedules and to do things like in school. By the time she must get into action, something always happens and she feels her day broken up." It didn't help that Kahlo and Rivera's relationship was never calm for long, with constant financial problems and numerous infidelities on both sides. Rivera's conquests included Kahlo's younger sister; Kahlo's included Leon Trotsky, who was in exile from the Soviet Union. She made many of her most famous paintings in two periods of intense activity: in 1937–38, following her affair with Trotsky, and in 1939–40, during her temporary separation and divorce from Rivera. (They remarried after about a year, although Kahlo would never again live in the San Ángel residence, preferring to stay in La Casa Azul, her family home in the suburb of Coyoacán.)

In 1943, at Rivera's suggestion, Kahlo began teaching at an experimental new painting and sculpture school where high school students from poor neighborhoods were given art supplies and free instruction. Kahlo enjoyed teaching, but inevitably it became yet another distraction from her own practice. In a 1944 letter, she described her routine as a teacher and artist:

I start at 8 A.M. and get off at 11 A.M. I spend half an hour covering the distance between the school and my house = 12 noon. I organize things as necessary to live more or less "decently," so there's food, clean towels, soap, a set-up table, etc., etc. = 2 P.M. How much work!! I proceed to eat, then to the ablutions of the hands and hinges (meaning teeth and mouth). I have my afternoon free to spend on the beautiful art of painting. I'm always painting pictures, since as soon as I'm done with one, I have to sell it so I have moola for all of the month's expenses. (Each spouse pitches in for the maintenance of this mansion.) In the nocturnal evening, I get the hell out to some movie or damn play and I come back and sleep like a rock. (Sometimes the insomnia hits me and then I am fuc-bulous!!!)

Throughout the 1940s, Kahlo also had to contend with endless medical problems stemming from her streetcar accident; by the end of her life, she had endured more than thirty surgeries, and starting in 1940 she had to wear a series of steel-and-leather or plaster corsets to support her spine. As Kahlo's health deteriorated, painting became more difficult; by the mid-1940s, she could neither sit nor stand for long periods of time. In 1950, the artist spent nine months in a Mexico City hospital, where she had a bone-graft surgery that became infected and required several follow-up surgeries. She made the best use of the time she could, once again employing the easel that allowed her to work lying on her back in bed. When the doctors permitted it, she would paint for up to four or five hours a day. "I never lost my spirit," Kahlo said. "I always spent my time painting because they kept me going with Demerol, and this animated me and it made me feel happy. I painted my plaster corsets and paintings, I joked around, I wrote, they brought me movies. I passed [the year] in the hospital as if it was a fiesta. I cannot complain."

Agnes de Mille (1905–1993)

De Mille was born in New York City and grew up in Hollywood, the daughter of the screenwriter and director William C. de Mille and the niece of the legendary filmmaker Cecil B. DeMille (who altered his last name to look better on movie marquees). Told she was not pretty enough to be an actress, the young de Mille resolved to become a ballet dancer instead, returning to New York after college and touring the United States and Europe as a dancer while also beginning to work in choreography, which was where she made her real contribution to the field. Beginning with *Rodeo,* in 1942, de Mille pioneered a distinctly American style of dance that incorporated folk idioms into modern dance and classical ballet. In 1943, she choreographed *Oklahoma!,* the first in a string of hugely successful Broadway musicals; by the end of the 1940s, she was the best-known choreographer in the world.

To develop a new work of choreography, de Mille needed "a pot of tea, walking space, privacy and an idea," she wrote in her 1951 memoir, *Dance to the Piper.* To begin, she would shut herself in a studio and listen to music—not from the musical or ballet in question (for musicals, the scores often wouldn't be written yet) but music that inspired her, especially that of Bach, Mozart, and the Czech composer Bedřich Smetana, "or almost any folk music in interesting arrangements," she wrote. Then the work began:

I start sitting with my feet up and drinking pots of strong tea, but as I am taken into the subject I begin to move and before I know it I am walking the length of the studio and acting full out the gestures and scenes. The key dramatic scenes come this way. I never forget

Agnes de Mille in rehearsal, 1964

a single nuance of them afterwards; I do usually forget dance sequences.

The next step is to find the style of gesture. This is done standing and moving, again behind locked doors and again with a gramophone. Before I find how a character dances, I must know how he walks and stands. If I can discover the basic rhythms of his natural gesture, I will know how to expand them into dance movement.

It takes hours daily of blind instinctive moving and fumbling to find the revealing gesture, and the process

goes on for weeks before I am ready to start composing. Nor can I think any of this out sitting down. My
body does it for me. It happens. That is why the choreographic process is exhausting. It happens on one's feet
after hours of work, and the energy required is roughly
the equivalent of writing a novel and winning a tennis
match simultaneously. This is the kernel, the nucleus of
the dance. All the design develops from this.

Once she had the kernel, de Mille sat down at her desk
and worked out the pattern of the dances, and at this point
she would listen to the score, if it existed. She made detailed
diagrams and notes of her own invention, "intelligible only
to me and only for about a week," she wrote. Then she was
ready to begin rehearsals, a process of several weeks. The
biographer Carol Easton writes:

> When a show was in rehearsal, Agnes saw little of her
> husband and even less of her child. She did not work
> at home—except in her head, before dawn. She had
> breakfast in a drugstore, away from the telephone and
> other interruptions, making notes while she ate. Morn-
> ings were for dance rehearsals, afternoons for the cho-
> rus. After that, to avoid interruption, she sometimes
> took a room at the Algonquin Hotel and worked there
> through dinner, returning to the theater to rehearse the
> actors until ten or eleven. When she got home, she made
> notes for the housekeeper about the next day before
> going to bed, usually with a headache.

After giving birth to her only child, a son, in 1946, de Mille
hired a full-time housekeeper who handled almost all of
the childcare duties, and she also hired the housekeeper's

husband, a chauffeur and general handyman. She could afford it: Following the success of *Oklahoma!,* de Mille's annual earnings could top $100,000 in a good year, or more than a million dollars in today's money. But her husband was never entirely comfortable with her success, and de Mille was aware that he had affairs on the side. She accepted this as something of an inevitability. When her friend the writer Rebecca West learned of her own husband's infidelity, de Mille sent her a letter of empathy and support. "I have yet to meet the man who can accept with grace and comfort creativity in his wife," she wrote. "Men can't. They want to. But they feel dwarfed and obligated. . . . That's how it is, darling. Gifted women pay. There are compensations."

For de Mille, the compensations came in the rehearsal room. Which is not to say the work was easy; to the contrary, it proceeded with excruciating slowness—two hours of rehearsal might yield just five seconds of a final dance. De Mille was so protective of the work in progress that she sometimes stationed a guard at the door of the rehearsal room. Inside, she sat leaning forward in a chair, burning "with the concentration of an acetylene torch," she said. Then she would spring to her feet to demonstrate a movement—only to stop abruptly and stand utterly still, in what one dancer called her "fish-out-of-water pose," as she mentally processed the next part of the dance. De Mille was, she admitted, "apt to be short-tempered and jumpy at these times," and her dancers learned to be patient—and to ply de Mille with cups of hot coffee, which she said comforted her. (By the end of a rehearsal, there would be a ring of empty cups surrounding her chair.) When she got stuck, "the tension could be *painful,*" one dancer recalled. "But when it was right," said another, "she was triumphant! You felt like a real collaborator. The kick wasn't just someone saying 'Well done,' but 'YES, THAT'S IT!' "

THE VORTEX

....

Louisa May Alcott [1832–1888]

Alcott wrote in fits of creative energy and obsession, skip-ping meals, sleeping little, and scribbling so furiously that she eventually had to train herself to write with her left hand to give her cramped right hand a break. "The fit was on strong and for a fortnight I hardly ate, slept, or stirred but wrote like a thinking machine in full operation," she noted while working on her first novel, *Moods.* A more detailed account of Alcott's writing binges can be found in her next and most famous novel, *Little Women,* in a passage about her heroine, Jo March, who has caught the writing bug at a young age, just as her creator had:

Every few weeks she would shut herself up in her room, put on her scribbling suit, and "fall into a vortex," as she expressed it, writing away at her novel with all her heart and soul, for till that was finished she could find no peace. Her "scribbling suit" consisted of a black woolen pinafore on which she could wipe her pen at will, and a cap of the same material, adorned with a cheerful red bow, into which she bundled her hair when the decks were cleared for action. This cap was a beacon to the inquiring eyes of her family, who dur-ing these periods kept their distance, merely popping in their heads semi-occasionally to ask, with interest, "Does genius burn, Jo?" They did not always venture even to ask this question, but took an observation of the cap, and judged accordingly. If this expressive article of dress was drawn low upon the forehead, it was a sign that hard work was going on, in exciting moments it was pushed rakishly askew, and when despair seized the author it was plucked wholly off, and cast upon the floor. At such times the intruder silently withdrew, and not until the red bow was seen gaily erect upon the gifted brow, did anyone dare address Jo.

She did not think herself a genius by any means, but when the writing fit came on, she gave herself up to it with entire abandon, and led a blissful life, unconscious of want, care, or bad weather, while she sat safe and happy in an imaginary world, full of friends almost as real and dear to her as any in the flesh. Sleep forsook her eyes, meals stood untasted, day and night were all too short to enjoy the happiness which blessed her only at such times, and made these hours worth living, even if they bore no other fruit. The divine afflatus usually lasted a week or two, and then she emerged from her "vortex," hungry, sleepy, cross, or despondent.

By all accounts, this was how Alcott herself worked—except that in place of a writing cap by which family members judged her availability for interruption, there was a "mood pillow" on the parlor sofa that served the same purpose. Alcott lived with (and financially supported) her parents for most of her adult life; during her writing fits, she generally holed up in her bedroom, working at the small half-moon desk that her father had built for her. But she was restless by nature and would sometimes move about the house as she daydreamed about her work. If she settled on the sofa, her

An illustration from Louisa May Alcott's Little Women, *depicting Jo in her "scribbling suit"*

parents or her sisters were occasionally tempted to interrupt her, but they knew from experience that breaking her concentration at a crucial moment would provoke the author's extreme consternation. So Alcott turned a bolster pillow into a kind of "tollgate for conversation," the biographer John Matteson has written. "If the pillow stood on its end, the family was free to disturb her," Matteson explains. "If the pillow lay on its side, however, they should tread lightly and keep their interjections to themselves."

Although *Little Women* contains the fullest description of Alcott's writing vortex, the novel was actually composed without her usual creative mania. Alcott never felt inspired by the project and wrote it only to please her editor and her father, both of whom saw the lucrative potential of popular children's books. This was in the late 1860s, when Alcott had just turned thirty-five, and by then she was already a seasoned writer of melodramatic short stories—"blood & thunder tale[s]," she called them, with titles like "The Maniac Bride" and "Pauline's Passion and Punishment"—which she published under the pseudonym A. M. Barnard. She wrote the stories for money, often while working other jobs and attending to myriad domestic obligations, and she had long yearned to make the leap into more serious literature; *Moods* had been her bid for a complex, nuanced work for adult sensibilities. But as with most matters in her life, Alcott deferred to her father on the "girl's book" he wanted her to write, and despite her lack of inspiration she worked fast, completing the novel's 402 manuscript pages in just two and a half months. Brisk sales prompted her publisher to ask for a second volume, which Alcott wrote even more quickly, aiming for a chapter a day. She thought she could finish the book in a month, and nearly managed to do so. "I am so full of my work I can't stop to eat or sleep, or for anything but a daily run," she wrote.

When the second volume was published, *Little Women* quickly became a sensation, and from then on the "girl's book" defined Alcott's life. Although its success finally gave her the financial independence to write full-time, it also curtailed her ambitions. Her audience would forever want more of the same, and after so many years toiling in obscurity, Alcott could not resist satisfying the demand. "Though I do not enjoy writing 'moral tales' for the young," she admitted in an 1878 letter, "I do it because it pays well." Meanwhile, a host of chronic health conditions prevented Alcott from working with the same intensity as she once had; in a letter from 1887, she lamented that she could "write but two hours a day, doing about twenty pages, sometimes more"—an enormously productive day for most writers, but, for Alcott, a cause for concern and self-reproach.

Radclyffe Hall [1880–1943]

"My daily life—I have no real life—this life is a dream, a dream of Duty," Hall wrote in a 1934 letter. By then she was the author of several collections of poetry and seven novels, including, most famously, 1928's *The Well of Loneliness*, a landmark of lesbian literature that was promptly banned as obscene in her native England. But she had not always felt duty-bound to writing. Born to wealthy but neglectful parents, Hall received a poor education and drifted throughout most of her adolescence and early adulthood, untethered to any vocation other than falling in and out of love with women whom she usually lost to marriage. That all changed with the first great love affair of her life, with the singer and composer Mabel "Ladye" Batten, who read voraciously, spoke several languages, and had no intention of sharing her life with an uneducated young dilettante. Determined to make herself worthy of Batten's love, Hall began writing short stories, and Batten submitted some of them to a publisher. To Hall's surprise, the publisher received them enthusiastically—but he insisted that Hall's talents would be better served by a novel, and suggested that she begin work on one right away.

Hall demurred; she was not yet ready to embark on such

Radclyffe Hall (standing) with Una Troubridge, 1927

a demanding project. But Batten's death in 1916—before which Hall had begun an affair with Batten's distant cousin, the sculptor Una Troubridge—injected a potent mixture of grief and guilt that stiffened her resolve. As Troubridge would later recall, Hall soon "launched upon an existence of regular and painstaking industry such as she had never before even dreamed of. The idle apprentice was metamorphosed by sorrow into someone who would work from morning to night and from night till morning, or travel half across England and back again to verify the most trifling detail."

In this enterprise Hall was lucky to have found Troubridge, who became her lifelong lover and literary amanuensis—and who stoically endured Hall's frequent struggles with "inspirational blackout," and the black moods that accompanied them. Hall was never an effortless writer; she labored ferociously over her books, and her process was halting in the extreme. In a biography of Hall written after her death, Troubridge records her writing methods:

> Whether she felt inspired or not, her method of work never varied. She never herself used a typewriter, in fact she never learned to type and the mere thought of dictating her inspiration to a typist filled her with horror. She always said that the written word was to her an essential preliminary and she wrote her work with pen or pencil, very illegibly, generally mis-spelt and often without punctuation. Sometimes she wrote in manuscript books but, especially in later years, often on loose sheets of sermon paper or indeed on paper of any kind, and to this day I will find scraps covered with sentences and sometimes discover "try outs" on a bit of blotting paper or an old cardboard box.

Hall chain-smoked as she worked, and she had a "neatness complex," she wrote, whereby "anything in the nature of untidiness fidgets me to death." Her writing wardrobe was unvarying. "I can never work in anything but old clothes, although these must always be very neat," Hall told a reporter. "I usually work in an old tweed skirt and my velvet smoking jacket, a man's smoking jacket by choice because of the loose and comfortable sleeves."

After she completed a first draft, Hall would ask Troubridge to read it back to her, and as the reading progressed the author would dictate corrections, which Troubridge would mark on the pages and incorporate into the next reading.

These readings had to be repeated many, many times until Hall was satisfied. "I have known a chapter worked on for weeks on end," Troubridge recalled. "I have often read one aloud a score of times." And if her reading evinced even a hint of flatness or boredom, Hall would seize on this as evidence of the writing's deficiency, and sometimes snatch the pages from Troubridge's hands and throw them into the fire. When, on the other hand, Hall was finally satisfied with the reading-aloud stage, she would next dictate the corrected draft to a typist, and then the process would begin all over again. In this manner, draft by painstaking draft, Hall would creep toward a final version, relying on Troubridge's endless readings aloud as her essential quality check.

As she got older, Hall only worked harder. In her later years, she gravitated increasingly toward writing first drafts at night, as a result of which, Troubridge recalls, "she never really got enough sleep. Not only had she always suffered from insomnia but after a night of intensive work—a stretch of perhaps sixteen hours on end during which she had reluctantly swallowed such food as I gave her, without leaving her desk—even when she finally almost fell into bed, within a couple of hours she would be wide awake, asking for her breakfast or going over her work." Once she developed her fanaticism for writing, Hall didn't know any other way to be. In a 1934 letter, she said, "I literally wear myself out over a book, too much I suppose, but there it is."

Eileen Gray (1878–1976)

The Irish-born, French-based architect and furniture designer helped revolutionize the look of modern homes but was proudly incompetent at running her own. "Oh, how I abominate housework," she once said—and she avoided this and other domestic obligations by employing a faithful housekeeper, Louise Dany, who attended to her needs from 1927 until Gray's death almost fifty years later. Gray also insisted on being driven everywhere. (In the 1910s, her favored chauffeur was the singer Marisa Damia, whose pet panther would join them on joyrides around Paris.) "Artists ought not to drive at all," she wrote in a letter to her niece. "First of all, they are too precious, secondly, driving prevents their thoughts wandering where they should, thirdly, it puts constant tension on their eyes." And Gray needed to preserve her eyesight for her work, which was really the only thing in her life that she cared about. As she wrote in her nineties, "Only work of some sort can help to give meaning to life even if it is really quite useless."

Isadora Duncan (1878–1927)

Duncan essentially invented modern dance and became an international star as a result, but her artistic triumph never made her wealthy; for most of her career she worried about how to pay her expenses, many times rehearsing in a freezing studio because she couldn't afford to heat it. (The problem may have been less about making money than holding on to it: According to the journalist Janet Flanner, Duncan "once

Isadora Duncan at the Acropolis of Athens,
circa 1910s or 1920s

gave a house party that started in Paris, gathered force in Ven-
ice and culminated weeks later on a houseboat on the Nile.")
During one of her European tours, Duncan started joking
with her sister that the solution, clearly, was to find a mil-
lionaire. Then, the morning after a performance in Paris, one
appeared—Paris Singer, heir to the Singer sewing machine
company fortune, a six-foot-three, blond, bearded arts
patron who had fallen for Duncan and come to sweep her off

her feet. Duncan was willing enough—but Singer soon proposed marriage, an institution she abhorred. Singer wanted the great dancer to live with him in London and on his estate in the English countryside. Duncan, accustomed to touring relentlessly before adoring crowds, wasn't sure she could tolerate such a settled life. What would she do with herself? Try it for three months, Singer proposed. "So that summer we went to Devonshire," Duncan wrote in her autobiography,

> where he had a wonderful château which he had built after Versailles and the Petit Trianon, with many bedrooms and bathrooms, and suites, all to be at my disposition, with fourteen automobiles in the garage and a yacht in the harbor. But I had not reckoned on the rain. In an English summer it rains all day long. The English people do not seem to mind at all. They rise and have an early breakfast of eggs and bacon, and ham and kidneys and porridge. Then they don mackintoshes and go forth into the humid country till lunch, when they eat many courses, ending with Devonshire cream.
>
> From lunch to five o'clock they are supposed to be busy with their correspondence, though I believe they really go to sleep. At five they descend to their tea, consisting of many kinds of cakes and bread and butter and tea and jam. After that they make a pretence of playing bridge, until it is time to proceed to the really important business of the day—dressing for dinner, at which they appear in full evening dress, the ladies very décolleté and the gentlemen in starched shirts, to demolish a twenty-course dinner. When this is over they engage in some light political conversation, or touch upon philosophy until the time comes to retire.

You can imagine whether this life pleased me or not. In the course of a couple of weeks I was positively desperate.

Duncan did not agree to marry Singer, or to ever again follow such a regimented lifestyle. She preferred to spend "long days and nights in the studio seeking that dance which might be the divine expression of the human spirit through the medium of the body's movement." Although, even for Duncan, not every day could be a joyous communion with art; sometimes she looked back on her life and was "filled only with a great disgust and a feeling of utter emptiness." But Duncan believed that this, too, was a part of the artist's life. "I have met many great artists and intelligent and so-called successful people in my life, but never one who could be called a happy being, although some have made a very good bluff at it," she wrote. "Behind the mask, with any clair-voyance, one can divine the same uneasiness and suffering."

Colette (1873–1954)

The French novelist began writing at the behest of her first husband, Henry Gauthier-Villars, a popular writer (and notorious libertine) who published under the nom de plume Willy. Suspecting that Colette's coming-of-age experiences would make compelling fiction, he urged her to write them down—and play up the more salacious bits—and then published the resulting novel, *Claudine à l'école,* under his own name. The book was a commercial and critical success, and Willy demanded more; according to Colette, he would lock

Colette at work, circa 1950

her in her writing room and wouldn't allow her to emerge until she had completed her daily quota of pages. "A prison is indeed one of the best workshops," Colette wrote many years later. "I know what I am talking about: a real prison, the sound of the key turning in the lock, and four hours' claustration before I was free again."

Colette eventually divorced Willy and began publishing under her own name, drawing on her numerous affairs with men and women for novels well stocked with sensual adventures; by the end of her life, she had written more than fifty books and had become a national institution in France, beloved especially for her novels *Chéri* and *Gigi*. Colette never enjoyed writing, but thanks to Willy's early "training," she forced herself to do it nearly every day. Her stepson Bernard—with whom Colette had a five-year affair, beginning when he was sixteen and she was forty-seven—had "the opportunity to watch her work early in the morning," he later recalled. "Wrapped up in a blanket, she attacked the blue pages she always wrote on. It was a great lesson for me, for she would fill four or five pages easily, then throw away the fifth, and so on in this manner until she was tired."

Colette didn't always write first thing. According to her third husband, "She was wise enough never to write in the morning, but to go out for a walk with her dog, whatever the weather. . . . She never worked in the evening except when pressed by circumstance." Rather, he said, it was "chiefly between three and six in the afternoon" that she composed her day's work. As she grew older and began suffering from arthritis, Colette preferred to write on the sofa, stretched out on her "raft" with a blue-shaded lamp (blue was her favorite color) hovering above her lap table. Writing for her meant, she wrote, "idle hours curled up in the hollow of the divan, and then the orgy of inspiration from which one emerges stupefied and aching all over, but already recompensed and laden with treasures that one unloads slowly on to the virgin page in the little round pool of light under the lamp." Once inspiration struck, she wrote fast, furiously filling page after page—although, the next day, she didn't necessarily approve of what she had written. "To write is to pour one's innermost self passionately upon the tempting paper," she wrote, "at such frantic speed that sometimes one's hand struggles and rebels, overdriven by the impatient god who guides it—and to find, next day, in place of the golden bough that bloomed miraculously in that dazzling hour, a withered bramble and a stunted flower."

Lynn Fontanne (1887–1983)

Fontanne and her husband, Alfred Lunt, created probably the greatest husband-and-wife acting team in theatrical history, working together in more than two dozen productions from 1923 to 1960. Their success was the result of mutual perfectionism and constant, almost obsessive rehearsal. "Miss Fontanne and I rehearse all the time," Lunt once said. "Even after we leave the theater, we rehearse. We sleep in the same bed. We have a script on our hands when we go to bed. You can't come and tell us to stop rehearsing after eight hours."

In his biography *The Fabulous Lunts,* Jared Brown describes the couple's rehearsal process inside their apartment on Manhattan's East 36th Street:

> They worked out a meticulous routine for their sessions at home. Memorization of lines came first. Since the apartment had three stories, with the dining room on the ground floor, the bedrooms on the second and a studio-living room on the third, Fontanne would take the top floor and Lunt the lowest. Each would thus be able to shout out the lines of the play without disturbing the other. . . . After both felt reasonably secure in their lines, they worked in the same room, sitting facing one another on two plain wooden chairs. With legs

Alfred Lunt and Lynn Fontanne, with a script, 1931

interlocked and eyes focused squarely on each other, they began to exchange dialogue. If one of them faltered or gave the wrong line, the other clapped his knees together and the scene began again. After several such sessions, their knees may have been bruised but they were letter-perfect in their lines.

Once the memorization was complete, rehearsals began, with Fontanne and Lunt playing each scene over and over again, each time modifying their characters' attitude and intentions. After multiple run-throughs, they would come to an agreement about which version had been most successful, and then they would begin yet another round of rehearsals, now stopping mid-scene as needed to discuss the finer points of each other's performance, making small modifications to gestures, looks, points of emphasis, relentlessly polishing every detail. Only after this extensive "homework" would the Lunts be ready to rehearse with the other actors in a production—and even then, they continued to rehearse by themselves at home afterward. "Over a period of weeks, each scene was repeated, with modifications, hundreds of times," Brown writes. And these were not gentle, supportive sessions—the Lunts were hard on each other. Indeed, Fontanne thought that this was probably the secret to their success. "I think that we are terrifically critical of each other," she once said. "And we've learned, the both of us, to take it."

Edna St. Vincent Millay (1892–1950)

"When I am working on a book I work all the time," the American poet told a reporter in 1931. "I always have notebook and pencil on the table at my bedside. I may wake up in the middle of the night with something I want to put down. Sometimes I sit up and write in bed furiously until dawn. And I think of my work all the time even when I am in the garden or talking to people. That is why I get so tired. When I finished [the poetry collection] 'Fatal Interview' I was exhausted. I was never away from the sonnets in my mind. Night and day I concentrated on them for the last year and a half."

Edna St. Vincent Millay at Steepletop, circa 1930s

By this time Millay had been living for several years at Steepletop, the abandoned berry farm that she and her husband purchased in 1925 and transformed into an elegant country estate with extensive gardens; an outdoor bar; a tennis court; a spring-fed pool, where guests were invited to swim in the nude; and a secluded writing hut for Millay (although she often wrote in the main house, lying in bed). Millay's husband, a Dutch coffee importer named Eugen Boissevain, had given up his business to run Steepletop, which proved a near-perfect arrangement for the poet. When a visiting reporter asked Millay how she managed such a large and complicated household, Millay explained that she had nothing to do with it:

Eugen does all that kind of thing. He engages the servants. He shows them around. He tells them everything. I don't interfere with his ordering of the house. If there is anything I don't like, I tell him. I have no time for it. I don't want to know what I'm going to eat. I want to go into my dining room as if it were a restaurant, and say, "What a charming dinner!"

It's this concern with my household that protects me from the things that eat up a woman's time and interest. Eugen and I live like two bachelors. He, being the one who can throw household things off more easily than I, shoulders that end of our existence, and I have my work to do, which is the writing of poetry.

Ignoring the household did not exactly come naturally to Millay. "I care an awful lot that things be done right," she said. "Yet I don't let my concern break in and ruin my concentration and my temper." She considered writing poetry an extremely delicate process and took pains not to let everyday worries disrupt it. "When you write a poem something begins to be a part of your thought and your life," she said, "and you become more and more conscious of it. It forms as if conjured out of steam." Once she had completed a first draft, she would work it over and over, often setting a poem aside for months or even as long as two years. "I put it away until it is cold," she said, "and I get a critic's point of view toward it as if it weren't mine at all, and only when it has satisfied my most searching analysis do I let it out."

All of this required tremendous energy, and while it appeared to guests that Millay and her husband were living a life of ease in the country, Millay was in fact pushing herself to the brink of collapse. "I can spade a garden and not get tired," Millay said, "but the nervous intensity attendant on writing poetry, on creative writing, exhausts me, and I suffer constantly from a headache. It never leaves me while I am working, and for that there is no cure save not to work. Doctors advise me to go away for a rest cure, but who wants to lie stretched on one's back idle for months at a time?"

Tallulah Bankhead (1902–1968)

"I have three phobias which, could I mute them, would make my life as slick as a sonnet, but as dull as ditch water: I hate to go to bed, I hate to get up, and I hate to be alone," Bankhead wrote in her 1952 autobiography. The first two phobias can be attributed, in part, to the Alabama-born actress's chronic insomnia; the last seemed to be congenital, and may have been tied up with her love of—even addiction to—conversation, although conversation for Bankhead was invariably a one-sided affair. Her preferred mode of being was monologue, to be carrying on an endlessly digressive mix of anecdotes, witticisms, and unintentional one-liners (e.g., "We're reminiscing about the future"; "I've had six juleps and I'm not even sober"). A friend of Bankhead's once measured her rate of words per minute, and estimated her daily output at just under seventy thousand (almost the length of this book). Another famously reported, "I've just spent an hour talking to Tallulah for a few minutes."

Bankhead claimed that she called everyone "dahling" because she could never remember names—just as she could never remember directions, addresses, or telephone numbers. But she had no trouble memorizing her lines during her five-decade theatrical career; indeed, onstage she was able to press her outsize personality into the service of flamboyant and fierce performances that made her one of her century's greatest leading ladies. Bankhead, however, dismissed acting as "sheer drudgery" and claimed it barely even qualified as a creative profession:

> The author writes a play, then is through with it, aside from collecting royalties. Four weeks of rehearsing and the director's work is done. Theirs are creative jobs. But how would the author feel if he had to write the same play over each night for a year? Or the director restage it before each performance? They'd be as balmy as Nijinsky in a week. Even the ushers traffic with different people every night. But the actress? She's a caged parrot.

Bankhead also loathed the strict timetable of the theater, the necessity to appear nightly from 8:30 to 11:00 p.m., without any room for error or improvisation. "Above the members of any other profession actors are slaves to the clock," she wrote. Not that she was ever tardy—another of Bankhead's phobias was being late to an appointment, and she generally arrived everywhere at least thirty minutes early. Before opening nights, she was struck with "pre-show terror," a rare lapse in her otherwise indefatigable persona. And although Bankhead disapproved of superstitions, she admitted to indulging in them on these occasions. "Ever since *The Squab Farm* [her first production] a framed picture of my mother had graced my dressing-room table on opening nights," Bankhead wrote. "Unfailingly I would drop on my knees just before curtain rise and pray: 'Dear God, don't let me make a fool of myself.' Then I would open a split of champagne and my maid and I would drink to our good fortune."

Birgit Nilsson (1918–2005)

Nilsson was one of the great opera singers of her era, renowned for her rich, powerful soprano voice and her definitive interpretations of the operas of Strauss and, in particular, Wagner. She grew up a farmer's daughter in southern Sweden, where she was encouraged to sing by a local choirmaster; after studying at Stockholm's Royal Academy of Music, Nilsson gradually built an international reputation and, from the late 1950s until her retirement in 1984, was constantly in demand. Asked how she maintained her instrument over such a long career, Nilsson demurred. "I do nothing special," she said. "I don't smoke. I drink a little wine and beer. I was born with the right set of parents." On another occasion, she was asked the secret to her success as Wagner's Isolde. "Comfortable shoes," she said.

The real secret to her success was discipline, which Nilsson said was particularly important for a singer. "A writer or painter can work when they feel the inspiration," she said. Singers aren't so lucky:

> A singer can awaken in the morning with a headache and feel very bad, and you'll be nervous and everything is against you, but you have to regain the strength for the performance that night. It's a very tough feeling. The more responsibility you feel, the more nervous and impossible you get. At times like that, you go very early to the theater and try little by little to get in shape. And most of the time those troubles are forgotten when you are onstage, and that's wonderful. I guess it's like giving birth to a child—when the child is there in your arms, it's wonderful and you forget the pain of before.

For many years Nilsson performed almost continually, traveling from one opera house to another, living in hotels for months on end. She didn't take vacations of any length, saying, "If you rest too long, it is harder to bring the voice back into shape." And although she and her husband, a Swedish businessman, maintained apartments in Stockholm and Paris, she did not consider either of them—or any place—her home. "I cannot be an artist and have a home," she once said. "You have to say 'No, thank you' to either one. I say 'No, thank you' to a home. I love my profession so much, and my husband is so understanding."

Despite her renown, Nilsson never relished the role of the diva off-stage. "I don't like that expression 'prima donna,'" she said. "I feel more like a working soprano." Her performance rituals were simple: Before going onstage, she performed a rapid series of vocal warm-ups that lasted three to four minutes and, according to eavesdroppers, sounded "perfectly awful." During intermission, she sucked on an orange; after a performance, she had an attendant bring her a glass of beer, a jigger of aquavit, and a Swedish herring from the personal supply she carried with her wherever she went.

Zora Neale Hurston (1891–1960)

In March 1951, Hurston wrote a letter to her literary agent thanking her for a $100 check and sharing some news about the novel she had recently started writing. "I have caught fire on the novel, and I am back at work on it already," Hurston wrote.

Zora Neale Hurston, 1938

I do not know whether you ever went down to the Matanza river in your pig-tail days to fish and caught a toad fish. You know if they are swallowed by a big fish, they will eat their way out through the walls of its stomach. That is like the call to write. You must do it irregardless, or it will eat its way out of you anyhow.

It's a pretty good metaphor for how Hurston worked. She never followed a writing routine or plan, and she went through "terrible periods" when she couldn't write at all. "Every now and then I get a sort of phobia for paper and all its works," she wrote in a 1938 letter. "I cannot bring myself to touch it. I cannot write, read, or do anything at all for a period. . . . Just something grabs hold of me and holds me mute, miserable and helpless until it lets me go. I feel as if I have been marooned on a planet by myself. But I find that it is the prelude to creative effort."

Once she was seized by a creative idea, everything changed. Hurston wrote her most famous novel, *Their Eyes Were Watching God,* in the fall of 1936, while on a Guggenheim Fellowship researching voodoo culture in Haiti. In the previous months she had been in Jamaica living with and studying the Maroons, descendants of escaped slaves, and the immersion in Jamaican and Haitian culture helped Hurston see her own country's race, class, and gender issues in a new light. Once she began *Their Eyes Were Watching God,* she worked with amazing speed. "It was dammed up in me, and I wrote it under internal pressure in seven weeks," Hurston wrote in her autobiography. "I wish that I could write it again."

Margaret Bourke-White (1904–1971)

Bourke-White was a pioneering photojournalist with a career of firsts: She was the first Western photographer allowed to enter the Soviet Union, the United States' first female war correspondent, and the first female staff photographer at *Life* magazine, where she was known by her colleagues as "Maggie the Indestructible" for her daring forays into sites of global conflict, from which she inevitably emerged unscathed and undaunted. Due to the nature of her work, Bourke-White could never really follow a fixed schedule as a photographer, instead adapting as needed to the assignment on hand. But she was also a gifted writer—publishing several books on her work and a lively autobiography, *Portrait of Myself*—and here she did follow extremely regular habits. Indeed, photography and writing proved an ideal pairing for Bourke-White: "I wanted to have a rhythm in my life: the high adventure—with all the excitement, the difficulties, the pressures—balanced with a period of tranquility in which to absorb what I had seen and felt," she wrote. And her house in Darien, Connecticut, "isolated by surrounding woods," proved the perfect setting for these periods of tranquility. "I am a morning writer," Bourke-White noted in *Portrait of Myself*.

The world is all fresh and new then, and made for the imagination. I keep an odd schedule that would be possible only for someone with no family demands—to bed at eight, up at four. I love to write out of doors and sleep out of doors, too. In a strange way, if I sleep under open sky, it becomes part of the writing experience, part of my insulation from the world.

For outdoor writing and sleeping, Bourke-White employed "a piece of garden furniture on wheels, with a little fringed half-canopy on top," she wrote. "It was wide and luxurious, and when it was made up with light quilts and a candle on each side, and reflected in the swimming pool, it was a child's dream of a bed made for a princess." Each night she would roll it to a different spot on her property and fall asleep as the sun set and the fireflies emerged. Just before daylight she would wake and begin writing, "and by the time the sun rose, I was sealed in my own planet and safe from the distractions of the day."

This last point was crucial: Bourke-White required long periods of solitude to write, with as few interruptions as possible. She was aware that this could be difficult for outsiders to accept. "I'm afraid my closely guarded solitude causes some hurt feelings now and then," she wrote. "But how to explain, without wounding someone, that you want to be wholly in the world you are writing about, that it would take two days to get the visitor's voice out of the house so that you could listen to your own characters again?" In fact, friends and colleagues were sometimes put out by Bourke-White's relentless focus on her work. "The very first time I met her I asked her if she would have lunch with me," the *Life* photographer Nina Leen once recalled. "She told me she was writing a book and there was no hope of a lunch for several years."

BOREDOM AND SUFFERING

Marie Bashkirtseff, circa 1876

Marie Bashkirtseff (1858–1884)

Bashkirtseff was a Russian-born painter and sculptor who kept a diary from age thirteen until shortly before her death of tuberculosis at twenty-five. During that time she studied painting in Paris (at a private academy; the famous École des Beaux-Arts did not admit women until 1897) and began to establish herself as a gifted young artist. "I hate moderation in anything," she wrote in 1876, the year she began to study art seriously. "I want either a life of continual excitement or one of absolute repose." In fact, she chose continual work, for years following more or less the same schedule: up at 6:00 a.m., drawing or painting from 8:00 to noon and from 1:00 to 5:00, with an hour-long meal break in between. Then she bathed and changed clothes, had dinner, read until 11:00 p.m., and went to bed. (Sometimes she would draw by lamplight in the early evening before dinner, extending her workday by an hour or so.) Occasionally, she grew fatigued of the relentless schedule, but, as she wrote in 1880, "when I spend the day without working I suffer the most frightful remorse." Learning that she had tuberculosis and would likely die young only increased Bashkirtseff's determination. "Everything seems petty and uninteresting, everything except my work," she wrote in May 1883. "Life, taken thus, may be beautiful."

Germaine de Staël [1766–1817]

"One must, in one's life, make a choice between boredom and suffering," Madame de Staël wrote to a friend in the summer of 1800. In her own life, Staël proudly chose suffering. The Swiss-French woman of letters was born into enormous wealth and status—her father was Louis XVI's minister of finance, her mother a central figure in the salons of Paris—but her outspoken opposition to Napoleon in the 1790s forced her into exile, much of it spent at her family residence in Coppet, Switzerland, which became an important meeting place and laboratory of ideas for many of Western Europe's leading intellectuals. There Staël also wrote numerous political and literary essays, although her productivity was not always apparent to her guests. "Madame de Staël worked a great deal, but only when she had nothing better to do;

the most trifling social amusement always had priority," one visitor noted. That's not quite true. In his biography of Staël, J. Christopher Herold provides a more nuanced portrait of her lifestyle in Coppet:

> Breakfast was between ten and eleven. Then the guests were left to their own devices, while Germaine devoted herself to her business correspondence, her accounts, the administration of her estate, and, if there was time, to reading and writing. To her guests it seemed that she was doing nothing, for she was able to busy herself with several matters at a time, and interruptions, which were continuous, did not set her back. She took notes while riding in her carriage, kept up running conversations while dictating letters, and worked at her books no matter where she happened to be or what was going on. Even to those closest to her it was a mystery how she could write so much when there seemed to be no time for writing. The secret was not in any special organization of time; rather, it was in absolute lack of organization. Most men expend the larger part of their time on trying to concentrate and on resting from the effort; between preparation and relaxation there is hardly time left for action. Madame de Staël, always concentrated, never at rest, was endowed with a brain that could, in an instant, adjust itself to whatever demanded her attention.

Because breakfast at Coppet was between 10:00 and 11:00 a.m., lunch wasn't served until about 5:00 p.m., and dinner not until 11:00 p.m. In between lunch and dinner, there was an evening walk or drive, or a gathering for music, conversation, and games. After dinner, conversation continued until the early morning, at least for Staël and her inner circle. Staël slept only a few hours a night—and then only thanks to a dose of opium—and she expected a similar level of stamina in her intimates. "Like all insomniacs," Herold writes, "she resented fatigue in others as a manifestation of disaffection." Staël's longtime lover, the politician and author Benjamin Constant, said that he had never known anyone "more continuously exacting without realizing it." He wrote, "Everybody's entire existence, every hour, every minute, for years on end, must be at her disposition, or else there is an explosion like all thunderstorms and earthquakes put together."

Marie de Vichy-Chamrond, Marquise du Deffand (1697–1780)

Madame du Deffand was an intimate friend and correspondent of Voltaire, Montesquieu, and Horace Walpole, and the hostess of a Parisian salon that stood at the center of the city's intellectual life for forty years. In his book *Written Lives*, Javier Marías summarizes Deffand's daily routine:

> Her life followed a slightly disorderly timetable: she would get up at about five o'clock in the afternoon and, at six, receive her supper guests, of whom there might be six or seven or even twenty or thirty depending on the day; supper and talk went on until two in the morning, but since she could not bear to go to bed, she was quite capable of staying up until seven playing at dice with [the British politician] Charles Fox, even though she did

not enjoy the game and was, at the time, seventy-three years of age. If no one else could keep her company, she would wake the coachman and have him take her for a ride along the empty boulevards. Her aversion to going to bed was due in large part to the terrible insomnia from which she had always suffered: sometimes, she would await the early morning arrival of someone who could read to her, and then, after listening to a few passages from a book, she could at last fall asleep.

The central event of Deffand's day was supper—"one of man's four aims," she wrote; "I have forgotten what the other three are"—and she continued hosting her evening supper parties right up until her death at age eighty-three. "Exert all your talents," she often told her cook, "as I more than ever require the aid of society to beguile the time." As Marías noted, she was especially loath to be left alone at night. After her visitors finally went home and her servants retired, Deffand wrote, "I am left to myself, and I cannot be in worse hands."

Dorothy Parker (1893–1967)

"If you have any young friends who aspire to become writers, the second greatest favor you can do them is to present them with copies of *The Elements of Style*," Parker once said. "The first greatest, of course, is to shoot them now, while they're happy." Parker was only half-joking, or maybe not even half. Despite becoming a much-sought-after writer, with high-profile, well-paying gigs at *Vanity Fair* and *The New Yorker,*

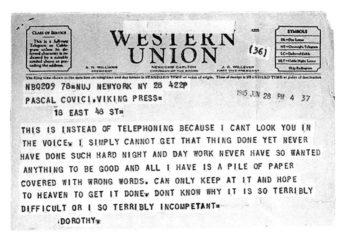

A 1945 telegram from Dorothy Parker to her editor

Parker loathed the writing process and barely managed to get her articles in on time. She never followed any particular writing routine, although when she was a reviewer for *The New Yorker* there was a kind of weekly routine, a push-and-pull act between the reluctant author and her editor, which Marion Meade describes in her biography of Parker:

> Almost from the outset, she set a precedent of being late with her copy, which was due at *The New Yorker* on Fridays. On Sunday mornings, someone from the magazine would telephone. Dorothy, reassuring, said that the column was finished except for the last paragraph and promised to have it for them within the hour. Throughout the day, the same routine would be repeated several times. Occasionally, she would claim she had just ripped up the column because it was awful. At that point, she would start writing.

She did this with all her editors. An editor at *The Saturday Evening Post* remembered the process this way: "You sit around and wait for her to finish what she has begun. That is, if she has begun. The probability is that she hasn't begun." An editor at *Esquire* confirmed that Parker "had a miserable time writing," and compared the process of extracting copy to a difficult childbirth, with the editor as obstetrician—the operation was, he said, a "high-forceps delivery." Parker hated it as much as her editors did, but she couldn't change. She was once asked by an interviewer what she did for fun. "Everything that isn't writing is fun," she replied.

Edna Ferber (1885–1968)

"I know of no professional writer who doesn't get to work every day as does a stenographer or a bus driver or a President of the United States," Ferber wrote in her 1963 autobiography, *A Kind of Magic.* "The difference is that the writer is accountable to no one but himself, which makes for a tough taskmaster; and the writer works as a rule seven days a week instead of the usual worker's five."

From the age of twenty-one until the end of her life, Ferber sat down at the typewriter every morning at 9:00 a.m. and aimed for one thousand words a day. Although she didn't always meet this mark, she often did, producing twelve novels, twelve short-story collections, nine plays, and two autobiographies in her fifty-year career. (In 1921, she won the Pulitzer Prize for her novel *So Big,* although she is probably better known for her novels *Show Boat, Cimarron,* and *Giant.*) The author's writing surroundings were unimportant; over the years, Ferber said, she had trained herself to work in virtually any conditions: "I have written in bathrooms and aboard ships; on jet planes and in woodsheds; on trains between New York and San Francisco or Paris to Madrid; in bed at home or propped up on a hospital contraption; in hotels; cellars, motels, automobiles; well or ill, happy or despairing."

There was one exception to this rule. When Ferber built her dream house in Connecticut, she had the opportunity to create her ideal workroom, a second-floor study with "caramel carpet, soft green walls, fireplace, bookshelves, armchair, desk-chair, desk, typewriter"—and three windows, facing east, west, and south, with expansive views of her thirty-five-acre estate. Soon, however, she dragged her desk away from the windows to face the room's one blank wall. She immediately felt better. "A room with a View," she declared, "is not a room in which a working writer can write."

Margaret Mitchell (1900–1949)

Mitchell began writing *Gone with the Wind,* her first novel, around 1928 and finally handed it over to a visiting editor in the fall of 1935. Though she had been a successful journalist before turning to fiction, Mitchell found novel-writing exceptionally difficult. "I do not write with ease, nor am I ever pleased with anything I write," she said in a letter, and she told an interviewer, "Writing is a hard job for me. Night after night I have labored and labored and have wound up with no more than two pages. After reading those efforts on the morning after, I have whittled and whittled until I had no more than six lines salvaged. Then I had to start all over again." She estimated that, with a few exceptions, each chapter of *Gone with the Wind* was rewritten "at least twenty times."

Mitchell wrote in the living room, wearing a green eye-shade and men's pants to simulate the newsroom conditions that had proved congenial in her earlier career. As she wrote, she felt the presence of "something strange, something headlong and desperate," she said. She didn't write every day, or on any kind of strict timetable; indeed, she frequently took weeks and months away from the book, often because of various accidents and ailments (some of which were certainly more mental than physical in nature—Mitchell was a dedicated hypochondriac). When she was working, Mitchell was obsessive about her privacy. "I not only did not ask anyone to assist me but I fought violently against letting even close friends read as much as a line," she said in 1936. Many of her friends didn't even learn of *Gone with the Wind*'s existence until it was nearly done, and they knew nothing about the plot until it was published. Once, when a friend showed up unannounced, surprising Mitchell at her typewriter, the author leapt from her seat and threw a bath towel over the table.

Even after the tremendous success of *Gone with the Wind*—which sold millions of copies, was made into a classic movie, and won the Pulitzer Prize in 1937—Mitchell was never tempted to write another book. "I wouldn't go through this again for anything," she said.

Marian Anderson (1897–1993)

Anderson was an American contralto who, in 1955, became the first black soloist to appear at the Metropolitan Opera, in New York. The conductor Arturo Toscanini said she had "a voice such as one hears once in a hundred years." In her autobiography, Anderson wrote about her method of learning a new song, a more complex and delicate process than audiences might imagine. "I like to hear the melody first, to get something from the music before I have begun serious work on the words," she wrote.

> Then I read the [words] apart from the music; I want to know what it is about. I want to know something about the way in which the song was written. I try to saturate myself in everything that relates to it. When I put words and music together I try to reach deeply into the mood. If I concentrate, and if there is nothing in the song to create unexpected difficulties, the task is not hard.
>
> It is not always easy, however, to concentrate; your mind has to be free of distractions. Household and family obligations have their rights, and do occupy my thoughts a great deal, and other calls on my time may intrude. No matter how study has gone during the day, I take the songs to bed with me. Just before one is ready to sleep there comes the time of complete relaxation, and one lives the mood of the music. Suddenly one is wide awake, completely lost in the spirit of the song, and in a few hours, while all is still around one, a great deal is accomplished.

"Music is an elusive thing," Anderson continued. Some weeks she worked on a song every day without making any

*Marian Anderson performing at the Lincoln Memorial,
Washington, D.C., 1939*

progress. "Then," she wrote, "suddenly there is a flash of understanding. What has appeared useless labor for days becomes fruitful at an unpredictable moment."

Leontyne Price (b. 1927)

When she was nine years old, Price was taken by her mother to Jackson, Mississippi, to hear Marian Anderson sing. From the moment Anderson opened her mouth Price knew exactly what she wanted to do with her life, and against long odds she achieved her dream, rising from the segregated South to the Juilliard School of Music in New York City

Leontyne Price in rehearsal, 1962

and, eventually, the Metropolitan Opera, becoming one of the Met's leading sopranos in the 1960s. According to the biographer Hugh Lee Lyon, Price's performance days followed an invariable routine: "On the day of a performance she gets up late and has a brunch consisting of a big glass of orange juice, two boiled eggs and *café au lait*," Lyon writes. "At five o'clock, she usually has a steak, baked potato, salad and coffee. Then Lulu Schumaker [her live-in housekeeper] prepares her a vacuum of hot broth to take with her to the opera house. She sips some of the broth between some of the scenes." More important than Price's daily routine, however, was her performance schedule, which needed to incorporate plenty of time off between dates. If at all possible, Price would not agree to more than two performances every eight to ten days. "Opera is a very tricky thing," she once explained. "It demands a lot. You need a day before a performance to prepare; the day of the performance to crack up, if you have to; and the day after to recuperate. How can you sing on either of those days? You blow your brains out and are exhausted which, believe me, I'll never do again. I much prefer to sing on my interest than my capital."

Gertrude Lawrence (1898–1952)

Lawrence was an English actress best known for her performances in Noël Coward's comedies and musicals—including 1930's *Private Lives,* which he wrote with her in mind—and also noted for her vivaciousness onstage and in person. (When a fan once asked Lawrence's doctor what vitamins she took to be so energetic, the doctor replied, "Vitamins should take Gertrude Lawrence.") In the fall of 1939, Lawrence gave a reporter a rundown of her typical workday:

> My day starts at 8 a.m. This usually shocks people when they hear it. The popular impression is that every actress sleeps until noon. So why do I get up so early? Well, I've loads to do. I have to exercise to keep in good

physical condition, and then a quarter of an hour for massage of feet and ankles to keep these useful appendages slim and unweary. Then, breakfast in bed. But no ham or eggs or marmalade or pancakes. Just fruit and coffee. Next, the morning mail . . . fan letters, letters about plays, business matters and lastly of course social correspondence. I have a secretary to help me, but even so dictating an answer to every single letter takes oftentimes until noon. Of course, personal letters I answer by hand. Then, while my secretary is typing, I relax before lunch by arranging flowers. . . . When these are all beautifully arranged in bowls and vases, it's usually lunch time. If there is half an hour to spare, my secretary and I play a game of chess. This is not only a splendid game but teaches you to concentrate. Lunch, which follows this busy morning, is a simple meal of vegetables and salad. Afterwards I sew for a while. I enjoy making old-fashioned samples, but usually there is not a very long time for this quiet occupation before my producer's representatives call. They visit me every day to discuss the problems that naturally arise in every production. After they leave me there are usually some new scripts to be read. After this I take Mackie my Highland terrier for a walk, thus giving both of us the necessary daily exercise. If I have shopping to do or visits to make, this is the time I do it—but always when I'm playing I make it a rule to be home in time for two hours' rest before going to the theatre, relaxing before the evening's work and making up for too brief sleep at night. I don't like to eat before I go to the theatre. After the performance I am usually very hungry, and I have a big meal usually with friends, for if I eat alone I seldom eat enough. It's well after midnight before I am home again and ready to go to bed. And this is what people call a glamorous and romantic life. There may be glamour and romance about certain phases of it, but let's nobody imagine that it isn't mostly hard and tireless work. I travel too much to have a real home, and I always say that a new play takes a year off one's life.

This description was from shortly before Lawrence married her second husband, the naval officer Richard Aldrich, who soon witnessed her pre- and post-performance rituals firsthand—and who discovered that Lawrence was indeed very hungry at the end of the night. He recalled, "At such times there was nothing she enjoyed more than steak tartare—the chopped raw beefsteak mixed with chopped green onion and a whole raw egg favored by stars of grand opera after an exhausting performance. With this she would drink a tankard of Canadian ale." Aldrich was frankly shocked. His new bride—"the exquisite, ethereal creature" he and so many others admired onstage—could, he wrote, "put away a meal I had hitherto associated only with ponderous Brunhildes and the drivers of transcontinental trucks."

Edith Head (1897–1981)

"To be a good designer in Hollywood, one has to be a combination of psychiatrist, artist, fashion designer, dress-maker, pin cushion, historian, nurse maid and purchasing agent too," Head once said. She would know: Over her six-decade career, Head designed costumes for more than eleven hundred films, was nominated for forty-five Academy Awards (and won eight of them), and became a style icon in her own

right, instantly recognizable by her short bangs, her monochrome two-piece suits, and the dark glasses she wore all the
time, indoors and out. Head started out in Paramount Studios' costume department as a twenty-six-year-old former
schoolteacher, and worked her way up the ranks, eventually
becoming the golden-age costume designer Travis Banton's
second-in-command. When Banton left Paramount in 1938,
Head took over the department. "There was no fanfare, no
dramatic transition, no popping of champagne corks, no
raise in salary," she remembered decades later. "I had been
working six days a week, fifteen hours a day, and I continued
this routine." Through the 1930s and 1940s, she worked on
thirty to forty films a year, often dressing all the stars, male
and female, for four or five films at once.

She succeeded due to her artistry and work ethic, but also
because of her skill at navigating the big personalities and
hot tempers of a Hollywood production; indeed, Head said
that she was "a better politician than I am a designer. I know
who to please." In an ideal world, she would have liked to be
more of a perfectionist about her work, but the realities of
Hollywood filmmaking simply didn't allow it. "Inside I was
a prima donna who insisted that a costume be made my way
or not at all," Head said; "outside I was the model employee,
easy to get along with and always on time." Working in Hollywood, she added, "I learned to suppress my artistic needs."

As for her signature wardrobe, that, too, grew out of necessity. When she took over Paramount's costume department,
Head quickly grasped the importance of letting the actors be
the absolute center of attention. "I never use color in the room
in which I work or my offices or my fitting rooms," she said.

And I never wear color myself. I mean *never.* I wear
beige, occasionally gray (my favorite shade is a beigy-

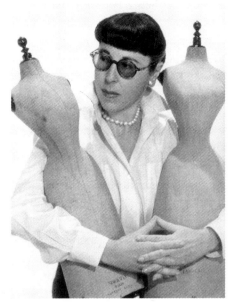

Edith Head, circa 1955

gray) or white or black. When I stand behind a glamorous star who's fitting a glamorous dress, I don't want to be an eye-catcher. I want the actors to concentrate on themselves. Any distraction such as pictures on the wall or the reflection of me in a very fashionable or brightly colored dress would only take their eye away from their image. I play down how chic I can look. An actor must be totally absorbed with how he or she appears.

"When I'm at the studio, I'm always little Edith in the dark glasses and the little beige suit," she said on another occasion. "That's how I survived."

Marlene Dietrich (1901–1992)

"Dietrich was not difficult; she was a perfectionist," recalled Edith Head, who dressed the German actress for several films beginning in the late 1930s.

> She had incredible discipline and energy. She could work all day to the point of exhaustion, then catch a second breath and work all night just to get something right. Once we worked thirty-six hours straight—from early Monday to late Tuesday—preparing a costume for her to wear on the set Wednesday night. . . . I was amazed at her stamina and determination.

Another costume designer who worked with Dietrich said that she "would come directly from the plane through the prop room and stand motionless for eight or nine hours a day in front of mirrors while we made the dresses *on* her." She was equally a perfectionist about film makeup, lighting, and editing, the finer points of which she had absorbed through her intense collaboration with the director Josef von Sternberg, who brought her to international stardom with the 1930 film *The Blue Angel* and six subsequent films. Away from the studio, Dietrich hardly relented; she held any form of idleness in contempt. "It is a sin to do nothing," she wrote. "There is always something useful to be done." Around the house, she regarded cooking and housework as among "the greatest occupational therapies," and went at them both with gusto. "The more plentiful the work," she wrote, "the less time to be neurotic."

Ida Lupino (1918–1995)

Born in England to a long line of performers, Lupino moved to Hollywood in the 1930s and initially made her mark as a worldly-wise actress in such films as *They Drive by Night, High Sierra,* and *The Sea Wolf.* But Lupino "never really liked acting," she once said. "It's a torturous profession and plays havoc with your private life." In 1949 she and her second husband founded an independent production company and Lupino began writing and directing a string of low-budget films that confronted such social taboos as rape, illegitimacy, and bigamy. In 1953, she released what may be her master-piece, *The Hitch-Hiker,* a tense thriller considered the only film noir by a woman. In the subsequent decades, Lupino made only one more feature film, but she was a frequent director for the small screen, lending her talents to scores of television series, including *Alfred Hitchcock Presents, Bewitched, Gilligan's Island,* and *The Twilight Zone.*

Of course sexism was an obstacle for Lupino, who tack-led it through relentless professionalism. "As soon as I get a script I go to work on it," she said. "I study and I prepare and when the time comes to shoot, my mind is usually made up and I go ahead, right or wrong." Whenever possible, she would use the weekend to prepare for the week ahead. "I go out on the back lot or to the sets on Saturday and Sunday," she said, "when it is nice and quiet, and map out my set-ups." (As a writer, she was not quite so organized. According to the biographer William Donati, "Ida would sometimes write for twenty-four hours straight, scribbling on anything at hand, from odd bits of paper to grocery bags.")

On set, Lupino also employed a calculated maternal façade; the cast and crew got into the habit of calling her

Ida Lupino in her director's chair, circa 1948

Mother, a nickname she encouraged. "Keeping a feminine approach is vital," she once explained.

Men hate bossy females. You do not tell a man; you suggest to him. "Darlings, Mother has a problem. I'd love to do this. Can you do it? It sounds kooky, I know. But can you do this for Mother? And, they do it. That way I got more cooperation. I tried to never blow up. A woman cannot afford to do that. They're waiting for it. . . . As long as you keep your temper, the crew will go along with you. I loved being called Mother.

Betty Comden [1917–2006]

Comden was one-half of the longest-running writing team in Broadway history; her sixty-year creative partnership with Adolph Green produced such hits as *On the Town, Wonderful Town, Bells Are Ringing,* and *Peter Pan,* and the duo also wrote the scripts for several Hollywood musicals, including 1952's *Singin' in the Rain.* Virtually every day, Comden and Green met in the living room of Comden's Manhattan apartment to work on their next show, although their meetings didn't always look much like work. "We stare at each other," Comden said in 1977.

> We meet, whether we have a project or not, just to keep up a continuity of working. There are long periods when nothing happens, and it's just boring and disheartening. But we have a theory that nothing's wasted, even those long days of staring at one another. You sort of have to believe that, don't you? That you had to go through all that to get to the day when something did happen.

The idea for *Bells Are Ringing* took them, Green said, "a year of sitting around." In interviews, they were sometimes pressed to describe their creative process in greater detail, to little avail. Comden once allowed that she tended to be the one who did the actual writing—on a pad of paper or, later, a typewriter—while Green paced about the room. But, she said, "at the end of the day we don't know who contributed what idea or what line."

Outsiders often assumed that Comden and Green were married to each other, but they were never romantically involved, and each enjoyed decades-long marriages to other people. ("Confusion still reigns," Comden wrote in her memoir, *Off Stage*. "I always say as long as we are not confused, everything is all right.") When asked what cemented their long working relationship, Green suggested the common element might have been hunger. Comden floated a different theory. "Sheer fear and terror," she said.

PURE NEGLECT

Zoe Akins [1886–1958]

Akins's youthful ambition was "to write seven good poems before I die," but the Missouri native also had "an indomitable hankering after the theatre," and it was there that she made her mark, eventually writing or adapting more than forty plays, eighteen of which appeared on Broadway; in 1935 she won the Pulitzer Prize for her adaptation of Edith Wharton's *The Old Maid.* She tended to write in streaks of fluency surrounded by long periods of idleness. "I write, when I write, very rapidly and to an end that is in certain view before I take up the pen," Akins explained in a 1921 essay for *The New York Times,* adding that she had several times written an entire act of a play in "one prolonged sitting." But she needed a lot of space around her writing time, which meant keeping her schedule as open as possible:

I prefer for an act of a play or a story or section of a novel to have a week ahead of me, in which all engagements are absolutely contingent upon my last-moment mood, and then loaf along the job, writing slowly and with my critical faculties very alert. But the appalling fact is that almost no one who leads a civilized life and whose friends are busy people can get a week ahead for such a program except, of course, by an unsettling change of surroundings—by going into the isolation of a strange place or by giving up much that he is anxious to enjoy and going on a sort of social diet that requires more strength of character than most of us—I, particularly—happen to have. Frankly, I've never been able to achieve any sort of order or method in my life or my work, and one result is that most of my friends have found me a procrastinator, an idler, a spendthrift of their time and my own and the most undependable and disappointing of associates. All of which is true. But somehow, sometime, the inevitable moment comes when renouncement is easy for the sake of that empty stretch of time down which one may travel with an idea. And once away upon that empty stretch all that makes life trivial as well as pleasant is left behind: fortunes of the individual are of no more importance, for the adventure of the artist has begun.

Agnes Martin (1912–2004)

"I have a vacant mind, in order to do exactly what inspiration calls for," the Canadian American painter said in 1997. Twenty-one years earlier, she had told another interviewer much the same thing: "Inspiration comes from a clear mind. Right straight through. We have nothing to do with it." But inspiration, for Martin, didn't simply arrive; it had to be courted, and it was essential that the artist create the proper physical conditions for it to flourish. "The most important thing is to have a studio and establish and preserve its atmosphere," Martin wrote.

> You must have a studio no matter what kind of artist you are. A musician who must practice in the living

room is at a tremendous disadvantage. You must gather together in your studio all of your sensibilities and when they are gathered you must not be disturbed. The murdered inspirations and loss of art work due to interruptions and shattered studio atmosphere are unassessable.

As for an artist's working hours—they should be long; otherwise, Martin wasn't particularly interested in work schedules. "I don't get up in the morning until I know exactly what I'm going to do," she said. "Sometimes, I stay in bed until about three in the afternoon, without any breakfast. You see, I have a visual image. But then to accurately put it down is a long, long way from just knowing what you're going to do." Again, the crucial component for Martin was vast stretches of uninterrupted time, with a near-total absence of competing obligations—and, most important, no meddling from neighbors or visitors. "When you're with other people, your mind isn't your own," she said.

This passion for solitude drove Martin to live alone for almost all of her adult life, and to spend decades in remote portions of New Mexico, where she interacted with only a handful of locals and, very occasionally, her gallerist in New York—who, by the 1970s, was selling her work for increasingly large sums. Still, Martin never upgraded her lifestyle beyond the most primitive living conditions. For years, she worked in a studio with no electricity or running water and slept in a camper mounted in the back of a pickup truck, where she had heat, a gas stove, an oven, and a refrigerator, but, again, no electricity or running water; instead of a toilet she used a chamber pot that she emptied into a hole dug a short distance away.

In the book *Agnes Martin and Me,* the photographer

Donald Woodman—who was Martin's neighbor, on-call handyman, and landlord-of-sorts between 1977 and 1984—provided more details of the artist's daily life in New Mexico:

> For as long as I knew her, Agnes's daily uniform was standard Bibb coveralls with which, depending on the weather, she wore either a long- or short-sleeved insulated t-shirt underneath. Her studio was heated with a woodstove, which was essential because she preferred to paint during daylight hours in the winter. As a painting progressed, she would sit for endless hours in a rocking chair and stare at the canvas, evaluating her work. She rarely allowed anyone into the studio to see work in progress—or even the finished paintings, which she kept stacked against a wall.
>
> Many a time I would see her sitting in the camper staring out the window—usually before she started a new series. On more than one occasion, she would call out through an open window, "I bet you think I'm not working, but I am! I am thinking about what I shall paint. I am meditating."

When she wasn't painting or meditating on her work, Martin liked to read paperback murder mysteries, which she would purchase by the bagful from a book exchange in Santa Fe. At one point she built a rudimentary swimming pool and swam in it daily, and she always grew vegetables in a garden plot outside her studio, although Woodman reports that her gardening technique was unusual: Rather than planting several different kinds of vegetables, she would choose one variety and fill the entire garden with it. "One year it was corn, another broccoli, then tomatoes, and so on," he writes. Occasionally Martin would invite Woodman over for dinner, which "might include eggs from her chickens (along with an occasional hen), peanut butter and jelly sandwiches, plus sliced, packaged meats like a ham roll in addition to the homegrown vegetables."

As all of the above suggests, Martin was more than just eccentric; she experienced schizophrenic episodes throughout her life, and many times she referred to the voices in her head that directed her painting. But Woodman, who probably had more firsthand experience of these episodes than anyone, was careful to note that her practice could not be reduced to the statement that "she painted what her voices told her to paint. It is more the opposite: that she had to quiet those voices in order to reach the core of what she wanted to paint, which took an incredible act of will." Martin herself affirmed the immense commitment required. "You're permanently derailed," she said. "It's through discipline and tremendous disappointment and failure that you arrive at what it is you must paint. . . . For months, the first paintings don't mean anything—nothing. But you have to keep going, despite all kinds of disappointments."

Katherine Mansfield (1888–1923)

The New Zealand–born writer was a master of the short story—and, judging by her published journals, also a master of the writerly arts of procrastination, self-doubt, and self-castigation. Mansfield tried to write every day but frequently failed to do so, heaping blame on herself while also wondering if it was really so bad for her to take a day off. "Well I must confess I have had an idle day—god knows why," Mansfield wrote in a representative example from 1921.

> All was to be written but I just didn't write it. I thought I would but I felt tired after tea and rested instead. Is it good or bad in me to behave so? I have a sense of guilt but at the same time I know that to rest is the very best thing I can do. . . . There is so much to do and I do so little. Life would be almost perfect here if only when I was *pretending* to work I always was working. But that is surely not too hard? Look at the stories that wait and wait just at the threshold. Why don't I let them in? And their place would be taken by others who are lurking just beyond out there—waiting for the chance.

Mansfield had a better excuse than most writers for taking a day off: Because of the tuberculosis that was diagnosed when she was seventeen (and that would ultimately kill her at age thirty-four), she needed the physical rest. And she also had to admit that her nonwriting days were, in the end, just as important as the more conventionally productive ones. "What happens as a rule is, if I go on long enough I *break through*," Mansfield wrote in her journal. "It's rather like tossing very large flat stones into the stream. The question is, though, how long this will prove efficacious. Up till now, I own, it never has failed me. . . ."

Katherine Anne Porter [1890–1980]

Porter lived a long life but published relatively little: twenty-seven stories and one novel, *Ship of Fools,* which took her twenty years to write. The Texas-born author had some good reasons for her modest output. For one, she didn't start writing seriously until her early thirties, after two failed marriages—the first to an abusive husband—and a string of "little dull jobs," including as an actress, a singer, a secretary, a newspaper reporter, and a ghostwriter. Along the way she nearly died during the 1918 outbreak of Spanish influenza, an experience that, she said later, marked a decisive turning point. "It just simply divided my life, cut across it like that," Porter told *The Paris Review* in 1963. "So that everything before that was just getting ready, and after that I was in some strange way altered, ready."

Porter published her first short story four years later, in 1922, and her first collection of stories in 1930, when she was forty. That book, *Flowering Judas,* was rapturously received by critics but sold little, a pattern that would hold true for her next two story collections, 1939's *Pale Horse, Pale Rider* and 1944's *The Leaning Tower and Other Stories.* Because her books never made much money, Porter had to piece together an income through speaking engagements, writing residencies, fellowships, and other temporary gigs, which she often cited as the reason she wasn't more prolific. "I think I've only spent about ten percent of my energies on writing," she said. "The other ninety percent went to keeping my head above water."

Outside observers didn't always find this excuse persuasive. The poet Marianne Moore called Porter the world's worst procrastinator, and Truman Capote's unfinished final

Katherine Anne Porter, 1947

novel includes a thinly fictionalized version of Porter, whose "prestige depended upon a controlled and limited output; and, in those terms, she was a royal success, the queen of the writer-in-residence swindle, the prizes racket, the high-honorarium con, the grants-in-aid-to-struggling-artists shit." There's no doubt that Porter courted a certain amount of distraction in her life, especially when it came to relationships. Shortly before her fortieth birthday, she told one acquaintance that she had had four husbands and thirty-seven lovers, and she continued adding to the latter tally throughout her life; according to the biographer Joan Givner, Porter "never did resist the temptation to abandon her work and throw herself single-mindedly into one more affair."

In her own defense, Porter always claimed that she needed long periods away from writing to do her best work. "It doesn't actually take me a long time to write," she told an interviewer in 1969. "I write at top speed, but there are long intervals because things form slowly, slowly, and I don't write until it's absolutely ready to go." This worked well for her short stories, which she would generally write in concentrated bursts of a week or so, often in a rented room someplace where she wouldn't be disturbed. With a novel, she couldn't rely on the same system, which explains the two decades that elapsed between her starting and finishing *Ship of Fools*. Porter finally completed the book by taking a three-year lease on a quiet, isolated house in Connecticut, where she worked with uncommon (for her) daily dedication. She told *The Paris Review*:

> I went up and sat nearly three years in the country, and while I was writing it I worked every day, anywhere from three to five hours. Oh, it's true I used to do an awful lot of just sitting there thinking what comes next, because this is a great big unwieldy book with an enormous cast of characters. . . . But all that time in Connecticut, I kept myself free for work: no telephone, no visitors: oh, I really lived like a hermit, everything but being fed through a grate! But it is, as Yeats said, a "solitary sedentary trade." And I did a lot of gardening, and cooked my own food, and listened to music, and of course I would read. I was really very happy. I can live a solitary life for months at a time, and it does me good,

because I'm working. I just get up bright and early—
sometimes at five o'clock—have my black coffee, and
go to work.

As much as she relished that solitary writing period, Porter
never considered making it a permanent condition. Her writing came from life, and she was dismissive of writers who
sought out long-term isolation. "Any such alienation from
society is death," Porter said in 1961. "You may live in an
attic, and you'll probably have fine company if you do, but
first you have to become a human being."

Bridget Riley (b. 1931)

"An artist feels a need 'to do something' about the very fact
of being alive, rather like a bird feels the need to sing," the
celebrated English painter said in 1998. But this does not
mean that Riley's artistic output is spontaneous or emotion-
driven—quite the opposite. The style of painting Riley has
practiced since the 1960s, when she electrified the London art
world with her so-called Op Art canvases—trippy black-and-
white paintings that toyed with and sometimes assaulted the
viewer's perceptual equipment—involves a lot of premedita-
tion, preliminary work, and the constant application of her
critical faculties. All of Riley's paintings begin as drawings,
and the artist makes numerous exploratory sketches for each
new painting, feeling her way by trial and error toward an
effective composition. "In a daydream way I have a sort of
hunger about what I am going to do, or rather about the sensation I want the painting to precipitate or convey," she said

Bridget Riley in her studio, 1979

in 1988. "It's actually bringing this sensation into existence that is the difficulty; what Cézanne called 'realization.' "

It is a slow process, which Riley regards as a good thing. Painting, she has said,

> takes and needs time and this is its great advantage. An artist needs enough time to reflect, to revise, to explore various directions, to make changes, to lay foundations. You have to build up a working routine—you have to

be able to surprise yourself and, above all, to make mistakes. And if you are a painter then you are fortunate because the practice of painting allows for all of this.

"Boredom is a tremendous indicator," Riley has said. "Your energy goes; it caves in on you; you can't do anything. That's very frightening but you must listen because you are being told that whatever it is you are doing is not quite right. It may only need a small adjustment or it may need more drastic treatment." Riley has learned to trust her intuition above all else: "It's not right if it doesn't *feel* right," she has said. Employing assistants who do most of the actual painting is an added advantage, Riley believes, because it allows her to be a spectator of her own work. "I am not at all interested in any sort of liberation from the working process; quite the reverse," she has said. "Holding myself at a certain distance enables me to be more engaged, not less. One of my assistants once said to me: 'We do the nice part, and you do the hard work.' It seems to me that it is in making the decisions—rejecting and accepting, altering and revising—that an artist's deeper, real personality comes through."

Julie Mehretu (b. 1970)

Born in Ethiopia and raised in Michigan, Mehretu studied art at Kalamazoo College and the Rhode Island School of Design before moving to New York in 1999. She is known for her densely layered paintings populated by abstract shapes, architectural drawings, and clusters of calligraphic markings—elements presented most dramatically in her twenty-three-by-eighty-foot *Mural* installed in the lobby of the Goldman Sachs building in lower Manhattan in 2009, a monumental project that required two years of work by Mehretu and her crew of up to thirty assistants. After completing *Mural,* Mehretu scaled back her enterprise to a core group of several assistants, many of whom have worked with her for years. "I don't have to manage them in any way," Mehretu said in 2016. "If anything, they manage me."

Mehretu lives on 118th Street and works in her studio on 26th Street, driving back and forth each day on the West Side Highway. "That drive along the river is part of my decompression into work," she said, "and then the drive back is a kind of release from the studio into life. Somehow the texture of the river, the color of the river, the color of the sky and clouds—it all becomes part of the movement from the studio to home and from home to the studio." Mehretu tries to get to the studio between 9:00 and 9:30 a.m., and the first thing she does is go through her emails, although she doesn't necessarily reply to them. ("I'm a bad avoider of email," she said.) Then she puts on her headphones—usually listening to podcasts or audiobooks—and starts moving around the studio, looking at the painting she's working on, trying to find an "entry point." And then, she said, "I usually just start working."

Mehretu works until lunch, typically eaten in the studio with her assistants. After lunch, she'll put her headphones back on and continue painting, or she'll sit in a chair and read for thirty minutes to an hour first. She tries to leave the studio by 5:30 or 6:00 p.m. so she can spend a couple of hours with her two young sons before they go to bed. In the past, Mehretu worked significantly longer hours, but she thinks that she's actually become more productive since having kids.

"I've been able to use my time much more wisely and much more potently," she said, "and I don't waste as much time." Occasionally, she will go back to the studio after her sons go to bed, but she tries to avoid doing that, using the evenings to recharge so she can work with maximum intensity during the day.

In the studio, some days feel like they fly by; other days, Mehretu said, "it doesn't go as smoothly and it feels like a grind." Occasionally, there will be a half-day or even an entire day where, she said, "you're just staring and staring and you can't find a point of entry." When that happens, she might go for a walk and visit a gallery or museum exhibition. But often staying in the studio is the most productive thing. Mehretu calls painting a "time-based medium," and emphasizes that viewers need to allow time with paintings, to let each painting work on them; a quick look is not sufficient. Mehretu spends "a lot of time" looking at her paintings, and in doing so she tries to "kind of disembody myself," she said. Sometimes, she added, "my head gets in the way and it messes things up"—so she has to put aside or squash down her everyday thoughts in order to really go into the work. There are no shortcuts. "When I had my first child, and I would be in the studio but I wouldn't be working, and I would just be staring—I felt really guilty about it," Mehretu said. "But then I realized it's such an important part of the process, and so much comes from that process of just connecting with the work in a way where you intuitively know it. . . . It's not a rational knowledge of the work. And that happens through that time-based experience of passing those hours with the work, I think. So I've become much more comfortable with that."

Rachel Whiteread (b. 1963)

The English sculptor gets up at 6:30 or 6:45 a.m., helps get her two sons out the door to school, and takes the bus a couple of miles to her London studio, arriving between 8:00 and 9:00 a.m. She works there—alone or with an assistant who comes in a few days a week—until sometime between 5:00 and 7:00 p.m. Whiteread's sculptures are often monumental works that involve complicated on-site logistics—she is probably best known for 1993's *House,* a concrete cast of the interior of a three-story Victorian terrace house in East London—so in the studio she usually works via drawings, using ink and paper to tease out ideas and to think about composition and color. Almost always, BBC's Radio 4 will be playing in the background while she works. At some point she'll stop for lunch, and she'll often spend an hour of the day reading, sitting in a comfortable chair away from her desk. (She has a library in the studio and reads "philosophy, psychology, novels, poetry—a little bit of everything," she said.) When Whiteread hits a creative block, which does happen, there is no magic formula for overcoming it. "You just carry on working and making drawings and just doing the same thing over again," she said. "I think it's important to keep on working that way, otherwise you can't get yourself out of it."

Alice Walker (b. 1944)

Walker wrote her third novel, *The Color Purple,* in the late 1970s, working on it weekdays between 10:30 a.m. and 3:00 p.m. while her daughter was at school. (Thanks to a

Guggenheim Fellowship, she was able to work full-time on the book, or at least all the time that her elementary-school-age daughter was out of the house.) She planned to give herself five years to finish the book, but after less than a year she found herself writing the last page. Walker wrote fast, but only because she spent so much time thinking about the book before she began writing—indeed, Walker has said that for new books she requires gestation periods of a year or two before she can actually put pen to paper. She uses that time to think deeply about the book, and to "just clear the horizon for one thing," which she considers an indispensable precondition for writing. As she put it in 2006, "In order to invite any kind of guest, including creativity, you have to make room for it."

If this makes Walker's process sound fairly straightforward, the reality is more complicated. In 1982, she published an essay about *The Color Purple*'s genesis that describes what it was like living with the novel's characters for the year or so leading up to that one year of writing. In the beginning Walker was settled in Brooklyn, but her characters, she wrote, found the big city disagreeable. "What is all this tall shit anyway?" they would ask. So Walker packed up and moved across the country to San Francisco—but here, too, her characters were unhappy; they needed a setting closer to the small town in Georgia where their story took place. So Walker moved again, this time renting a small cottage in an apple orchard in Boonville, California, a couple hours north of San Francisco. There, her characters finally started talking to her. "We would sit wherever I was sitting, and talk," Walker wrote. "They were very obliging, engaging, and jolly. They were, of course, at the end of their story but were telling it to me from the beginning." But then Walker's daughter,

Rebecca—who had been staying with her father, Walker's ex-husband, on the East Coast during all these moves—came to join the author and her characters in Boonville. At first, it was an uneasy détente. The characters, Walker wrote, "just quieted down, didn't visit as much, and took a firm Well, let's us wait and see attitude." Fortunately, they soon returned—Walker's characters decided that they "adored" her daughter, especially the novel's protagonist, Celie. Walker writes, "So, just when Rebecca would arrive home [from school] needing her mother and a hug, there'd be Celie, trying to give her both."

Rebecca Walker later became a writer herself, and her version of this story is considerably less rosy; in her telling, being the child of an author who was so deeply absorbed in her characters' lives was profoundly destabilizing. (As an adult, she eventually stopped speaking to her mother entirely.) For her part, Alice Walker has been unapologetic about the choices she made in order to realize her life's work. "I don't know if I've ever cared much what others think," she said in 2014. "I've always felt quite singular, even as a child. That I must stay on track to keep my purpose."

Carole King (b. 1942)

The American singer-songwriter—who has written or cowritten more than one hundred pop hits, and whose 1971 album *Tapestry* is one of the best-selling albums of all time—is a die-hard morning person. "I'm one of those really inconsiderate early-morning people that nocturnal people hate," King wrote in her 2012 memoir, *A Natural Woman*. "Never giving a thought to whether someone might be sleeping in the next room, I rattle the cereal box, clink the spoon while stirring my tea, and yell at the top of my lungs to a dawdling child, 'Hurry up or you'll miss the bus!' "

As a songwriter, however, King has had to learn to be a bit more relaxed, and let the process move on its own timeline. In a 1989 interview, she shared her secret to avoiding writer's block:

I have found that the key to not being blocked is not to worry about it. Ever.

If you are sitting down and you feel that you want to write and nothing is coming, you get up and do something else. Then you come back and try it again. But you do it in a relaxed manner. *Trust* that it will be there. If it ever was once and you've ever done it once, it will be back. It always comes back and the only thing that is a problem is when you get in your own way worrying about it.

King added that, in her experience, the creative channel usually opened up again after an hour or so; but sometimes it took a day or a week or even a few months. No matter what, she didn't worry about it. The key, she wrote in her memoir, was to let the subconscious mind work away at the problem, without the ego trying to assert control. "When the ego is in charge, that's when the work is coming *from* you," she wrote. "You may still be doing good work but the ego allows doubt to creep in." By contrast, "when the thing you're creating comes *through* you, you know it, and it's much better than good enough."

Andrea Zittel (b. 1965)

Zittel is an American artist who since 2000 has lived and worked in the high desert of Joshua Tree, California. Because of the extreme climate—with summer highs surpassing 100 degrees Fahrenheit and winter lows slipping below freezing—Zittel's morning routine shifts with the season. In the summer, she is awake and out the door as the sun is rising, beginning her day with a forty-minute hike with her dog. Returning to her residence—a former homestead cabin that she has expanded and updated over the years—Zittel feeds her chickens, waters plants, and performs other outdoor chores before meditating, taking a shower, making breakfast, and getting dressed. In the winter, Zittel's morning schedule reverses: She meditates, showers, and eats breakfast first; then, once the sun has raised the outdoor temperature, she heads out on her hike and does chores. "It's really all about establishing a flexible routine," Zittel said in 2017. "Having a pattern helps ensure that you fit everything into a limited amount of time, but too much of a pattern and you get stuck."

Zittel is rarely alone on her property; her art practice is just one part of a larger enterprise named A–Z West, which also encompasses residency and work-trade programs, and which often hosts group tours of the numerous structures on the sixty-acre site. (In addition to Zittel's residence, there are permanent sculptural installations, multiple workspaces, and a dozen capsule-like "Wagon Stations" just big enough for one person to sleep in.) To avoid getting constantly swept up into the various activities happening at A–Z West, Zittel reserves Mondays and Fridays as personal studio days; in between, she has "three really intense days" in the main studio with her various assistants and collaborators. (Weekends she generally takes off.) And in her personal life, Zittel does as much as possible to pare down decision-making. One of her longstanding beliefs is that creating a set of rigid personal rules can be a way to break free of external societal rules. The most visible manifestation of this approach is Zittel's wardrobe. "Each season I wear a 'uniform'—usually this is an outfit that feels comfortable and looks good that I'll wear for three months straight," she explained. The uniforms evolve every season, and they are for the most part handmade by the artist. Zittel has long fantasized about achieving a similar level of streamlined simplicity in her eating habits, but so far, she said, this has eluded her: "Cooking is one of the few dilemmas that I'll probably never fully solve."

Meredith Monk (b. 1942)

Monk is a composer, singer, director/choreographer, and creator of new music-theater works, operas, films, and installations. Starting in the mid-1960s, she pioneered what has become known as "extended vocal technique," a complex vocabulary of vocal sounds that go beyond the conventional singer's repertoire, expanding the possibilities of the human voice. To develop a new performance, Monk works in alternating periods of solitude and time with others. Her home base is Manhattan, in the TriBeCa loft she has rented since the early 1970s (and that she shares with Neutron, the box tortoise she has kept as a pet since 1978); but her solitary work periods take place at a property she owns in New Mexico, in her "tiny" house in upstate New York, or at the MacDowell Colony in New Hampshire, where she has gone for working retreats several times over the years. When she's in retreat mode, Monk gets up at about 7:00 a.m., meditates for thirty minutes or longer, eats breakfast, reads for a little while, and devotes the remainder of the morning to, in her words, "maintaining my instrument as a singer and mover." This means a series of physical exercises, another series of vocalizing exercises, and piano practice. Then she has lunch, reads a little more, and spends the afternoon conceiving a new performance. This is slow, uncertain work. "I like to start from zero with every piece, even though it's very risky and even terrifying at the beginning," Monk said in 2017. "At some point the fear gives way to interest and curiosity. Over the years I've learned how to tolerate hanging out in the unknown. Discovery begins there."

During this process Monk mostly works at the piano, trying out new musical and vocal ideas. She notates what she's working on in music notebooks, but primarily she uses a four-track tape recorder to capture what she has found. ("God forbid if there gets to be a point where these four-track recorders don't exist anymore," Monk said. "Because I've really tried the digital devices, and they're just too slow for me.") When she's working on an interdisciplinary piece, Monk often draws, makes charts of the various elements, or creates maps of the spatial aspects to help consider an overall structure. A typical afternoon work session lasts about four hours; afterward she has dinner, catches up on correspondence, and sees friends, reads, or watches films. For Monk, these periods of solitary work, particularly at MacDowell, are "so luxurious," she said. "Because you might have a bad day, but then you know that you have the next day. It's that amazing sense of having time and space to really think."

In New York, by contrast, Monk's routine revolves around

rehearsals for upcoming performances. She uses the morning to do an abbreviated version of her retreat day: meditation, vocalizing, piano practice, and solitary work, for about three or four hours altogether. (For a long time she would do her composing at home, but her TriBeCa neighborhood is currently undergoing "wall-to-wall construction," so she has been using a practice room at a local music school instead.) In the afternoon or early evening, Monk's ensemble joins her in her loft for rehearsals. These typically last four hours, and they begin with a physical and vocal warm-up. Monk usually writes down what she wants to accomplish in the rehearsals, and she will sometimes videotape or tape-record them, so she can see or hear what the group has done. Bringing the work she has developed in solitude to the ensemble inevitably changes it, and she uses her morning work sessions to go back and rethink the material and make adjustments. At all stages of the process, Monk strives to become "totally at one with the material," she said. "That is the ultimate goal both in the creative process and in performing." When this happens, she said, "Your consciousness is very pinpointed, focused. Simultaneously, you're absolutely open and deeply relaxed. I don't mean not having any energy; I'm talking about the deepest level of relaxation, a sense of spaciousness, awareness of what's going on in the moment. It's the same thing when you're performing with other people. My ensemble works so much on listening with every ounce of our beings."

Grace Paley (1922–2007)

Paley was a political activist, a teacher, and a writer—of poetry, essays, and three volumes of vivid, highly compressed short stories that are unlike anything else in American fiction. In 1976, an interviewer asked Paley how she managed to write so brilliantly alongside her political work, her teaching, and her responsibilities as a wife and mother. "I remember somebody once asking that and I gave my usual wise-guy remark: pure neglect," she replied.

> . . . But really, I think that any life that's interesting, lived, has a lot of pulls in it. It seems to me natural that I'd be pulled in those ways. When you've got children, you don't want to just hand them over to somebody. It's interesting how children grow and you deprive yourself if you give too much of it away. I don't mean that you don't want to be free, you do, you want all that. But that's again a pull, you're pulled, and it's only one life for Christ's sake. And you are privileged somehow to do as much as you can. I wouldn't give any of it up. And I've talked a lot about this with women's groups because I think that in whatever is gained, that everything, that the world should be gained. But that nothing should be given up. I think a good hard greed is the way to approach life.

Paley's stories usually began, she said, with a sentence—a single sentence that was "absolutely resonant" and suggested a character and a setting. But moving forward from there was slow work. "I'm almost invariably stuck after one page or one paragraph—at which point I have to begin thinking about what the story could possibly be about," she said. "I begin by writing paragraphs that don't have an immediate relation to a plot. The sound of the story comes first." And the thing that carried it forward was pressure—not deadline pressure, but an inner pressure to do justice to that initial storytelling impulse. "Art comes from constant mental harassment," Paley said. "You're bugged."

A BALLOON, A SPACESHIP,
A SUBMARINE, A CLOSET

Susan Sontag (1933–2004)

"Somewhere along the line, one has to choose between the Life and the Project," Sontag said in a 1978 interview. There was never any doubt in her mind about which was the right choice for her. Ever since discovering Modern Library books as a girl browsing a stationery and greeting-card store in Tucson, Arizona, Sontag was determined to escape "that long prison sentence, my childhood" for the world of the writers and intellectuals she idolized. "It never occurred to me that I couldn't live the life I wanted to lead," she said many years later. "It never occurred to me that I could be stopped. . . . I had this very simple view: that the reason people who start out with ideals or aspirations don't do what they dream of doing when they're young is because they quit. I thought, well, I won't quit."

Sontag wasted little time chasing her ideals. She graduated from high school at fifteen, entered the University of Chicago at sixteen, married at seventeen, and gave birth to a son a year and a half later. Her husband was a sociology instructor eleven years her senior, who proposed ten days after their first meeting. Although Sontag was initially thrilled with their life as university intellectuals, the marriage lacked passion, and in 1959 she ended it, moving with her seven-year-old son to New York to start over. Despite having very little money, Sontag refused alimony or child support. She took a temporary job as an editor at the journal *Commentary,* then a series of teaching jobs. Within a few years, she had published a novel and was writing the essays that would make her name.

Sontag succeeded, in large degree, thanks to her seemingly boundless energy: From the moment she arrived in New York, she wanted to read every book, see every movie, go to every party, have every conversation. One friend recalled, only half jokingly, that she "watched twenty Japanese films and read five French novels a week"; another said that, for Sontag, "aiming for a book a day was not too high." Her son, David Rieff, later wrote: "If I had to choose one word to describe her way of being in the world it would be 'avidity.' There was nothing she did not want to see or do or try to know." Sontag herself recognized the value of this avidity. "More than ever—and once again—I experience life as a question of levels of energy," she wrote in her journal in 1970, adding a few paragraphs later: "What I want: energy, energy, energy. Stop wanting nobility, serenity, wisdom—you idiot!"

Sontag's relentless curiosity helped give her writing its density of references and its unmistakable air of authority, but it also made it hard for her to actually sit down and write. Even though she believed that writing every day would be best, Sontag was never able to do so herself; instead, she wrote in "very long, intense, obsessional stretches" of eighteen or twenty or twenty-four hours, often motivated by an egregiously neglected deadline that she finally couldn't ignore any longer. She seemed to need the pressure to build to an almost intolerable level before she could finally begin to write—largely because she found writing incredibly difficult. "I am not at all the kind of writer who writes very easily and very rapidly and only needs to correct or change a bit," she said in 1980. "My writing is extremely painstaking and painful, and the first draft is usually awful." The hardest part, she said,

was to get that initial draft; after that, at least she had something to work with, and she would rework it many times,
going through ten to twenty drafts, regularly taking months
to complete a single essay. And she only got slower as time
went on: It took Sontag five years to complete the six essays
for her landmark 1977 book, *On Photography.*

Another obstacle for Sontag was simply being alone: She
was an extremely gregarious person who loved conversation
and had no real desire for solitude, a trait that she knew was
bad for a writer. She said in 1987:

> Kafka had a fantasy of setting up shop in the sub-
> basement of some building, where twice a day some-
> body would put something to eat outside the door. He
> said: One cannot be alone enough to write. I think of
> writing like being in a balloon, a spaceship, a subma-
> rine, a closet. It's going someplace else, where peo-
> ple aren't, to really concentrate and hear one's own
> voice. . . . It's up to me not to answer the phone, or not
> to go out to dinner. I need a lot of turning inwards. It's
> an effort to find that solitude, because I'm not actually
> a very reclusive person. I like being with people, and I
> don't particularly like being alone.

Of course, when she was starting out, she wasn't alone:
Sontag wrote her first novel, *The Benefactor,* and her early
essays while caring as a single parent for her young son—and
also juggling several jobs, numerous romances, and her vora-
cious cultural life. How did she manage it all? Partly it was by
eschewing some of the traditional obligations of motherhood,
such as cooking, which she never pretended was a priority.
"I didn't cook for David," she joked with an interviewer in

Susan Sontag, Paris, 1972

1990. "I warmed for him." (In another interview, she said that David "grew up on coats"—that is, the coats on the beds at all the parties she brought him along to.) As for her writing binges, Sontag later told the writer Sigrid Nunez that she simply made it work. "When I was writing the last pages of *The Benefactor*, I didn't eat or sleep or change clothes for days," Sontag said. "At the very end, I couldn't even stop to light my own cigarettes. I had David stand by and light them for me while I kept typing." (Nunez adds: "While she was writing the last pages of *The Benefactor*, it was 1962, and David was ten.")

This was before Sontag began taking Dexamyl, an anti-depressant medication that combined an amphetamine (to elevate mood) and a barbiturate (to counter the amphetamine's side effects). According to Sontag's son, she became dependent on Dexamyl for writing in the mid-1960s and continued using it until the 1980s, "though in diminishing doses." She was open about the drug's utility for a writer. In a 1978 interview, the magazine *High Times* asked Sontag if she ever used marijuana for her writing. "I use speed to write, which is the opposite of grass," she replied. Asked what it did for her, Sontag said: "It eliminates the need to eat, sleep or pee or talk to other people. And one can really sit 20 hours in a room and not feel lonely or tired or bored. It gives you terrific powers of concentration. It also makes you loquacious. So if I do any writing on speed, I try to limit it."

Sontag generally wrote first drafts by hand, lying stretched out on her bed, then moved to her desk to type up successive drafts on the typewriter or, later, the computer. Writing for her meant losing weight, it meant backaches and headaches and pains in her fingers and knees. Sontag talked about wanting to work in a way that was less physically punishing, but she never seriously tried to change her habits; she seemed to need the process to be a little self-destructive. "To write is to spend oneself, to gamble oneself," she wrote in her journal in 1959, and she thought that it was only by pushing herself for long hours that she arrived at her best ideas. Besides, she had to admit that on some level she found it all "thrilling." She liked to quote Noël Coward: "Work is more fun than fun."

Joan Mitchell (1925–1992)

The American painter developed a remarkable ability to evoke natural landscapes through abstract compositions—

"You have a feeling that her paintings show a location, even though you don't know where it is," the poet John Ashbery once observed—and yet she mostly painted at night, working by fluorescent light. Living in a one-room studio in New York's East Village in the 1950s, Mitchell generally wouldn't get up until the early afternoon and often wouldn't start painting until sundown. She would prepare to work by lowering the needle on a record, usually jazz or classical music, played loud. The music made her "more available" to herself, Mitchell said—and it signaled to others that she "was in her 'painting mode' and was not to be disturbed," one former neighbor recalled.

By then Mitchell would have had a few drinks; she started drinking at about 5:00 p.m. most days, steadily guzzling beer, Scotch, bourbon, gin, or Chablis—she wasn't picky. But she was sensitive about the cliché of Abstract Expressionist painters drunkenly flinging paint onto their canvases, and according to the biographer Patricia Albers, "at least once she made a younger artist swear never to tell anyone that she or her colleagues touched a drink in the studio." This was far from the truth; Mitchell once admitted to another friend that "if she did not drink she could not paint."

Mitchell painted in fits and starts, making several decisive brushstrokes, then retreating from the canvas to the opposite end of the studio, looking at what she had done, changing the record, looking some more, and finally reapproaching the canvas for another few brushstrokes—or not. She progressed slowly, sometimes spending months on a single painting. "The idea of 'action painting' is a joke," Mitchell said in 1991. "There's no 'action' here. I paint a little. Then I sit and look at the painting, sometimes for hours. Eventually the painting tells me what to do."

Joan Mitchell, Vétheuil, France, 1992

In 1959, after losing the lease on her East Village apartment, Mitchell moved to Europe with her companion Jean-Paul Riopelle, a Montreal-born painter. The couple settled in Paris for several years; then, in 1967, Mitchell used a modest inheritance from her grandfather to purchase a two-acre country estate in Vétheuil, a tiny village about thirty-five miles northwest of Paris. (Monet lived there in the 1870s, although Mitchell resented the association.) Mitchell, Riopelle, and their five dogs moved there in 1968. "How goes your work day, Joan?" a visiting critic asked her several years later. "Get up in the morning?" "Not always," Mitchell answered with a laugh. She continued:

Lunch at one. With Hollis [her assistant and friend] or by myself. Afternoon, I do the crossword puzzle and listen to a couple of shrink programs. . . . People call up with their problems, and that sort of makes you feel better you don't have *that* problem.

Then, winter, the light goes down around four-thirty. I dog-feed then, or I can't see in the kennel. Later, in summer. Then Jean-Paul comes home around seven-thirty to nine for supper. We eat. Look at television. Then I might paint. Or I might *not* look at television—and paint. Ten to four I paint. Something like that. Except the bad times.

The bad times, Mitchell continued, were when she couldn't feel anything, and "everything looks the same no-color. I fight it. It's not a cyclical thing—seems to be my water level. I don't play around with it, though. I hear music, try to be active, walk to town. If I get into the work, then it's not there. That's the only fun I have. When I'm in it, I don't think about myself."

In 1981, she and Riopelle separated and Mitchell continued to live in Vétheuil alone, albeit with the companionship of her dogs and a steady stream of friends and visitors. Although Mitchell was notoriously prickly in person, she loved to entertain, hosting long, boozy dinners most nights. Afterward, she would wash the dishes and then walk—or stagger—to her studio, housed in a former game room directly behind the house, toting along, according to Albers, "her survival bag bulging with a jug of Johnnie Walker, two or three books of poetry, and perhaps a few letters." The studio was her private sanctuary; she kept it locked at all times and slept with the key under her pillow. (When the studio toilet broke, she procrastinated on getting it fixed because she couldn't bear to let the plumber inside.) It felt, one friend remembered, "like a place that an animal goes to for safety."

In fact, it may have been the opposite—the place that a tough, combative artist went to let down her defenses and take risks. "No one can paint—write—feel whatever without being vulnerable," she once said. And, she added, "one has to be very strong to be vulnerable."

Marguerite Duras (1914–1996)

For Duras, writing was less a process of invention than of discovery—or, perhaps more accurately, of confrontation. Writing meant uncovering something that, she felt, already existed inside her unconscious, whole, waiting to be revealed. She found the process daunting, even terrifying—no doubt because her fiction often drew on her traumatic childhood. (Duras may be best known for her 1984 novel *The Lover,* about a fifteen-year-old French girl's affair with an older, wealthy Chinese man—a barely fictionalized retelling of her own experience growing up in an impoverished family in French Indochina.) "It's like a crisis I handle as best I can," Duras said of her writing process. "It's a kind of subjugation. When I'm writing I'm frightened; it's as though everything were crumbling around me. Words are dangerous, physically charged with powder, poison. They poison. And then that feeling that I mustn't do it." Not surprisingly, writing wasn't something she did regularly or on any kind of timetable; instead, when a book idea came to her, it obsessed her and took over her life. She wrote her 1950 novel *The Sea Wall* in eight months, "working at her desk without a break from five in the morning to eleven at night," according to the biographer Laure Adler. At night she drank, seeking oblivion. "I'm a real writer, I was a real alcoholic," she said in 1991, after she finally dried out for good. "I drank red wine to fall asleep. Afterwards, Cognac in the night. Every hour a glass of wine and in the morning Cognac after coffee, and afterwards I wrote. What is astonishing when I look back is how I managed to write."

Penelope Fitzgerald [1916–2000]

In the 1980s, Fitzgerald offered some writing advice to her son-in-law's sister, who was trying to compose poetry while working as an administrator of a writers' colony in West Yorkshire, England. "I hope you'll be completely ruthless," Fitzgerald told her, "take the best typewriter for yourself, neglect all the friends who come to stay, the hens, the course members, etc, in favour of the writing, otherwise it's not possible to get it done." Fitzgerald was writing from personal experience. She had been a star student at Oxford in the 1930s, and was widely expected to go on to a brilliant literary career; as it turned out, she didn't publish her first book, a biography, until she was fifty-eight years old. Eleven more books—nine novels and two biographies—followed over the subsequent twenty years, and her last novel, *The Blue Flower,* made Fitzgerald an unlikely literary celebrity at age eighty. But in between Oxford and her first book there was a long period of family crises, financial strain, and drudgery, and for much of that time Fitzgerald pretty much resigned herself to never achieving her ambitions. "I've come to see art as the most important thing but not to regret I haven't spent my life on it," she noted to herself in 1969.

Initially, Fitzgerald's writing career had looked bright. After graduation, she found work as a film and book reviewer, a BBC scriptwriter, and the coeditor, with her husband, of the monthly culture magazine *World Review,* for which she wrote numerous editorials and essays. But the *Review* folded, and her husband's attempt to resume his delayed legal career fizzled; meanwhile, he began drinking heavily. By then the Fitzgeralds had three young children, and the family was living beyond its means; soon they found themselves hurtling toward poverty. In 1960, they moved onto a rickety houseboat moored in the Thames, the cheapest available housing option in London, although it proved just barely habitable— the barge was chilly and damp; as the tide rose it leaked, and as the tide went out it settled unevenly in the mud, putting their living quarters on a slope. It eventually sank, along with most of the family's possessions.

The same year they moved onto the houseboat Fitzgerald began teaching to earn money, and she would continue to do so for twenty-six years, until she was seventy. She took up teaching because it was the obvious choice for a middle-aged woman with a good education and few other options, but she did not enjoy it. "Faced by piles and piles of foul A level scripts I have a sensation of wasting my life, but it's too late to worry about this anyway," she wrote in a letter from the time. In reality, she wasn't quite as despairing as that letter makes it sound, or at least not all the time. A few years into her new career, Fitzgerald began to write in small spurts, making notes on the backs of student papers and filing drafts alongside her pupils' exams, stealing time whenever she could—"during my free periods as a teacher in a small, noisy staff room, full of undercurrents of exhaustion, worry and reproach."

But it wasn't until 1971 that Fitzgerald was finally able to properly resume—or, really, begin—her literary career. She was fifty-four, and her youngest child was about to leave home; meanwhile, her rocky marriage had settled into a friendly companionship. For the first time in decades, Fitzgerald had the time and mental space to write. She began researching her first book, a biography of the Victorian painter Edward Burne-Jones, in the evenings after work, chiding herself for not having the energy to work even longer hours. "I'm very annoyed with myself that I can't manage to do more in the evening," she wrote to her daughter Maria in 1973. "All this dropping off must cease. After all I hardly ever go out so I should be able to get more done. One must justify one's existence."

It took her four years to finish the biography, but doing so unleashed a long-delayed outpouring. In the next five years she published six more books, including a series of short novels that drew on the trials of her middle age. (The Booker Prize–winning *Offshore,* for instance, is a fictionalized version of the family's years aboard the ill-fated houseboat.) If she never quite felt that she had lived up to her full potential, she at least knew that she had found her proper subject matter as a novelist. "I have remained true to my deepest convictions," Fitzgerald said in 1998. "I mean to the courage of those who are born to be defeated, the weaknesses of the strong, and the tragedy of misunderstandings and missed opportunities, which I have done my best to treat as comedy, for otherwise how can we manage to bear it?"

Barbara Hepworth (1903–1975)

"I am basically and primarily a carver and the properties of stone and wood and marble have obsessed me all my life," the English abstract sculptor said in 1961. Hepworth's process began with the raw material on hand, and she came to her sculptural ideas by relating herself to the "life" in a piece of wood or stone. She always visualized the completed work before she started carving. "I think one goes around sort of brooding," Hepworth explained in 1967. "And then suddenly it flashes into one's mind complete."

Hepworth did not see her working process as particularly magical or mysterious. "I have always thought of my profession as an ordinary work-a-day job," she said, although she did allow that being an abstract sculptor is "emotionally exhausting work." Hepworth usually worked an eight-hour day, and she felt that the longer she worked, the better the results. "You have to work long unbroken hours in order to see any real progress," she once told a visiting interviewer. "A block of stone like this, for instance, will not look very much different until a great deal of time has been spent on its carving. I like to start work around eightish in the morning and keep going until about six in the evening."

This was in 1962, when Hepworth was fifty-nine and her four children were grown. While she was raising the children, her working habits could never be quite so consistent. "I had to have a very strict discipline with myself so that I always did some work every day, even if it was only 10 minutes," she said of the years when her children were young.

It's so very easy to say "Well, today's a bad day; the children aren't well, and the kitchen needs scrubbing . . .

Barbara Hepworth at her studio, 1952

but maybe it will be better tomorrow." And then you say to yourself that it may be even better next week, or when the children are older. And then you lose touch with your development. I think the ideas can go on developing behind the scenes if you keep in close touch with what you are doing even if you have interruptions. You actually mature faster. You may do fewer carvings, but they could be maturing at the same rate as if you had all the time to work.

Indeed, Hepworth insisted that having children didn't hold her back as an artist, and that she felt no resentment about their demands on her time. (It may have helped that Hepworth's first and second husbands were also artists with flexible schedules, and were able to help with the child-rearing, at least to some extent.) "We lived a life of work and the children were brought up in it, in the middle of the dust and the dirt and the paint and everything," Hepworth said. "They were just part of it."

From 1939 until the end of her life, Hepworth lived and worked in St. Ives, Cornwall, near the southwestern tip of England, and she worked outdoors as often as the weather allowed, which was most of the year. "Light and space are the sculptor's materials as much as wood or stone," she said. She generally worked on multiple sculptures at a time, and as she grew older she employed several assistants to help her with the work, although she still carved daily right up until her death, at seventy-two, in an accidental fire at her studio. She compared sculpture to playing poker. "I don't actually play cards, but I gamble fearfully on my work," she said. "You have to play your hunch. You must have a passion, an obsession to do something. My idea is to play it hard. Nothing really matters except doing the next job."

Stella Bowen (1893–1947)

Bowen was an Australian painter who studied art in London, where she became friendly with the city's literary avant-garde, including Ezra Pound, T. S. Eliot, and the novelist Ford Madox Ford, whom she fell in love with and married in 1918, when she was twenty-four and he was forty-four. The next year they moved to a cottage in rural Sussex, where Ford—already celebrated as the author of *Ladies Whose Bright Eyes* and *The Good Soldier*—resolved to make a living as a pig farmer, and where Bowen gave birth to a daughter in 1920. After a few years (and the utter failure of Ford's farming ambitions), they fled the cold, wet winters for the south of France and, later, Paris. Throughout this time Ford wrote fiction, and for a year he edited the *Transatlantic Review*. Bowen, meanwhile, struggled to find time for painting while caring for their daughter and—far more wearying—attending to her husband's many needs. Ford, Bowen later wrote, "had a genius for creating confusion and a nervous horror of having to deal with the results." Bowen was the "shock absorber" in their relationship: She paid the bills, prevented Ford from learning the full extent of their debts, and shielded the sensitive writer from interruptions; when Ford was finishing a book, he required that no one speak to him or show him the mail until after he had finished his morning's work. Despite all this, Ford wondered why Bowen could never work as steadily as he did. She wrote in her memoir, *Drawn from Life*:

> Ford never understood why I found it so difficult to paint whilst I was with him. He thought I lacked the will to do it at all costs. That was true, but he did not realise that if I *had* had the will to do it at all costs, my life would have been oriented quite differently. I should not have been available to nurse him through the daily strain of his own work; to walk and talk with him whenever he wanted, and to stand between him and circumstances. Pursuing art is not just a matter of finding the time—it is a matter of having a free spirit to

bring to it. Later on, when I had more actual free time, I was still very much enslaved by the terms of my relationship with Ford, for he was a great user-up of other people's nervous energy. . . . I was in love, happy, and absorbed. But there was no room for me to nurse an independent ego.

For a time in Paris, Bowen and Ford managed to find a mutually beneficial work arrangement, sharing a studio with an upper platform where Ford could write while Bowen painted on the main floor below. During this time, their five-year-old daughter stayed with a governess in a cottage in Guermantes, about twenty miles outside Paris. She went to school there during the week, and Bowen and Ford spent the weekends with her, an arrangement that proved suitable to everyone, although Bowen missed her daughter terribly. But this period of peaceful coworking proved to be only an interlude; Bowen soon learned that Ford had been having an affair with a younger writer, a thirty-four-year-old unknown named Ella Lenglet (who, at Ford's suggestion, adopted the pen name Jean Rhys; see page 320). Bowen and Ford separated in 1928, and despite the many complications that ensued, Bowen was finally able to concentrate on her painting; three years after their separation, she had her first solo exhibition. Unfortunately, money problems prevented Bowen from giving art her full attention for very long, and forced her to focus on commissioned portraits. By the time Bowen wrote her memoir in 1940, she could take some satisfaction in having carved out a career as a well-regarded painter, but she could not help but feel that she could have accomplished more had she not poured so much energy into others' needs. "If you are a woman, and you want to have a life of your own, it would probably be better for you to fall in love at seventeen, be seduced, be abandoned, and your baby die," she wrote. "If you survived this, you might go far!"

Kate Chopin (1850–1904)

Chopin grew up in St. Louis, married at twenty, and moved with her husband to New Orleans, where he ran a cotton brokerage; over the next nine years, she gave birth to six children. In 1882, Chopin's husband died of malaria, and a few years later she moved the family back to St. Louis, where she began writing fiction, publishing her first story in 1889 and her first novel, *At Fault,* in 1890. Over the next decade, she wrote approximately a hundred short stories, and gained an increasingly wide readership through publication in several national magazines, including *The Atlantic Monthly* and *Vogue.* Chopin never wrote to any kind of timetable, and she didn't even keep a separate writing room; according to her daughter, she preferred to write with her children "swarming about her." In an essay for the *St. Louis Post-Dispatch* from November 1899—six months after the publication of her most famous novel, *The Awakening*—Chopin addressed some common questions about her writing process:

> How do I write? On a lapboard with a block of paper, a stub pen and a bottle of ink bought at the corner grocery, which keeps the best in town.
>
> Where do I write? In a Morris chair beside the window, where I can see a few trees and a patch of sky, more or less blue.

When do I write? I am greatly tempted here to use slang and reply "any old time," but that would lend a tone of levity to this bit of confidence, whose seriousness I want to keep intact if possible. So I shall say I write in the morning, when not too strongly drawn to struggle with the intricacies of a pattern, and in the afternoon, if the temptation to try a new furniture polish on an old table leg is not too powerful to be denied; sometimes at night, though as I grow older I am more and more inclined to believe that night was made for sleep.

According to the biographer Per Seyersted, Chopin "spent only an average of one or two mornings a week on the physical act of writing," and by all accounts she wrote only when seized by inspiration. "There are stories that seem to write themselves," Chopin said, "and others which positively refuse to be written—which no amount of coaxing can bring to anything." Chopin's son Felix observed firsthand how "the short story burst from her: I have seen her go weeks and weeks without an idea, then suddenly grab her pencil and old lapboard (which was her work bench), and in a couple of hours her story was complete and off to the publisher." Chopin claimed that she made virtually no revisions, which she considered unnecessary and even counterproductive. "I am completely at the mercy of unconscious selection," she wrote. "To such an extent is this true, that what is called the polishing up process has always proved disastrous to my work, and I avoid it, preferring the integrity of crudities to artificialities."

Harriet Jacobs (1813–1897)

Jacobs was born a slave in Edenton, North Carolina. After years of enduring the sexual predations of her master, she managed to escape to the North—but first she spent nearly seven years hiding in her grandmother's house, in a nine-by-four-foot garret whose sloped ceiling reached three feet at its tallest point, and from which Jacobs could emerge only at night, for brief periods of exercise. This was but one of the harrowing experiences recounted in Jacobs's autobiography, *Incidents in the Life of a Slave Girl,* published under the pseudonym Linda Brent in 1861. Jacobs almost didn't write the book; when the Quaker abolitionist Amy Post first suggested the idea, she resisted, loath to revisit her traumatic past. But Jacobs decided it was her duty to try to be "useful in some way" to the antislavery cause, and she set out to record her life.

The actual writing was not a problem; as a child, Jacobs was taught by her mistress to read, write, and sew. But finding the time to write was a serious challenge. By the 1850s, Jacobs was no longer a fugitive—her employer, Cornelia Willis, had purchased her freedom in 1852—but she was still obliged to work for a living, and was employed as the Willis family nursemaid, traveling with them between New York and Boston. In 1853, the year she started her book, the Willises relocated to Idlewild, their new estate in the Hudson River valley. There, Jacobs felt increasingly isolated, and she was exhausted by her twenty-four-hour-a-day, seven-day-a-week job caring for the Willis family's five children, including a new baby born that summer. She could find the time to write only at night, while the children slept. "I have not yet written a single page by daylight," she confided in a letter to Post,

". . . with the care of the little baby the big Babies and at the household calls I have but a little time to think or write." In another letter she complained that if she "could steal away and have two quiet Months" to herself, she "would work night and day though it should all fall to the ground." At other times, however, she struck a more sanguine tone: "The poor Book is in its Chrysalis state and though I can never make it a butterfly I am satisfied to have it creep meekly among some of the humbler bugs."

Over the years, the book crept toward completion; by continuing to write "at irregular intervals, whenever I could snatch an hour from household duties," Jacobs gradually recorded her life, and in March 1857, after four years of work, she finished the book. (Working on the preface, she noted that she had "been interrupted and called away so often—that I hardly know what I have written.") Publication was another challenge, involving years of further work, and when the book finally came out, Jacobs's story was overshadowed by the outbreak of the Civil War, and then largely forgotten for decades. Its rediscovery in the late twentieth century finally restored Jacobs's autobiography to the stature it deserves, as a triumph of perseverance and truth-telling in the face of unimaginable adversity.

Marie Curie (1867–1934)

Marie and Pierre Curie announced the existence of polonium and radium in papers published in July and December 1898; to prove their discoveries beyond a doubt, they next set out to isolate the elements in their pure form. Over the course

Marie Curie in her laboratory, Paris, 1913

of their earlier research, the married scientists had hypoth-
esized that pitchblende ore contained minute quantities of
the new elements. But attempting to separate them from the
pitchblende would require an arduous process. It was Marie
who resolved to attempt it regardless of the difficulty; Pierre
confided to a friend that he would never have done so on
his own: "I would have gone another way," he wrote. Many
years later, Marie and Pierre's daughter Irene (born the year
before the Curies' discovery) agreed that her mother was the
motivating force behind the project. "One can discern," Irene
wrote, "that it was my mother who had no fear of throwing
herself, without personnel, without money, without supplies,
with a warehouse for a laboratory, into the daunting task
of treating kilos of pitchblende in order to concentrate and
isolate radium."

The Curies' lack of institutional support or adequate facilities has become legendary. After the Sorbonne declined their request for a workroom, the couple found a cavernous hangar at the school where Pierre taught; it was previously used as a dissection room by medical students, until it was deemed unfit even for that purpose. The space was barely furnished, the roof leaked, and the only source of heat was an ancient cast-iron stove. "It looked like a stable or potato cellar," a visiting chemist wrote, "and if I had not seen the worktable with the chemistry equipment I would have thought it was a hoax." But at least the hangar opened onto a courtyard, which proved indispensable for storing the tons of pitchblende residue the Curies ended up needing for their work.

From the beginning, Pierre concentrated on the physics side of the problem, while Marie took charge of the chemistry—which required periods of backbreaking labor. "I had to work with as much as twenty kilograms of material at a time," she wrote, "so that the hangar was filled with great vessels full of precipitates and liquids. It was exhausting work to move the containers about, to transfer the liquids, and to stir for hours at a time, with an iron bar, the boiling material in the cast-iron basin." In the early stages of the process, she sometimes spent the entire day standing over the boiling material, stirring it with an iron rod that weighed as much as she did; "I would be broken with fatigue at the day's end," she wrote.

Nevertheless, the Curies were content; it was "the heroic period of our common existence," Marie wrote. "In spite of the difficulties of our working conditions, we felt very happy," she later recalled. "Our days were spent at the laboratory. In our poor shed there reigned a great tranquility: sometimes, as we watched over some operation, we would walk up and down, talking about work in the present and in the future; when we were cold a cup of hot tea taken near the stove comforted us. We lived in our single preoccupation as if in a dream."

In an 1899 letter to her sister, Marie elaborated on their daily routine during this period:

> Our life is always the same. We work a lot but we sleep well, so our health does not suffer. The evenings are taken up by caring for the child. In the morning I dress her and give her her food, then I can generally go out at about nine. During the whole of this year we have not been either to the theater or a concert, and we have not paid one visit. For that matter, we feel very well.

The experiment proceeded with excruciating slowness. As the Curies entered their third year of work, money began running low. Pierre added another class to his teaching load and Marie became a physics professor at an academy for young women, with a ninety-minute commute each way, significantly reducing the time she could spend in the laboratory. Worried about their health, a friend and fellow scientist wrote to Pierre:

> You hardly eat at all, either of you. More than once I have seen Mme. Curie nibble two slices of sausage and swallow a cup of tea with it. . . . It is necessary not to mix scientific preoccupations continually into every instant of your life as you are doing. . . . You must not read or talk physics while you eat.

The couple ignored his warning. Finally, after forty-five months of labor, Marie succeeded in isolating a decigram of pure radium and determining its atomic weight, officially proving the element's existence. The following year the Curies were awarded the Nobel Prize for Physics (along with Henri Becquerel, who first discovered radioactivity). The Curies at first declined the invitation to deliver a speech in Stockholm, pleading too much work; however, in 1905, they reluctantly made the trip in order to claim the prize money, which they used to hire their first laboratory assistant. Although the money was helpful, the publicity unleashed by the Nobel announcement proved an unwelcome distraction for the Curies, who wanted only to continue their scientific work. Writing home to her brother the day after the Nobel ceremony, Marie said that they were continually beset by journalists and photographers, and inundated with invitations, which they always declined. "We refuse with the energy of despair," she wrote, "and people understand that there is nothing to be done."

RESIGNATION AND RELIEF

George Eliot (1819–1880)

Mary Anne Evans published seven novels under the pen name George Eliot, including *Middlemarch,* widely considered one of the greatest novels in the English language. But writing never came easily to her; with each new novel, Eliot was convinced that her creative powers had deserted her and she would never meet the standard set by her earlier work. Rereading her 1866 novel *Felix Holt* while struggling through *Middlemarch,* Eliot told her longtime companion George Henry Lewes that she "could never write like that again and that what is now in hand is rinsings of the cask!"

This was in 1872. That summer, to give her an opportunity to work without interruption, Lewes and Eliot moved from London to the countryside and kept their address a secret from everyone but Eliot's dentist and one close friend. This strategy of retreat had worked in the past; in the country, Eliot generally devoted the morning to writing and spent the afternoon walking with Lewes, and in this manner made steady if painful forward progress. It didn't help that Eliot was often in ill health while writing—or perhaps writing brought on these periods of illness. During the composition of *Middlemarch,* she suffered from severe tooth and gum aches; while working on 1876's *Daniel Deronda,* her symptoms were closer to depression. "I had hardly a day of good health while it was in progress," she wrote. That Eliot finished the novels despite near-constant suffering is a testament both to her own tenacity and to the steadying influence of Lewes, who had first encouraged Eliot to write fiction and who went out of his way to provide her with favorable conditions for her work. "We have so much happiness in our love and uninterrupted companionship," Eliot wrote, "that we must accept our miserable bodies as our share of mortal ill."

Edith Wharton (1862–1937)

In her autobiography, *A Backward Glance,* Wharton described her life as divided into two "equally real yet totally unrelated worlds," which went along "side by side, equally absorbing, but wholly isolated from each other." On the one hand, there was the real world of her marriage, her home, her friends and neighbors; on the other, the fictional world she created each morning in bed, writing longhand on sheets of paper that she dropped onto the floor for her secretary to retrieve and type up. Wharton always worked in the morning, and houseguests who stayed at the Mount—the 113-acre estate in Lenox, Massachusetts, where Wharton penned several novels, including *The House of Mirth* and *Ethan Frome*—were expected to entertain themselves until 11:00 a.m. or noon, when their hostess would emerge from her private quarters, ready to go for a walk or work in the garden. If guests needed to speak to the author during the morning, however, Wharton was willing to receive them in her bedroom. The historian Gaillard Lapsley was one such visitor, and he later wrote a memorable description of Wharton in bed, "flanked by night tables charged with telephone, travelling clock, reading light." She would be wearing, he continued,

Edith Wharton with Mimi and Miza, circa 1889–90

a thin silk sacque with loose sleeves, open at the neck and trimmed with lace and on her head a cap of the same material also trimmed with lace which fell about her brow and ears like the edging of a lamp shade. . . . Edith's mask stood out sculpturally beneath it. She would have her writing-board perilously furnished with an inkpot on her knee, the dog of the moment under her left elbow on the bed strewn with correspondence, newspapers and books.

The "dog of the moment" referred to one of the numerous canines Wharton owned over her lifetime, which included

Spitzes, Papillons, a poodle, a Pekingese, and a pair of long-haired Chihuahuas named Mimi and Miza. Dogs had been a tremendous comfort to Wharton since her earliest childhood; and when, in her last years, Wharton made a list of the "ruling passions" of her life, dogs ranked second only to "Justice and Order," and were followed by books, flowers, architecture, travel, and "a good joke."

Evenings at the Mount, Wharton would read to her guests from the novel she was writing, or from the work of one of her favorite authors. Although she was happy to share her writing in progress, she never had much to say about the writing process itself. A guest at the Mount recalled that "very little allusion was made to it, and none at all to the infinite pains that she put into her work or her inexhaustible patience in searching for the material necessary to perfect it." One unspoken requirement was that she follow the same schedule each day, with as little variation as possible. As Wharton wrote in a 1905 letter, "The slightest interruption in the household routine completely de-rails me."

Anna Pavlova (1881–1931)

"On the day of a performance most ballerinas cannot eat a thing," the Russian prima ballerina once declared. "Not I! At five o'clock I have a cup of bouillon, a cutlet and a custard dessert. During the performance I drink water with breadcrumbs, which is most refreshing. After the ballet I have a bath as soon as possible. Then I go out to dinner, as by that time I have an unmerciful hunger. When I get home I drink tea."

This description comes from Pavlova's days as a young

ballerina-in-training; as she matured, she became one of the greatest dancers of her era, serving in the Imperial Russian Ballet and briefly with Serge Diaghilev's Ballets Russes. She also became the first ballerina to tour the world, acting as a sort of missionary of the art form on her travels to North and South America, New Zealand and Australia, India, China, and Japan, among other destinations. According to Pavlova's husband and manager, Victor Dandré, while she was on tour, "the whole of Pavlova's life was regulated by the clock and nothing was allowed to interfere with the routine." The dancer rose at about 9:00 a.m., and by 10:00 she was at the theater to begin her extensive preparatory exercises, first at the barre and then onstage. These lasted for ninety minutes to two hours, after which Pavlova was joined by her company for rehearsal. At 1:00 p.m., rehearsal ended and everyone went back to their hotel for lunch. After lunch, Pavlova had a window of about thirty minutes to see anything of interest in the town they were visiting; then she rested for ninety minutes before returning to the theater at about 6:00 p.m.

At the theater, Pavlova would begin to put on her makeup, which she applied herself, then pause for a final round of practice onstage. After this she donned her wig and costume, finished applying her makeup, and endured the final moments of pre-performance anxiety. "She was always in a state of great agitation before the actual entry before the footlights," Dandré writes. During the interval between acts, Pavlova would, if necessary, change her costume, wig, and makeup, and she would drink a cup of weak tea. She never received anyone in her dressing room between acts, but once the performance was over she enjoyed greeting locals backstage. Returning to the hotel afterward, Pavlova would have a light supper and more tea, and then spend an hour reading or in conversation before bed. She repeated the routine every performance day, with no variation. "People imagine we [ballerinas] lead a frivolous life; the fact is we cannot," Pavlova said after her first tour. "We have to choose between frivolity and our art. The two are incompatible."

Elizabeth Barrett Browning (1806–1861)

One of the most famous courtships of English literary history began in 1845, when the publication of Elizabeth Barrett's *Poems* inspired Robert Browning to write a letter to the poet beginning, "I love your verses with all my heart, dear Miss Barrett," and ending with a declaration of love for the poet herself. The two had not even met—but several months and many letters later they did, and the following year they were married. Their courtship and marriage were kept a secret from Elizabeth's domineering father, and soon after their wedding the Brownings left England for Italy. In 1847, they settled in Florence, where they had a son, nicknamed Pen, and where they would live until Elizabeth's death in 1861. Their apartment, Casa Guidi, became a center of British society in Florence, and a productive workplace for the two poets. In her biography of Barrett Browning, Margaret Fuller describes the couple's working schedule during "the happy winter" of 1852–53, an especially calm and creative period for them both:

> She and Robert both got up at seven and were dressed and breakfasting by nine. Then Wilson [the maid] took Pen out while both poets used "the bright ribbands of

morning time" to write until three o'clock when they dined. Robert worked in the little sitting room and Elizabeth in the drawing room. The dining room was between them, with the doors firmly closed. Robert sat at a desk writing lyrics for a collection to be called *Men and Women;* Elizabeth sat in an armchair with her feet up writing *Aurora Leigh,* the long prose poem she had contemplated for so many years. Neither showed each other the day's output nor did they discuss it. Elizabeth had firm ideas about this: no matter how close people were, their intimacy should not extend to work. "An artist must, I fancy, either find or *make* a solitude to work in, if it is to be good work at all," she once wrote to [her friend Henry] Chorley, and meant it.

The 3:00 p.m. meal was probably more of a snack; according to the biographer Julia Markus, both Brownings "favored a poet's food group and seemed to exist on coffee, a bit of bread, chestnuts, and grapes. The two of them were once seen sharing a squab!" Afterward, the poets rested or went for a walk, and then received visitors for tea. (To protect their working hours, the Brownings gave their staff instructions that they would not receive visitors before 3:00 p.m.) In the evening, Robert often socialized outside the home while Elizabeth stayed in. Her health had always been frail; as a teenager, she began suffering intense head and spinal pain of unclear origin, and later she also developed lung problems, possibly tuberculosis, which left her with a chronic cough. At age fifteen, she began taking a daily dose of laudanum, a tincture of opium dissolved in alcohol that was a popular cure-all in Victorian England. Elizabeth used it primarily to sleep at night, but she also took it during the day when she felt "irritable" to "steady the action of the heart." In 1845, she reported that she took forty drops of laudanum a day; although it's impossible to know the exact strength of her prescription, it seems safe to assume that this was a large (perhaps very large) dose.

When Robert urged her to give up laudanum, Elizabeth protested that she merely used it to balance her nervous system: "My opium comes in to keep the pulse from fluttering & fainting," she said. "I don't take it for 'my spirits' in the usual sense,—you must not think such a thing." She claimed that she never used the drug for writing and didn't need it for her poetry except in the most literal sense: It was "perfectly true," she said, "so far, that life is necessary to writing, & that I should not be alive except by help of my morphine."

Virginia Woolf [1882–1941]

In a 1925 essay for *Vogue,* Woolf praised the Irish novelist George Moore for "eking out a delicate gift laboriously." She could have been describing her own writing process, which was always halting, difficult, unpredictable. "A good day—a bad day—so it goes on," Woolf wrote in her diary in June 1936. "Few people can be so tortured by writing as I am. Only Flaubert I think." Like Flaubert, Woolf's work habits were regular and orderly: For most of her life, she stuck to a daily routine of writing from 10:00 a.m. to 1:00 p.m., and she used her diary to keep track of her output and chide herself for unproductive days. "She structured her working life by self-imposed routines which were essential to her," the biographer Hermione Lee has written. "Writing (fiction or reviews) was done in the first part of the morning; just before or after

Virginia Woolf in the garden at Monk's House,
East Sussex, England, 1926

lunch was for revising (or walking, or printing). After tea was
for diary or letter-writing; the evenings were for reading (or
seeing people)." She never wrote at night. "How great writers
write at night, I don't know," Woolf noted in her diary. "Its
[*sic*] an age since I tried, & I find my head full of pillow stuff-
ing: hot; inchoate."

The regular schedule was encouraged by Woolf's husband, Leonard, who had additional reasons for preferring a
steady, calm life. Shortly after their marriage in 1912, Virginia

suffered a prolonged and harrowing mental breakdown—one of several in her life—and from then on Leonard assumed the role of his wife's guardian, caretaker, and quasi-parent, cajoling her into following doctors' orders; supervising her social life to make sure she didn't get overexcited; keeping track of her diet, her writing, and even her menstrual periods; and deciding, after consultations with several doctors and with Virginia's sister, Vanessa Bell, that they should forgo having children, under the belief that a pregnancy could ruin Virginia's fragile mental health. Many biographers have interpreted Leonard's behavior as overly controlling, but there's no doubt that he believed in her writing and created conditions favorable for it to flourish. "L. thinks my writing the best part of me," Virginia wrote in a letter. "We're going to work very hard." They certainly did that. "Neither of us ever took a day's holiday unless we were too ill to work or unless we went away on a regular and, as it were, authorized holiday," Leonard wrote. "We should have felt it to be not merely wrong but unpleasant not to work every morning for seven days a week and for about eleven months a year."

Regardless of whether such a routinized lifestyle was really necessary for her mental health, Woolf found that it was ideal for fiction writing, which she thought required a kind of sustained dreaminess. "I hope I am not giving away professional secrets if I say that a novelist's chief desire is to be as unconscious as possible," she said in a 1933 speech.

He has to induce in himself a state of perpetual lethargy. He wants life to proceed with the utmost quiet and regularity. He wants to see the same faces, to read the same books, to do the same things day after day, month after month, while he is writing, so that nothing may break the illusion in which he is living—so that nothing may disturb or disquiet the mysterious nosings about, feelings around, darts, dashes and sudden discoveries of that very shy and illusive spirit, the imagination.

Walks were essential to this state. In London, Woolf engaged in her hobby of "street haunting"; in the country, she was "extremely happy walking on the downs. . . . I like to have space to spread my mind out in," she wrote. Elsewhere she described herself as "nosing along, making up phrases," and wrote that, in the country, she "slip[ped] easily from writing to reading with spaces between of walking—walking through the long grass in the meadows, or up the downs." Baths also played a part in her creative process. The Woolfs' servant Louie Everest recalled hearing the author talking to herself during her post-breakfast bath: "On and on she went, talk, talk, talk: asking questions and giving herself the answers. I thought there must be two or three people up there with her."

Real company was more problematic. "The truth is, I like it when people actually come; but I love it when they go," Woolf wrote, and friends remembered her as an inattentive and borderline rude host. The novelist E. M. Forster recalled what it was like being a guest at Monk's House, the Woolfs' country retreat in East Sussex: "I was irritated at being left so much 'to myself,'" he wrote. "Here are Ws, who read, Leonard the *Observer,* and Virginia the *Sunday Times,* and then retired to literary studies to write till lunch." But Woolf was wise to protect her working hours from interruption. "I wake filled with a tremulous yet steady rapture," she wrote in a 1930 letter, "carry my pitcher full of lucid and deep water across the garden, and am forced to spill it all by—some one coming."

Vanessa Bell (1879–1961)

If Virginia Woolf was the artist as a detached, self-contained observer, drawing creative sustenance from solitary contemplation, then her older sister, Vanessa Bell, was very nearly the opposite: the artist in the midst of messy life, working alongside her children, her lovers, and their friends, bringing her creativity to bear on everything and everyone in her orbit. As a painter and decorative artist, Bell developed her own distinctive style of portraiture, still-lifes, book-jacket designs, and interior décor; and in her personal life, she famously flouted convention with an unorthodox arrangement of lovers and ex-lovers, all of them reconciled with one another—and frequently sleeping under the same roof—thanks to Bell's seemingly innate charisma, vitality, and what one former lover called her "marvelous practical power."

It was these qualities that, starting around 1906, put Bell at the center of the legendary Bloomsbury group of writers, artists, and intellectuals—Cyril Connolly called her "the unwobbling pivot of Bloomsbury"—but perhaps their fullest expression was at Charleston, the remote estate that she leased in 1916 (discovered for her by Woolf, whose own country cottage was about four miles away). Bell and her family would live in Charleston's rambling three-story farmhouse full-time for the next three years and use it as a holiday retreat for decades afterward. For visitors, it was an idyll, a continuation of Bloomsbury ideals in rural Sussex. As one visitor recalled, "Charleston in its heyday [was] an enchanted place—a place of such potent individuality that whenever I stayed there I came away grateful to it, as it were, for giving me so much pleasure, so many rich and varied visual sensations, such *talk,* such an awareness that lives were being intensely and purposefully led there."

Vanessa Bell, 1911

In addition to Bell, Charleston's regular inhabitants included her husband, Clive, who after about 1914 had become her spouse in name only, as both embarked on their own extramarital affairs while remaining friends; her lover Duncan Grant, with whom she shared a decades-long partnership despite his homosexuality; Grant's lover the novelist David "Bunny" Garnett; Bell's three children, two of whom were fathered by Clive, while the youngest was Grant's (although she didn't yet know it); and a rotating cast of visiting friends, often including the art critic Roger Fry (with whom Bell had had a years-long affair before she fell in love with Grant), the novelist E. M. Forster, the economist John Maynard Keynes, and Virginia and Leonard Woolf. There was also a live-in cook—a crucial personage whose labors prevented Bell's art from being completely subsumed by housework.

On a typical morning in Charleston, the family would gradually assemble in the dining room for breakfast. Grant would eat porridge while the others fetched their own eggs and bacon from the kitchen, where they were kept warm on the stove. When the mail arrived, Clive would seize *The Times* and carry it off to his study, and Bell and Grant would head to their shared painting studio, which they had built onto the house where a chicken coop had been. Although many artists cannot abide anyone else in their workspace, Bell and Grant were content to paint in the same room, often listening to classical music on the gramophone as they worked. Bell's son Quentin described them as "like two sturdy animals side by side in a manger, munching away contentedly, not needing to talk to each other but just happy in the presence of the other." (Bell eventually craved her own space, however, and after 1925 she worked in a private studio on the top floor of the house, in what was formerly a spare bedroom.)

To Woolf, Bell was a sort of genius of the everyday, an enviably grounded person with the courage to grab what she wanted from life. After spending the day with Bell and Grant, she wrote, "I never saw two people humming with heat and happiness like sunflowers on a hot day more than those two." They "pour out pure gaiety and pleasure in life," Woolf continued, "not brilliantly or sparklingly, but freely quietly luminously." Despite all the vivid portrayals of her as a woman of great common sense, happiness, and creativity, Bell herself remains something of an enigma; she lives on in others' glowing descriptions, but her own innermost thoughts have remained largely private. To her intimates, she sometimes expressed doubts about the very qualities that others admired in her, and worried that amid all her activities she may have diluted her artistic gift. She said to Woolf, "I have spilt myself among too many stools."

Maggi Hambling [b. 1945]

Hambling is an English painter and sculptor best known for her evocative, sometimes controversial portraits; her oil paintings of breaking waves and violent seas; her public monument to Oscar Wilde, installed in London's West End in 1998; and her 2003 beachfront sculpture *Scallop,* a tribute to the composer Benjamin Britten. She has followed the same daily routine since the 1970s. "Work can make me feel higher or lower than any other part of life," Hambling said in 2017. "I can only be brave, take risks, encourage my work to travel into unknown territory, because the pattern of each day is constant."

Hambling is wide awake at 5:00 each morning, "full of optimism," and with a cup of tea she goes straight to her studio. Once she's in the studio, however, her optimism begins to flag. "As with Hamlet, uncertainty soon sets in," Hambling said. "Doubt is my constant companion. The first thing I do every day is to draw in a sketchbook to renew the sense of touch, much as a pianist practices scales." Then comes strong coffee, which helps her "be at the ready" in case her fickle muse arrives. "Perhaps it is no coincidence that she shows up only after days of seriously considering giving the whole thing up," Hambling said. She likes to paraphrase Brancusi: "It is not difficult to make a work of art, the difficulty lies in being in the right state to do it."

In addition to coffee, Hambling depends on cigarettes for her work, an association that was formed at any early age:

> My first experience of painting in oils, aged fourteen, was on the edge of a field in Suffolk. It was boiling hot and insects stuck to the painting, the palette, the rags, knives and brushes. My art teacher came to inspect and told me a cigarette was the only solution. From that moment on smoking and making art became inseparable. I gave up for five years aged fifty-nine because I said I would—that was the age at which my father gave up. . . . Five years later the installation of a large bronze wave sculpture was challenging my sanity. And it was my birthday. Once again a cigarette was the only solution. So work and smoking have remained inseparable.

At 9:00 a.m. Hambling takes a brief break for "a disgustingly healthy muesli and twelve vitamin pills." Later, at 1:00 p.m., she has lunch, takes her Tibetan terrier, Lux, for a walk, and switches on the television to satisfy her tennis addiction. Her other TV addiction is to the long-running evening soap opera *Coronation Street*—"and I am often sound asleep on the sofa before the end of it at 9:00 p.m.," she said.

But between tennis and *Coronation Street,* at about 6:00 p.m., "the whiskey beckons," and Hambling goes back into the studio to "have a chat" with whatever she's been working on. "I can even be pleased for a moment," she said. "But next morning, I simply cannot see why." She destroys a good deal of her work, going at canvases with a Stanley knife and burning the remnants in a bonfire. (Her feeling at those moments? "Resignation and relief.") Even after six decades of steady work, she continues to feel tremendous uncertainty about the process, which in her estimate is a good thing. "Everything has to be an experiment," Hambling once said in a documentary about her work. "Otherwise it's dead."

Carolee Schneemann (b. 1939)

The pioneering performance artist has lived in the same eighteenth-century stone house in upstate New York since 1964. When she wakes in the morning, she immediately starts writing, sitting in bed, trying to capture the residual images and thoughts from her dreams. "I'm usually very permeable in the morning," Schneemann said in 2017, "so there's the dream residual sense, and sometimes that relates directly to making work. And then there's the scattershot of all the daily debris that's always waiting." Schneemann makes notes on whatever scraps of paper are left around the bed, and she doesn't worry too much about organizing or tracking the results. "They float around, and I try to put them together, and then they just accumulate," she said. "If something seems really consequential I try to get it typed up, put it in the computer."

If she doesn't have any pressing engagements, Schneemann will write in bed like this for an hour or two. Then she gets up, feeds her two cats, makes herself breakfast, and gets to work. Schneemann has two studios—the "little studio" comprises a few rooms and the hallway in the upstairs of her house, and the "big studio" is a separate building across the field from her front door, where Schneemann's assistant comes to work four days a week from 10:00 a.m. to 5:00 p.m. Schneemann usually joins her assistant there, and spends most of those hours on office work—the sundry correspondence, logistics, and administrative tasks that have ballooned as her paintings, assemblages, performances, photographs, and films have become increasingly recognized and celebrated in recent years. The actual making of new work happens outside office hours, whenever Schneemann can carve out the time. "I'm fighting all the time," she said, "just fighting, fighting, fighting to have everything moved away so that I can just concentrate on work. And every month it gets worse. The more appreciation I get, the less control I have over my time. The more bills, the more debt, the more taxes, the more people that need attention."

Schneemann is most likely to get concentrated studio time in the evening, although she can no longer work as late as she once could. "I still expect to go to two in the morning, but I probably manage to go to midnight," she said. She works every day, weekends included. Asked if she ever takes a weekend off, Schneemann laughed. "What a ridiculous thought!" she said. "Take a weekend off? How about a vacation? How about a little holiday? How about retiring? No—whatever it is, it's pretty constant." Aside from attending to office chores and caring for her cats, the one thing that keeps her away from making art is housework; although she's fine with the big studio being messy, she keeps her house meticulously clean. "I'm the kind of artist who has to do the dishes before she can work," she said. "It's very annoying, but that's how it is."

Marilyn Minter [b. 1948]

"I'm pretty much an obsessive worker," the New York–based painter said in 2017. "I love to work, and it gives me incredible energy. I would pay somebody to do what I do if I wasn't getting paid for it." Weekdays, Minter goes to bed at about 2:00 a.m. and gets up at 9:30 or so. "I've never been able to get up early and never will," she said. First thing, she has "lots of coffee" in bed with her husband and their dogs, and reads for about an hour. Then she gets ready to go from her downtown Manhattan apartment to her studio in Midtown, always walking or taking the subway. Before leaving home, she'll often talk on the phone with one of her several studio assistants, to begin figuring out her priorities for the day, which vary widely. Minter's paintings all begin as photographs, which are then combined and manipulated in Photoshop to create the image to be painted, so on any given day the artist may be staging a photo shoot, editing images, painting, or some combination of the above. As often as possible, she tries to find some time to paint each day. "When I really want to chill, I paint," she said. "That's the most therapeutic. Because the painting technique that I invented [involving layers and layers of translucent enamel paint] is very labor-intensive and it's almost like knitting. It's very satisfying."

Minter usually finishes work in time to have dinner with her husband and spend a couple hours together unwinding and reading before bed. She takes the weekends off. "On weekends, I devote my life to my husband," Minter said. "We compromise—I'm not allowed to work." When she is working, Minter never gets creative blocks, at least not since a long period of drug and alcohol addiction, during which her art, she said, "just turned to shit." Getting clean and sober in 1985 was the decisive turning point in her career. "I've been excited ever since," she said.

Josephine Meckseper (b. 1964)

"The great thing about being an artist is that you can create time and are not ruled by it," Meckseper said in 2017. The German-born, New York–based artist has long experience making time conform to her preferences: As a young girl, she loved to sleep late and, as a result, refused to go to school before 10:00 in the morning. "I posted a note on my door not to wake me until 9:30 a.m.," she said. "I always made my own hours." (It probably helped that Meckseper grew up with artist parents in Worpswede, Germany, a fabled artists' colony cofounded by Meckseper's great-uncle, the painter and architect Heinrich Vogeler.)

As a young artist, Meckseper continued to sleep late, preferring to work at night and get up at noon or later. Nowadays, she's back to waking at 10:00 a.m. "I find that my mind produces the best ideas in the morning," she said. "I don't like to venture into the real world too early in order to preserve that moment of immaculacy." While at home she showers, eats breakfast, exercises, and drinks her first two espressos of the day. At about noon, Meckseper walks the two blocks from her apartment to her studio, on the fourth floor of an industrial building on Manhattan's Lower East Side, where she has her third espresso and a quick briefing with her assistants. Then she sets about "addressing various aspects of conceptualizing and executing my works." Since these encompass large- and small-scale installations, paintings, photographs, and films, her workday is extremely varied; on any given afternoon, she may be looking at 3-D models or technical drawings, examining material samples, or meeting with fabricators, production designers, cinematographers, or other collaborators.

At 2:00 p.m., Meckseper stops for lunch, always the same salad and iced coffee delivered by bicycle from a local café. After lunch, she continues working at the studio until 8:00 p.m. If she needs a break, which happens about once a year, she will walk to a park in nearby Chinatown "to watch the crowds of people milling around, playing badminton, or performing traditional dances," she said. "I find peace within worlds that are completely different from my own." After work, she has dinner with friends before going to sleep at 1:00 or 2:00 a.m.

This schedule is not something Meckseper has to work at maintaining; indeed, she doesn't really think of it as a schedule at all. "For me, everything revolves around the creative process rather than the other way around," she said. "There is no need for a routine or schedule, because the ideas and the work fill out the space automatically." Similarly, Meckseper never finds herself stuck or blocked—if anything, the opposite is the case: "I often have too many ideas and need to restrain myself in order to finish a specific project." (She does, however, feel that she is most productive on rainy days, and wishes that it rained in New York more often.) Otherwise, there is only one requirement for her creative process: "No matter what, it is virtually impossible for me to work without drinking coffee—perhaps five espressos a day. It both fuels me and calms me down."

Jessye Norman (b. 1945)

"I do not tend to subscribe to rituals before going onstage," the American opera singer wrote in her 2014 autobiography.

> Indeed, I learned early in my performance life that these things need to be kept to a minimum if I am to get the job done well. Surely, as a very young singer in Berlin's Deutsche Oper, I did take notice of how the more experienced singers looked after themselves and their voices, and I even tried to incorporate some of their customary pre-performance rites into my own preparation. I remember one singer intimating that a raw egg mixed into a cup of tea was just the elixir she needed prior to a performance. That concoction held no magic for me. I did, however, try the "tea and honey" ritual that is the habit of many singers, and I used to prepare this mixture in a thermos and take it with me to performances. Once, while I was rushing out of a hotel in Vienna to sing a recital, my old-fashioned thermos, with its glass interior, fell out of my bag and crashed onto the floor. The noise of the shattered glass astonished me. What would I do? My tea was ruined! Would I be able to sing? How could I go onstage now? Right then and there, I halted that "ritual," which had become simply a mental crutch.

From then on, Norman's only pre-performance drinks have been water and fruit juices, and no special administration method is required. "Hydration; that is all that is needed," she wrote.

Maggie Nelson (b. 1973)

Nelson is the author of several books of poetry and prose, including *The Argonauts, The Art of Cruelty,* and *Bluets,* nonfiction books that combine autobiography, academic theory, and art, literary, and cultural criticism. Approached for an interview about her writing habits, Nelson warned that she's "a dull subject." As a young poet, she made a point of writing every day, she said, but now she no longer finds that necessary. "I think I'm just a project-oriented person," she said. "When I'm in the project, I'll probably write more than every day—like all the time, kind of feverishly. But if I'm not in that mode, there's no point in going to the computer and pecking away."

Nelson does not write full-time; she is also a professor at the University of Southern California, and so the rhythm of her days is largely dictated by her teaching schedule and other academic commitments. Her teaching often informs her writing—indeed, Nelson said, a lot of her writing starts as intensive "reading cycles," during which she'll make notes with a mechanical pencil in the margins of books. When she reaches the end of a cycle, she'll go back through the books and type up all her notes and see where she is. At some point, she knows it's time to start writing. "It's kind of cheesy, but I'll just start writing sentences in my head," she said. "And then it seems like I've hit some kind of tipping point where the research should be over and the writing part should happen."

Nelson generally writes at her home in Los Angeles, sitting at the kitchen table, on the back porch, or in the prefab Tuff Shed that she had installed as a writing hut in her backyard (on the advice of her former writing teacher Annie Dillard), although she says that she doesn't use the shed quite as much

as she thought she would. Asked whether she finds it difficult to fit the writing in around her academic work, Nelson
admits it can sometimes be a challenge—but hardly an insurmountable one. "I use the time that I have," she said.

Nikki Giovanni (b. 1943)

The Knoxville, Tennessee–born poet grew up in Cincinnati
and began writing seriously as a student at Fisk University, in
Nashville. After graduating, she borrowed money to publish
her first volume of poems, *Black Feeling, Black Talk,* which
sold more than ten thousand copies in its first year. Giovanni
used the proceeds to publish her second collection, *Black
Judgement,* and from then on she made a living as a poet
and an activist, relying on book sales, speaking engagements,
and teaching gigs to support herself; she didn't have her first
"real" job until 1987, when she joined the faculty of Virginia
Tech, where she is still a professor. Nowadays, the septuage-
narian poet teaches two days a week and writes when she is
moved to do so. She has never been a nose-to-the-grindstone,
two-hours-a-day kind of writer. "I never had that kind of
time," Giovanni said in 2017. "You have to realize, my generation was the Black Power generation. We were always on
the go, we always had something to do, someplace we needed
to be. So we got used to writing on the go."

Giovanni gets up at 6:00 or 7:00 a.m. "The first thing I do is
putter around the house," she said. "And if I've had an idea,
or something running through my head, I'll get some coffee
and sit down and putter in front of the computer." But many
days she doesn't write, and she doesn't worry about it either

way. "The only thing that I do every day is I read something," Giovanni said. "Even if it's just the comics pages, I read something. And I say that to my students: I think it's way more important to read something than it is to write."

Giovanni regularly makes notes as she's going about her days, and her writing often grows from those notes. "I don't ever feel pressure to write," Giovanni said. "I get interested." The feeling she has when sitting down at the computer is, she said, along the lines of "Oh, wouldn't it be nice, let's see where this goes." The tricky part is recognizing the difference between what's worth pursuing and what isn't—and not worrying over writing that falls into the latter category. "When it doesn't work, I just let it go," she said.

Giovanni can write at any time of day, but she feels that she's at her best at night. "All things being equal, I'm a late-night person," she said. "Because it's quiet and there's nothing else going on; even the dog goes to sleep. So if I have my way, I'll write from 10:00 or 11:00 until 2:00 in the morning, something like that." Asked if she's ever had writer's block, she laughed. "Never," she said. "If you have writer's block, you're not reading enough. And you're not thinking enough. Because there's no such thing as writer's block. What that really means is you don't have anything to say. And everybody goes through a period of not having anything to say; you have to accept that." Asked whether she often has periods of not having anything to say, Giovanni laughed again. "Very seldom."

AN ABNORMAL LIFE

....

Anne Bradstreet (1612–1672)

The eighteen-year-old Bradstreet arrived in what is now Massachusetts in 1630, with her new husband, her father, and a group of their fellow Protestant dissenters, among the first wave of settlers in the New World. Two years later she wrote her first poem, "Upon a Fit of Sickness," while convalescing from a long illness. The following summer Bradstreet became pregnant, and for the next six years she would not pen another line. But from 1638 to 1648, Bradstreet wrote more than six thousand lines of poetry—as the biographer Charlotte Gordon notes, "more than almost any other English writer on either side of the Atlantic composed in an entire lifetime." And, Gordon continues, "for most of this time, she was either pregnant, recovering from childbirth, or nursing an infant." (Bradstreet eventually had eight children.) The poet thought about her verse throughout the day, while minding the children, cooking family meals, or supervising the one or two female servants who performed the heaviest household chores—but she wrote exclusively at night, while the family and servants slept, the only hours when she could be alone. As she wrote in a letter, "The silent night's the fittest time for moan."

Emily Dickinson (1830–1886)

The only complete record of Dickinson's daily routine comes from a letter she sent to a friend in November 1847, when she was a sixteen-year-old student at Mount Holyoke Female Seminary, seven miles from her home in Amherst, Massachusetts. "I will tell you my order of time for the day, as you were so kind as to give me your's," Dickinson wrote.

> At 6. oclock, we all rise. We breakfast at 7. Our study hours begin at 8. At 9. we all meet in Seminary Hall, for devotions. At 10¼. I recite a review of Ancient History, in connection with which we read Goldsmith & Grimshaw [a pair of history textbooks]. At .11. I recite a lesson in "Pope's Essay on Man" which is merely transposition. At .12. I practice Calisthenics & at 12¼ read until dinner, which is at 12½ & after dinner, from 1½ until 2 I sing in Seminary Hall. From 2¾ until 3¾. I practise upon the Piano. At 3¾ I go to Sections, where we give in all our accounts of the day, including, Absence—Tardiness—Communications—Breaking Silent Study hours—Receiving Company in our rooms & ten thousand other things, which I will not take time or place to mention. At 4½, we go into Seminary Hall, & receive advice from Miss. Lyon in the form of lecture. We have Supper at 6. & silent-study hours from then until retiring bell, which rings at 8¾, but the tardy bell does not ring untl 9¾, so that we dont often obey the first warning to retire.

Although the letter provides a vivid portrait of student life at a nineteenth-century New England religious school,

Emily Dickinson, circa 1846–47

it does not reveal much about Dickinson's personality, and nothing about her eventual habits as a writer. Regretfully, no such detailed account of Dickinson's writing day exists. It's not even known exactly when Dickinson began composing poetry, although it was certainly by 1858, when the twenty-eight-year-old embarked on a project to recopy and organize her existing poems into small, hand-sewn booklets. These were not for distribution—Dickinson frequently enclosed individual poems or fragments of poems in her letters, but she did not share her eventual forty booklets with anyone, and they were discovered only after her death. Nor did she write with the idea of publication in mind, noting in a letter that it was "foreign to my thought, as Firmament to Fin." Only ten of her nearly eighteen hundred poems were published in her lifetime, none of them at her instigation.

As for what is known of Dickinson's writing habits, evidence suggests that she wrote mostly at night—both letters and poetry—while the rest of the household slept. Except for the year she spent at Mount Holyoke, Dickinson always lived with her family, which comprised her conservative, overprotective father; her anxious, sickly mother; a sister who never married; and a brother who married in 1856 and moved to an Italianate mansion next to the Homestead, the large brick Federal house Dickinson's grandfather had built, and where the poet lived for the first nine years of her life and from 1855 to her death. (In between, financial difficulties forced her father to sell his portion of the house, but he was later able to repurchase the entire property.) There, her large upstairs bedroom had windows looking out over Main Street and toward the Evergreens, her brother's residence a few hundred yards away. The room had a small writing table in the corner and a Franklin stove to keep Dickinson warm on chilly nights while she wrote by candlelight.

Famously, after 1865 Dickinson was housebound, rarely or never leaving the grounds of the Homestead. It is possible that she suffered from agoraphobia, or that an eye ailment in the 1860s prompted her seclusion; Dickinson's sister suggested, however, that it was their mother's illness in the years leading up to 1865 that contributed to the poet's withdrawal: "Our mother had a period of invalidism, and one of her daughters must be constantly at home; Emily chose this part and, finding the life with her books and nature so congenial, continued to live it." Whatever the reason, it is true that Dickinson found her seclusion congenial; she enjoyed a rich private world concentrated on her reading and writing, and a wide-ranging correspondence. She still interacted with her family daily and took part in the household chores (apparently, baking and dessert-making were her special province). She avoided most visitors but would occasionally receive a guest at home, and she spent hours tending her spacious garden, although she was known to bolt indoors if any adults approached. Children, however, she welcomed, gardening peacefully while they played nearby—or, if she was in her room, silently lowering from her window a basket of gingerbread for them to enjoy.

Visitors who did get to meet "the myth," as locals took to calling her, remember Dickinson as soft-spoken and childlike in demeanor, but with a strange intensity. After years of correspondence with Dickinson, the critic and scholar Thomas Wentworth Higginson visited her at the Homestead for an hour in August 1870. Years later, he recalled, "The impression undoubtedly made on me was that of an excess of tension, and of an abnormal life." The day after his meeting, he wrote in a letter to his wife: "I never was with any one who drained my nerve power so much. Without touching her, she drew from me. I am glad not to live near her."

To write, Dickinson seemed to need to harness that nervous energy, which she could not do on command. As a result, she wrote in waves of literary activity rather than through any kind of everyday practice. In her most fertile period, from 1862–63, she composed hundreds of poems; then, for years, she hardly wrote at all. As she said in an 1862 letter, "I had no Monarch in my life, and cannot rule myself, and when I try to organize—my little Force explodes—and leaves me bare and charred—"

Harriet Hosmer (1830–1908)

"I am as busy as a whole hive of bees, one bee is not sufficient to represent all the irons I have in the fire," the American neoclassical sculptor wrote from her studio in Rome in 1870. Ever since arriving in the Eternal City as an eager apprentice eighteen years earlier, Hosmer had been perpetually at work, sculpting most days from dawn until dinner. "She was never idle," her friend Cornelia Carr remembered. "Her busy brain was unceasingly at work on favorite designs, and she was happy in plans for future activity." Her dedication did not leave much time for a personal life; indeed, Hosmer swore off any romantic attachments at a young age, believing that they were too compromising for a female artist. "I am the only faithful worshipper of Celibacy, and her service becomes more fascinating the longer I remain in it," she wrote in the summer of 1854, four years after arriving in Rome. "Even if so inclined, an artist has no business to marry. For a man, it may be well enough, but for a woman on whom matrimonial duties and cares weigh more heavily, it is a moral wrong, I think, for she must neglect her profession and her family, becoming neither a good wife and mother nor a good artist. My ambition is to become the latter, so I wage an eternal feud with the consolidating knot."

Fanny Trollope (1779–1863)

Trollope married at thirty and, over the next nine years, gave birth to four sons and three daughters. Meanwhile, her husband failed first as a lawyer and then as a farmer, and the family's financial situation grew dire. In an effort to forestall destitution, Trollope, her husband, and their three youngest sons sailed to America, where they helped to establish a utopian colony in Memphis and opened a bazaar for fancy imported goods in Cincinnati. Neither venture made any money, and after three years the family returned to England—but the trip planted the seed of a much more lucrative enterprise. While still in America, Trollope began making notes for a travelogue, on the hunch that her fellow British citizens would enjoy reading about the "so very queer" people in the New World. She was right; when it was published in 1832, *Domestic Manners of the Americans* was a best seller. With its success, Trollope had found her calling, and over the next twenty-five years she would publish five more travelogues and thirty-four novels.

Two of Trollope's sons also grew up to become writers: Thomas Adolphus Trollope published more than forty volumes of travel writing, history, and fiction, and Anthony Trollope became one of the great novelists of the Victorian era, with forty-seven novels and many volumes of short stories, biography, and reportage. Anthony also became famous for his industriousness, writing for three hours every morning before going to his day job as a civil servant at the General Post Office (and, if he finished a book during his morning writing stint, immediately taking out a clean sheet of paper and beginning the next book). But he was merely doing his best imitation of his mother, who had set a high bar. "Of the mixture of joviality and industry which formed her character, it is almost impossible to speak with exaggeration," Anthony wrote in his *Autobiography*. "The industry was a thing apart, kept to herself. It was not necessary that any one who lived with her should see it. She was at her table at four in the morning, and had finished her work before the world had begun to be aroused." After that point, Trollope resumed her duties as the family matriarch, running the household (with the help of a pair of servants) and attending to the needs of her husband and children. Nevertheless, according to Anthony, she always remained cheerful in the face of her myriad responsibilities. "She had much, very much, to suffer," he wrote. "Work sometimes came hard to her, so much being required . . . but of all people I have known she was the most joyous, or, at any rate, the most capable of joy."

Harriet Martineau (1802–1876)

Often cited as the first female sociologist, Martineau was also one of the first female journalists. Over her long career, she produced countless essays on economics and social theory, as well as travel writing, an autobiography, and several novels— her best known is 1839's *Deerbrook*—and she earned enough money to support herself solely by writing, a rare feat for a woman in Victorian England. Naturally, she worked incredibly hard. "From the age of fifteen to the moment in which I am writing, I have been scolded in one form or another, for working too hard," Martineau noted in her autobiography. But the fact was, she continued, that she "had no power of choice" when it came to her intellectual labor: "I have not done it for amusement, or for money, or for fame, or for any reason but because I could not help it. Things were pressing to be said; and there was more or less evidence that I was the person to say them."

This makes it sound as though Martineau never suffered from a moment of writer's block; in fact, the opposite was the case. It was only her intimate experience with being blocked, and her realization of how to overcome that miserable state,

An engraving of Harriet Martineau, circa 1873

that had enabled her to write so much. "I can speak, after long experience, without any doubt on this matter," she wrote in her autobiography.

I have suffered, like other writers, from indolence, irresolution, distaste for my work, absence of "inspiration," and all that: but I have also found that sitting down, however reluctantly, with the pen in my hand, I have never worked for one quarter of an hour without finding myself in full train; so that all the quarter hours, arguings, doubtings, and hesitation as to whether I should work or not which I gave way to in my inexperience, I now regard as so much waste, not only of time but, far worse, of energy. To the best of my belief, I never but once in my life left my work because I could not do it: and that single occasion was on the opening day of an illness.

This discovery came as a tremendous relief—merely by forcing herself to work for those first fifteen minutes, Martineau found that she was spared from "those embarrassments and depressions which I see afflicting many an author who waits for a mood instead of summoning it," and from then on she could write whenever she chose.

As for her writing hours, Martineau was (perhaps not surprisingly) a devoted morning person. "I never pass a day without writing; and the writing is always done in the morning," she wrote. In London, her typical schedule was to get up and make coffee at 7:00 or 7:30 a.m. and go immediately to work, which she continued until 2:00 p.m. (In her descriptions of her day, there is no mention of lunch.) Then she received visitors at home for two hours before going out for a one-hour walk. Returning home, she changed into evening dress and read the newspaper. Then a friend's carriage would arrive to take Martineau to dinner and one or two evening visits. She tried to get home by midnight or half past, in order to answer letters or read before going to bed at 1:00 or 2:00 a.m. This means that on an average day she wrote for five and a half or six hours and slept the same amount at night. But after her morning coffee, Martineau did not drink any additional caffeine during the day, and she was dismissive of the popular idea that most writers relied on caffeine or alcohol or opiates to fuel their working hours. "Fresh air and cold water are my stimulants," she said.

Fannie Hurst (1885–1968)

"Writers, like teeth, are divided into incisors and grinders," the nineteenth-century English journalist Walter Bagehot once wrote. Hurst fell decisively into the latter group. Although she published more than three hundred short stories during her lifetime, as well as nineteen novels and several plays—making her one of the most widely read female authors of the twentieth century, and one of the highest-paid American writers of either sex—Hurst never found the writing process congenial. In her autobiography, she wrote of "that stubborn hiatus between the idea and the written word. The concept lively and boiling in my mind, the words coming in slow and painful trickle onto paper, there to torture with their inadequacies." She continued, "That monkey on my back has never relinquished hold in all the years. The urge to write versus the torturous process of getting it said." Despite the torture, Hurst wrote for several hours a day, every day, for pretty much her entire adult life. "My own workaday routine, five to six to seven hours at the desk, holds with the years," she wrote. "Like woman's work, the author's work is never done."

Emily Post (1872–1960)

Post became a household name following the publication of *Etiquette,* her 1922 bible of proper social conduct, which she updated twice a decade for the rest of her life while also writing a syndicated newspaper column and answering a ceaseless influx of letters from readers seeking her advice on all manner of household, workplace, and polite-society dilemmas. Fortunately, Post liked to work. "We used to tell her that when she had a job in hand she was like a bird dog on a scent," her son, Ned, wrote in a biography of his mother.

Throughout her life, Post woke at 6:30 a.m. and, while still in bed, set immediately to the day's tasks, continuing to work without pause until noon. Her son writes:

> She had improvised an arrangement which enabled her to get her own breakfast as early as she wished and while remaining in bed. A thermos of hot coffee, another small one of cream, butter in an iced container, zwieback and the dark buckwheat honey she loved were placed on a tray on her bedside table every night. She would breakfast and then, remaining in bed, write, edit copy, and plan her correspondence against the time her secretary would arrive. No telephone calls, no visitors, no household interruptions were permitted to break in on her working time. After twelve she rose, dressed, and was ready and hungry for luncheon punctually at one.
>
> She preferred to have friends come to her to having lunch at other houses or at the Colony Club of which she was a charter member. She flatly refused to lunch in restaurants. She liked to drive in the afternoon, but would never consent to having a car of her own. She welcomed a guest or two at tea, which was always a part of her day's ritual, and she frequently had guests for dinner, or dined out with friends of old standing and at houses where conversation flourished. She did not play bridge and she hated gossip and never indulged in it.

The reason Post refused to dine in restaurants was because she ate extremely rapidly, devoting no more than ten to fifteen minutes to mealtimes when she was at home; anything more, she felt, was a waste of her work hours. Of course, it helped that Post was always able to employ several domestic servants, and never had to prepare meals herself, something she was more or less incapable of. (The breakfast tray described by her son was prepared by the household staff the night before.) As Post once admitted to an interviewer, "If I were forced to cook for myself, my diet would be bread and water."

Janet Scudder (1869–1940)

Scudder was an Indiana-born sculptor whose whimsical fountains and statues became hugely popular in the early twentieth century, championed by the Beaux-Arts architect Stanford White and installed in the Metropolitan Museum of Art and the gardens of John D. Rockefeller and other members of the wealthy elite. Before achieving this success, however, Scudder endured an arduous apprenticeship, with studies in Cincinnati, Chicago, and Paris, and a period of near poverty in New York as she sought out commissions from architects and other clients. In her autobiography, *Modeling My Life,* Scudder describes her first summer in New York, when she was a twenty-six-year-old unknown living alone in a shabbily furnished studio on Union Square that she rented for fourteen dollars a month:

These long hot days began with a frugal breakfast— milk and bread; then I would put the studio in order,

Janet Scudder, circa 1920

removing all traces of the bedroom it was at night and turning it into a workshop. The rest of the morning I usually spent in drawing, though many mornings I felt I should profit more by looking at the work of others and tramped up to the Metropolitan Museum, where I spent hours in studying the sculpture and in painting. . . . At lunch time I returned to the studio and prepared the simple meal that never varied and that did not take any time or skill to prepare—a can of baked beans and a glass of milk. I had heard that there was a great deal of nourishment in beans; at any rate I found them the most filling thing I could buy for fifteen cents. In the afternoon I went about from one architect's office to another's—always with hope and always in vain. . . . After an afternoon of rebuffs, footsore, hot and weary, I would usually—not every day but almost every other day—drop into a friendly little restaurant on Sixth Avenue, where, for twenty-five cents, I could have dinner, my only square meal. And it was square, there is no doubt about that—all put on the table at once, from soup to ice cream, each little dab in its own bird-bath dish, the meat growing cold and the ice cream melting before I could finish the soup. On those evenings when I felt twenty-five cents was too much to spend on dinner—having already wasted ten cents on street cars that day—I would dine in my studio on the same old menu of baked beans and milk. But the hardest part of the day to get through was the long summer evening. Can anything be more utterly dismal than a summer evening in a city without a soul to speak to! If the air was unbearably stifling, I would often wander out to Union Square and sit there on a bench for an hour or two—which invariably increased my depression and loneliness. Those other benches were filled with derelicts and loafers—the failures of life. I was too young then to feel any surge of sympathy towards them; they only filled me with disgust and an even greater desire for work—hard, satisfying work that would fill my empty life to overflowing. When I could stand it no longer I would leave the bench, walk slowly back to the studio and creep into my couch bed without turning on the light.

Scudder's perseverance eventually paid off. Through the father of a wealthy art-school friend, she landed a commission to design the seal for the New York Bar Association, which opened the door to other jobs—and to a more congenial diet. Scudder wrote in her autobiography, "I can never see a tin of baked beans now without having an alarming sinking sensation."

Sarah Bernhardt (1844–1923)

For decades, Bernhardt was the most famous actress in Europe, lauded by critics, greeted by adoring crowds wherever she went, and endlessly discussed in the press, which tracked her every movement and dubbed her the Eighth Wonder of the World. After watching her perform in London in 1880, the American psychologist William James wrote to his wife that "Bernhardt last night was the *finest* piece of acting I've ever seen—as if etched with the point of a needle—and altogether she is the most race-horsey, high-mettled human being I've ever seen—physically she is a perfect skeleton." Bernhardt's notorious thinness was only one part of her legend. There was also the ornate rosewood coffin that she was said to sleep in, and which she supposedly carried along on tour (in fact, she did keep such a coffin as a macabre set piece in her bedroom but did not normally sleep in it); the hat she wore festooned with a pair of leathery bat wings, and the stuffed vampire bat that she kept in her bedroom, along with a human skeleton and the aforementioned coffin; the pet alligator that she acquired while on tour in America, and which she named Ali-Gaga; and her insistence on being paid only in gold coins, which she carried around in an old chamois leather bag or a small suitcase, from which she reluctantly

Sarah Bernhardt posing in her coffin, circa 1873

doled out payments to her performers, her servants, and her creditors. Although she hated to part with a single coin, she spent lavishly on her household, employing eight to ten servants, two carriages, and several horses, and constantly hosting luxurious dinner parties at which she herself ate virtually nothing.

But to her contemporaries in the theater Bernhardt's most striking characteristic was her prodigious, seemingly unlimited energy, which allowed her to work around the clock without ever appearing to tire. "No person I have ever known had such amazing energy as Bernhardt," the theatrical producer George Tyrell said. "Something seemed to burn within her like a consuming flame, which at the same time did not burn her out. The more she did the more inspiration she found." In 1899, the poet and dramatist Edmond Rostand—whose play *L'Aiglon* gave Bernhardt one of her signature roles—described the actress's typical workday, starting with her afternoon arrival at the theater:

A brougham stops at a door; a woman, enveloped in furs, jumps out, threads her way with a smile through the crowd attracted by the jingling of the bell on the harness, and mounts a winding stair; plunges into a room crowded with flowers and heated like a hothouse; throws her little beribboned handbag with its apparently inexhaustible contents into one corner, and her bewinged hat into another; takes off her furs, and instantaneously dwindles to a mere scabbard of white silk; rushes on to a dimly lighted stage and immediately puts life into a whole crowd of listless, yawning, loitering folks; dashes backward and forward, inspiring every one with her own feverish energy; goes into the prompter's box, arranges her scenes, points out the proper gesture and intonation, rises up in wrath and insists on everything being done over again; shouts with fury; sits down, smiles, drinks tea, and begins to rehearse her own part. . . .

According to Rostand, these rehearsals could draw tears from the other actors who paused to watch Bernhardt—but the remainder of her pre-show ritual was more likely to draw groans of frustration from the theater's crew, whom Bern-hardt relentlessly pestered and bullied in her manic rounds backstage, making the decorators redo their work to her lik-ing, showing the costumier exactly how to dress her, supervis-ing the lighting artists' work and reducing the electrician to "a state of temporary insanity." Finally, Rostand continues, Bernhardt

> returns to her room for dinner; sits down to table, splen-didly pale with fatigue; ruminates over her plans; eats with peals of Bohemian laughter; has no time to finish; dresses for the evening performance while the manager reports from the other side of the curtain; acts with all her heart and soul; discusses business between the acts; remains at the theater until after the performance, and makes arrangements until three o'clock in the morning; does not make up her mind to go until she sees her staff respectfully endeavoring to keep awake; gets into her carriage; huddles herself into her furs and anticipates the delights of lying down and resting at last; bursts out laughing on remembering that someone is wait-ing to read her a five-act play; returns home, listens to the piece, becomes excited, weeps, accepts it, finds she cannot sleep and takes advantage of the opportunity to study a part!

"This is the Sarah I have always known," Rostand con-cludes. "I never made the acquaintance of the Sarah with the coffin and the alligators. The only Sarah I know is the one who works." Bernhardt must have appreciated the homage. "Life engenders life," she once said, "energy creates energy. It is by spending oneself that one becomes rich."

Mrs. Patrick Campbell (1865–1940)

One of the great actresses of Edwardian England, Campbell had no real interests outside the theater, which didn't leave her much time for them anyway. "The life of the stage is a hard one; the sacrifices it demands are enormous," she wrote. "Peaceful normal life is made almost impossible by the ever over-strained and necessarily over-sensitive nerves—caused by late hours, emotional stress, swift thinking, swift feeling. . . ." Campbell's dedication to her profession could make her a difficult collaborator; no one who worked with her was unfamiliar with "the exacting perfectionism, the terrible sarcasms, the bursts of fury, the will that dominated and dwarfed everyone around her," in the words of the biographer Margot Peters. Away from the theater, Campbell's perfectionism was toned down only slightly; at home, she aspired to simple bourgeois comforts for herself and her two children, and she could grow cross when this vision proved elusive. "Her neatness amazed me," one acquaintance remembered. "Somehow one expected so great an artist to be careless about detail, but she was meticulously neat in all her habits. Domestic details maddened her, and I can see her now, entering [her daughter's] bedroom, her great tragic eyes smouldering, and declaiming passionately—'They tell me there is no more toilet paper in the house. How can I be expected to act a romantic part AND remember to order TOILET PAPER!' "

A SUBTLE AND DEEP-LAID PLAN

....

Niki de Saint Phalle (1930–2002)

In the spring of 1959, Saint Phalle, her husband, and their two children went on a weeklong vacation with the painter Joan Mitchell and her companion, Jean-Paul Riopelle (see page 133). The two couples had become friends in Paris, where they were all living and working. Saint Phalle, then twenty-eight, was painting while taking care of her children; her husband, Harry Mathews, was a writer working on his first novel; and Mitchell and Riopelle were well-established artists. One night at dinner during their vacation, Mitchell turned to Saint Phalle and said, "So you're one of those writer's wives that paint." The remark, Saint Phalle wrote years later, "hurt me to the quick. It hit me as though an arrow pierced a sensitive part of my soul."

Returning to Paris, Saint Phalle decided that if she wanted to be taken seriously as an artist, she would have to make a more drastic commitment. Since marrying Mathews at eighteen, she had worked as a model, attended drama school, suffered a nervous breakdown, and discovered a talent and passion for art. But she had never had the opportunity to give all her energy and attention to one thing. In 1960, still smarting from Mitchell's comment, she left her husband and two children, ages nine and five, so that she could "live her artistic adventure to the full without the perfect balance that I found between my work, Harry and the children." She intended to remain single but soon began a relationship with the Swiss

Niki de Saint Phalle with some of her sculptures, circa 1971

artist Jean Tinguely that would last until his death in 1991. Her real commitment, however, was to her work. "My secret jealous lover (my work) is always there and waits for me," she wrote.

He is tall, elegant, and like Count Dracula wears a black cloak. He whispers in my ear that I don't have much time left for what I have to do. He is jealous of every moment I don't spend with him. He is even jealous of my closed bedroom door. Sometimes he flies through the open window of my room at night, in the shape of a giant bat. I tremble when he embraces me with his wings. For a moment I defend myself in my long white nightshirt. His teeth sink into my soul. I am his.

Only a couple years into her artistic adventure, Saint Phalle became famous for her "shooting paintings," made by attaching bags or cans of paint to assemblages and shooting them with a rifle, a pistol, or a miniature cannon, splattering paint over the artwork. A few years later, Saint Phalle began working primarily as a sculptor, and in 1978 she embarked on the Tarot Garden, a monumental sculpture garden that she built in Tuscany over the course of twenty years. After the site's largest sculpture, a house-size female figure, was completed, Saint Phalle moved into its interior, turning one breast into her bedroom and the other into her kitchen. (The only two windows were built into the sculpture's nipples.) "I enjoyed living the life of a monk, but it wasn't always pleasant," she later wrote of her seven years living inside the sculpture. "There was a large hole in the ground where I kept my provisions, and I cooked on a tiny camping stove. Every hot night I woke up to find swarms of insects from the marshes buzzing round me, as in a childish nightmare."

Wealthy friends had provided the land for the Tarot Garden, but financing the construction over so many years was a constant struggle, and the artist resorted to a variety of means (including selling her own perfume, called Niki de Saint Phalle). But she also relied on scores of unpaid helpers, whom she lured onto the project through her immense personal charisma. She was aware of the effect she had on others, and used it to her advantage. "Enthusiasm is a virus and a virus that I am able to propagate very easily because enthusiasm enables me to do anything I want, no matter how difficult it is," she wrote. Whether the work was in the best interest of her friends and collaborators was not her concern. "People are very important," Saint Phalle wrote. "They are essential but they are not the most important. The most important remains the work, the total obsession, the virus."

Ruth Asawa (1926–2013)

Asawa was a Japanese American artist who learned to draw in an internment camp during World War II and pioneered a unique style of looped-wire sculpture in the 1940s, while attending Black Mountain College in North Carolina. There she studied with Anni and Josef Albers and Buckminster Fuller, befriended Merce Cunningham and Robert Rauschenberg, and met her future husband, Albert Lanier. In 1949 she joined Lanier in San Francisco, where he was working as an architect and where Asawa continued her sculpture experiments while raising an eventual six children, born between 1950 and 1959. Asawa came from a large family herself—she was the fourth of seven children born to Japanese immigrant farmers in California—and she never saw children as an impediment to her artwork; rather, she felt that art should be a part of daily life, and she made her sculptures with the kids around her, whenever she could squeeze it in between other chores. "My materials were simple," she said, "and whenever there was a free moment, I would sit down and do some work. Sculpture is like farming. If you just keep at it, you can get quite a lot done."

Lila Katzen (1932–1998)

The Brooklyn-born sculptor began her career as a painter but, around 1960, moved into three-dimensional work, creating immersive environments from plastic, water, and fluorescent lights, and later building monumental sculptures in Cor-Ten steel. Katzen knew that she wanted to be an artist from a young age—"I was going to be an artist even when I was in kindergarten," she said—and over the years she became adept at carving out time for her work despite all manner of obstacles. After high school, Katzen couldn't afford to attend art school full-time, so she lived at home with her mother and stepfather, worked during the day, and took night classes. Because her stepfather was "adamant about my not working at home," Katzen recalled later, she would do so only after he went to bed, setting up her work and painting until 2:00 or 3:00 a.m., then putting everything away and airing out the room before going to sleep.

Katzen married at nineteen, and after college moved with her husband to Baltimore. As she began to establish herself as an artist she was also the mother and chief caretaker of two small children. At the time, Katzen used the upstairs of her house as her studio, and she worked when her kids napped or after they went to bed at night. In the 1970s, the art historian Cindy Nemser asked her how she managed it all. "I worked from eight in the evening to two in the morning," Katzen said.

> I also set up a schedule of work knowing that I wanted to put in a forty-hour week. I felt that I had to do that. In the beginning it was very hard and I used to chalk out the hours that I got out of the week. This week I only got four hours. Well that is very bad. This week I got eight hours. That is better, but it is nothing. And I made up my mind that even if I didn't do anything, even if I just sat there or if the things were messes or if I destroyed things (and I went through real rituals of making nothing and destroying lots of stuff that I had made), regardless of anything, that time was going to be

spent in the studio. That is the way I did it. . . . When they napped, I would nap too or I would go upstairs and work.

If Katzen was working and her kids woke up and needed something to do, the artist would yell, "Here are some crayons and paper," and throw them down the stairs.

Helen Frankenthaler (1928–2011)

"A really good picture looks as if it's happened at once," the Abstract Expressionist painter said. "It's an immediate image . . . it looks as if it were born in a minute." Of course, Frankenthaler might have abandoned ten versions of a painting before she arrived at the one that felt spontaneous and true. And getting to that image required more than just practice or experimentation, she thought—it came from a marshaling of all the painter's resources. "One prepares, bringing all one's weight and gracefulness and knowledge to bear: spiritually, emotionally, intellectually, physically," Frankenthaler said. "And often there's a moment when all frequencies are right and it hits."

To find those moments, Frankenthaler worked in fits and starts—periods of fertile activity followed by stretches of labored, unsatisfactory painting, or nothing at all. "I tend to focus on a body of work intensely and one day put down the brush and feel emptied out," she said. "I realize that I need to shift gears before I paint again." A small break could be refreshing, Frankenthaler said, but a long one was frightening:

Helen Frankenthaler in her studio, 1969

I will often get back to painting after a break and panic and not know where I left off. I seem to start at day one again. I sit around and sharpen pencils, make phone calls, eat handfuls of pistachios, take a swim. I feel I should, must, will paint. It is agony. It is boredom. I become impatient and angry with myself, until I reach a point of feeling I must start, make a mark, just make a mark. Then, hopefully, I slowly get into a new phase of work.

The artist followed a somewhat similar rhythm in the kitchen. She said that she had more energy and painted best when she ate healthy—but she also needed the "catharsis" of the occasional junk-food binge. "My usual regime is no fat, no salt, no butter, no sugar, no bread, no cream, but home-made skim-milk yogurt," Frankenthaler told the authors of a 1977 cookbook. But when she had denied herself for long enough, she would indulge in chocolate, ice cream, or one of a variety of snack foods: "Processed cheese, kosher dill pickles, peanut butter, cheap sardines, and bologna—junk food; these are things that I periodically crave and give in to."

Eileen Farrell (1920–2002)

One of the most celebrated American singers of the twentieth century, Farrell was a classically trained soprano who successfully performed both classical and popular music over the course of her sixty-year career. When she sang at the Metropolitan Opera in New York City, Farrell had a pre-performance routine that she always followed. At about midday, she went into the music room of her home in Staten Island and sang through the entire opera she would be performing that evening. "Some people think this is crazy," Farrell wrote in her 1999 memoir, "but I say if you're going to be singing high Cs that night, you'd better make sure they're in place that afternoon." In the late afternoon, she took the Staten Island Ferry to Manhattan and caught a taxi to the Met. Although many opera singers are careful to eat a very light meal, or nothing at all, before singing, Farrell was not so dainty. "There was a little restaurant across the street where I would always go for a six-o'clock dinner," she wrote.

> I usually had the same thing—a steak, baked potato, green salad, and hot tea with lemon. Rich, creamy des-

serts really clog up your throat, so I would order a dish of Jell-O, which went down very easily. Then I'd go across the street, hit my dressing room, and get into my makeup and costume. The only thing I insisted on having in my dressing room when I arrived was a big bottle of warm Coca-Cola. Once I was in my costume, I would drink a few glasses of warm Coke and start to belch. It's amazing what this can do for the voice, and as Miss Mac [her longtime voice teacher] always used to tell me, "It saves wear and tear on the rectum."

In the early 1950s, the renowned opera singer Beverly Sills sang with Farrell in New York—and was scandalized by the belching she could hear coming from Farrell's dressing room. "Those weren't discreet burps," Sills later recalled. "They were more like symphonies."

Eleanor Antin (b. 1935)

Antin began her career as a painter but soon moved into conceptual art, becoming a pioneering figure in video, performance, and installation art. She is best known for the elaborate fictional personae whose lives she led, in costume, for days or weeks at a time. These alter egos included a king, a nurse, and, most famously, Eleanora Antinova, the legendary black prima ballerina of Serge Diaghilev's Ballets Russes, whom Antin invented in the mid-1970s and whose persona she explored for more than a decade through performances, installations, films, plays, and memoirs. Creating fictional selves like Antinova has allowed the artist to, in her words, "get out of my own skin to explore other realities." But it has also required paring back her own life to the very basics. As she said in a 1998 interview, "Because the one thing that matters most to me in my life, and what I've spent most of my life doing, is making art, I've had to make the rest of my life fairly simple."

I teach, I have a husband whom I really love, I have a son, now a daughter-in-law, and I have friends, so I'm lucky. But often I don't have too much time for them. I work very hard. I get five hours of sleep a night—if I'm lucky—but I'm always working, there's just not much time left for anything else. So I live in my head, making up stories. I really prefer spending my life in what you might say—with not a little touch of irony—is a "traditional" woman's way of living, like those eighteenth- and nineteenth-century women who were stuck in their roles and their class because they couldn't escape, so they wrote romantic novels. But in my case I've *chosen* that way. My personae / historical fictions, are actually all the lives that I'm not going to live because I *chose* not to. . . . To me, the uninvented life, to paraphrase the cliché, is hardly a life.

Antin figured all is out relatively early in her career—as she said in a 1977 interview, "It seems to me you have to have your personal life organized so that it takes as little of your time as possible. Otherwise you can't make your art. And if you're an artist, I don't care what they say, you should be married to an artist. If not, forget it. If you aren't married to an artist, what would you talk about?"

Julia Wolfe (b. 1958)

Wolfe is a New York–based composer who won the 2015 Pulitzer Prize for her oratorio *Anthracite Fields,* which evokes the lives of nineteenth- and twentieth-century Pennsylvania coal miners. She works at home in the TriBeCa loft she shares with her husband, the composer Michael Gordon, with whom she cofounded (along with David Lang) the new-music collective Bang on a Can in 1987. The married composers each have small studios on opposite ends of the loft, and although their schedules do not always overlap, "there's a good chunk of the day when we're both working in our little caves," Wolfe said in 2017. Her ideal working day begins at 7:30 or 8:00 a.m., when she gets up and takes the family dog out for a walk along the Hudson River. Then she has breakfast and coffee and gets to work. When Wolfe is on a deadline, she'll work on a new composition around the clock, often right up until bedtime at 11:00 p.m. or midnight, but she considers the morning her prime window of opportunity. "I just feel like my mind is clear," she said. "I'm not a fuzzy morning person—I mean, I'm physically fuzzy; I don't find that I want to exercise. But in terms of just putting my mind to work, it's the best time."

If she doesn't have other commitments, Wolfe will compose from about 9:00 a.m. until the early afternoon. In her studio, she has an upright piano, a small desk with a large-screen computer monitor, and bookshelves with scores, music books, CDs, and notebooks; she uses the notebooks to write down ideas about the piece she's working on (and she generally works on one piece at a time, preferring a long immersion in a single composition). She doesn't have email access on her desktop computer, and though she can—and often does—check her email on a laptop computer she keeps in the studio, she tries to put off dealing with it until later in the day.

In the afternoons, Wolfe may have teaching duties—she is a professor of music composition at New York University's Steinhardt School—or she may work with her colleagues at Bang on a Can's Brooklyn headquarters, or host a rehearsal at home. (Since the family dog wails at high-pitched sounds, this requires a trip to the local doggie daycare first.) Sometimes in the late afternoon she'll take a walk, a fruitful activity for her work. But perhaps the most crucial component of her working life is the feedback that she and her Bang on a Can cofounders routinely trade among themselves. The three of them are in the habit of running musical ideas by one another, sometimes holding the phone up to their computer speakers to play something and get a quick second opinion. This is not mere positive reinforcement; all three composers are opinionated, and they do not go easy on one another—which, Wolfe said, is what makes the arrangement so valuable. "There's this very tough dialogue that's going on pretty regularly," she said. "And I really cherish that. I think that kind of dialogue lights a fire under you."

Charlotte Bray (b. 1982)

The Berlin-based British composer usually wakes up at 7:00 a.m., has coffee and breakfast, and gets immediately to work in her home office. "I find I'm most creative in the morning, so I try to not do anything other than think about composing in the morning," she said in 2017. Many days, this requires a conscious application of willpower. "I have to deliberately not let myself do other things when I need to compose," Bray said. "Very often, I need to just sit looking at the music for a few minutes first, and try to empty my head." She'll tell herself, "This is what I'm doing now." Typically, Bray will compose until lunchtime, at about 1:00 p.m. Then, if she's on a deadline—or if the work is going particularly well—she'll "carry on a bit" after lunch. But normally the afternoon is for the administrative chores she avoids thinking about in the morning—in particular, dealing with the emails that have been piling up while she works.

When she's composing, Bray moves among the piano, the cello—her main instrument—and her desk, where she'll usually sketch ideas by hand first; she won't switch to the computer until about two-thirds of the way into the process. Unless she's traveling, Bray works six mornings a week, and doesn't often find herself stuck or blocked; even so, new compositions proceed slowly. A good morning's work might yield thirty seconds to a minute of music, but then the next few days are often spent reviewing and fine-tuning those ideas. (A twenty-minute cello concerto will take Bray about six months to complete.) Although she works in a very methodical, orderly fashion, Bray said that the process doesn't feel at all straightforward. "Personally, I need a routine, and I need to make myself do it," she said. "It's not like I expect it to just come naturally."

Hayden Dunham (b. 1988)

The Texas-born, Los Angeles–based artist's sculptural assemblages grow out of her fascination with materials—with how they transform from one state to another and how they interact with the human body, in a literal sense and in more esoteric ways. "That's why I'm interested in making physical objects," Dunham said in 2017. "I really believe that objects can carry energy, and that they can change internal human dispositions."

Dunham's creative process is guided by her own disposition on any given day. She typically wakes up at about 7:00 a.m. and stays in bed until 7:30, when she heads into the kitchen of her combined studio/residence to make a "tonic" whose ingredients vary depending "on what I need for that day," she said. "I might wake up and feel really airy and need to be grounded—so then I might put apple-cider vinegar or greens in the tonic, to sort of weigh me down. Then there are other days where I wake up and feel heavy, so I need something light. It's a kind of check-in. The liquid reflects how I'm doing, almost like a mirror."

Next, Dunham heads out to the small backyard behind her building, to write for about twenty minutes. "It's basically just putting the pen on the piece of paper and trying to let something come through you," she said. Then she eats breakfast—often oatmeal—before getting dressed for the day. "I always dress up for work," she said. "I never work in sweatpants or something like that. I'll wear heels; I usually look very formal when I'm working. Because I think that also helps shift my energy. . . . It's another way of thinking about how you are, the state that you're in, if you're able to do this type of work, how your day would be best spent based on your internal composition."

And then she gets to work. For the first part of the day, this often involves a lot of running around Los Angeles, picking up or dropping off objects or materials for her work, or meeting with suppliers or other collaborators. The making part of the equation usually starts at about 4:00 p.m., by which time

Dunham is back in her studio and ready to focus on constructing a new sculpture or modifying one in progress. There is also time pressure by now: Dunham will have made dinner plans, so the late afternoon is "crunch time," and she'll work up to the last minute before she has to leave for dinner (or before guests begin to arrive, if she's hosting). After dinner, she will often go back to work, but that time is usually reserved for computer-based tasks. Bedtime is at about 11:00 p.m.

Dunham usually skips lunch, but she may make a smoothie in the afternoon, and she continues to drink variations on her morning tonic as needed throughout the day. If she feels stuck in her work she'll sometimes use "treats" to kick-start things. "Earl Grey is a treat," she said. "Chocolate is a treat. . . . Marshmallows are a treat." Another thing she uses to get out of a rut is dancing. "If I get into a weird zone during the day or I feel stuck, I'll make a choreographed dance routine," she said. "Sometimes I'll record it and sometimes I won't." Other types of exercise don't particularly appeal to her. "I don't take walks and I don't exercise," she said. "I don't like it. I want to like it, but I don't."

Dunham stresses that this schedule applies only when she's in Los Angeles—she travels frequently, and has also made work in London, New York, and Texas—and that it could be completely different by the next week. "I think my time isn't organized by day or by hour," she said. Indeed, she works seven days a week, and doesn't consider weekends any different from weekdays. She will occasionally take days off from making her sculptures, but that's a decision she'll make the morning of. Once again, it's her internal state that's the deciding factor; she needs to be in "an energetic disposition" in order to handle her artworks properly. Ultimately, she sees herself less as her sculptures' maker and more as their facilitator. "It's like I'm working for the objects," she said. "I'm just trying to support them in the things that they need in order to communicate as efficiently as they can."

Isabel Allende (b. 1942)

Allende starts each new book on January eighth, the day in 1981 that she began writing the letter to her dying grandfather that eventually became her first novel, *The House of the Spirits*. "To have a starting date, which started as a superstition because it was a lucky day for me, is now a matter of discipline," the Chilean American author said in 2016. "I have to organize my life, my calendar, everything around that day. I know that on January eighth I'm cut away from everything, sometimes for months."

This period of seclusion, during which Allende refuses trips, lecture invitations, interviews, and other impositions on her time, lasts only until the first draft is done; after that, she is less strict about her time, although she still writes every morning, weekends included, from shortly after waking until lunchtime. "I'm a morning person," she said. "I get up at 6:00, sometimes before. . . . I have my coffee with my dog, and then I get dressed and I put on makeup and high heels, even if nobody is going to see me—because it puts me in the mood of the day. If I stay in pajamas I won't do anything."

Allende works in a two-room home studio in the attic of her house in the San Francisco Bay Area. One room contains all of Allende's research for her book-in-progress, and all of her beads—the writer is also an avid maker of bead necklaces, which she loves to give away to friends. In the other room she has an altar and a big desk with a computer that's not connected to the Internet. "It's just for the writing," she said. "It only contains the book and the research."

At lunchtime, Allende stops writing, has a quick meal at home, and begins attending to the myriad demands of being the world's most widely read Spanish-language author, which usually starts with a review of emails forwarded by her assistant. The remainder of the afternoon is less structured. If there's not much going on, Allende may write all afternoon, or continue the research that undergirds all of her books, fiction and nonfiction. Otherwise, the only other essential component of her day is a twice-daily walk with her dog, during which she avoids thinking about her writing project. In the evening, she makes herself a simple dinner and goes to bed at 10:00 or 11:00 p.m. "I have this fantasy that after a working day I will sit down and have a wonderful meal with a glass of wine and listen to music," she said. "Forget it. I have time to wash my face and drop in bed."

Although she writes for several hours a day, seven days a week, Allende's current schedule is relaxed by her standards. When Allende was writing *The House of the Spirits,* she was also working full-time as a school administrator and raising her two children, "so I would write only at night, although I'm not a night person, and on the weekends." (She worked at a portable typewriter on her kitchen counter.) When she finally quit that job to dedicate herself to writing full-time, Allende maintained an intense schedule, writing Monday to Saturday from 9:00 a.m. to 7:00 p.m., and sometimes until later if she was deep into a particular scene. Allende admits now that she may have been putting too much pressure on herself, a consequence of being raised by her grandfather, a disciplinarian who impressed on her the necessity of hard work. "That was very good for me, because it carried me through many ups and downs in my life," Allende said. "But now that I'm finally stable and at peace and I have a very good life, and I have written so many books, I don't feel that I have the duty to keep forcing myself to do stuff." On the other hand, she doesn't see herself retiring; even after more than twenty books she still enjoys the process. "That's why I do it," she said. "Of course I love telling a story. I love it."

Zadie Smith (b. 1975)

In interviews over the years, the London-born novelist has said that she doesn't write every day—and although she sometimes wishes she had that compulsion, Smith also recognizes the value of writing only when it feels necessary to her. "I think you need to feel an urgency about the acts," she said in 2009, "otherwise when you read it, you feel no urgency either. So, I don't write unless I really feel I need to." Even when Smith does feel that urgency, she writes "very slowly," she said in 2012, "and I rewrite continually, every day, over and over and over. . . . Every day, I read from the beginning up to where I'd got to and just edit it all, and then I move on. It's incredibly laborious, and toward the end of a long novel it's intolerable actually."

Smith has also been vocal about the difficulty of writing in a world of infinite digital distractions, and in the acknowledgments section of her 2012 novel *NW* she thanked two pieces of Internet-blocking software, called Freedom and Self Control, for "creating the time." She does not use social media, and as of late 2016 she did not own a smartphone, and had no plans to acquire one. "I still have a laptop, it's not like I'm a nun," Smith said, "I just don't check my email every moment of the day in my pocket."

Hilary Mantel (b. 1952)

The Booker Prize–winning author of *Wolf Hall* and *Bring Up the Bodies*, as well as several other novels and a memoir, Mantel finds fiction writing an all-consuming and thoroughly unpredictable activity. "Some writers claim to extrude a book at an even rate like toothpaste from a tube, or to build a story like a wall, so many feet per day," the English author wrote in 2016.

> They sit at their desk and knock off their word quota, then frisk into their leisured evening, preening themselves.
>
> This is so alien to me that it might be another trade entirely. Writing lectures or reviews—any kind of non-fiction—seems to me a job like any job: allocate your time, marshall your resources, just get on with it. But fiction makes me the servant of a process that has no clear beginning and end or method of measuring achievement. I don't write in sequence. I may have a dozen versions of a single scene. I might spend a week threading an image through a story, but moving the narrative not an inch. A book grows according to a subtle and deep-laid plan. At the end, I see what the plan was.

Mantel writes every morning as soon as she opens her eyes, seizing the remnants of her dream state before it dissipates. (Sometimes she wakes up in the middle of the night and writes for several hours before going back to sleep.) Her writing days tend to fall into one of two categories: "days of easy flow," which "generate thousands of words across half a dozen projects," and "stop-start days," which are "self-conscious and anxiety ridden, and later turned out to have been productive and useful." She writes by hand or on the computer, and considers herself "a long thinker and a fast writer," which means that a lot of her writing day is spent away from her desk, on the thinking part. When she does sit down at the computer, Mantel will sometimes "tense up till my body locks into a struggling knot," she wrote in 2016. "I have to go and stand in a hot shower to unfreeze. I also stand in the shower if I get stuck. I am the cleanest person I know."

To other writers who get stuck, Mantel advises getting away from the desk: "Take a walk, take a bath, go to sleep, make a pie, draw, listen to music, meditate, exercise; whatever you do, don't just sit there scowling at the problem," she has written. "But don't make telephone calls or go to a party; if you do, other people's words will pour in where your lost words should be. Open a gap for them, create a space. Be patient." Over the course of her career, Mantel has learned extraordinary patience: She first began considering a series of novels based on the life of Thomas Cromwell in her twenties but didn't begin writing the first of them, *Wolf Hall*, until thirty years later. (When she finally began writing it, however, she worked with tremendous speed, cranking out the four-hundred-page book in five months, working eight to twelve hours a day.)

"Sometimes people ask, does writing make you happy?" Mantel told a visiting reporter in 2012.

But I think that's beside the point. It makes you agitated, and continually in a state where you're off balance. You seldom feel serene or settled. You're like the person in the fairy tale *The Red Shoes;* you've just got to dance and dance, you're never in equilibrium. I don't think writing makes you happy. . . . I think it makes for a life that by its very nature has to be unstable, and if it ever became stable, you'd be finished.

Catherine Opie (b. 1961)

As a student at the San Francisco Art Institute in the early 1980s, Opie worked for her room and board at a residence club in the city, "a druggie, fucked-up place," she said in 2016. In those days, Opie got up at 2:30 a.m., worked at the front desk from 3:00 to 8:00 a.m., had breakfast, and went to school. After school, she had a job at an early-childhood education program at the YMCA. She worked there until about 7:00 p.m., then went home, had dinner, and forced herself to go to bed at 9:00—or else she would skip sleep entirely, instead pulling an all-nighter in the school's darkroom until it was time to go back on the night shift at 3:00 a.m.

The long hours paid off: Opie is now one of America's preeminent photographers, probably best known for her portraits of San Francisco's queer community, although she has also made photo series on surfers, Tea Party gatherings, America's national parks, Los Angeles's freeways, teenage football players, and the inside of Elizabeth Taylor's Bel-Air mansion. Her schedule is more forgiving than it was in her student days, but not that much more; in addition to running a busy art practice, Opie is a tenured professor at UCLA, which doesn't leave much free time in her week. "I suppose that I would actually like to *not* have a daily routine," Opie said. "I would like to have more wandering. But because I'm a professor, a mother, and an artist that runs a full studio, I end up having to have a really incredibly rigid routine."

As of fall 2016, her routine meant waking up at 5:50 a.m. weekday mornings, getting her teenage son out the door for school, and going to work out or take a tennis lesson. Then, Monday through Wednesday, she goes to UCLA to teach; Thursday and Friday, she heads to her studio. Either way, she is busy until the evening. After work, she has business dinners a few nights a week; otherwise, she's home with her family. Because her schedule is so packed, she can generally make new bodies of work only during summer, spring, and winter breaks from school. "There hasn't been any point where I haven't been able to make work," she said. "It's just, you schedule that like you schedule the rest of your life. It doesn't happen by chance."

That said, she is looking forward to retirement and the freedom it will bring—Opie and her wife talk about buying an RV and "roaming around National Parks just for the hell of it"—but teaching has also been incredibly important to her, both because she believes in building and mentoring a community of artists and because it gets her out of her own head, which she thinks is essential for an artist. "It's important to remember that at times there's a certain kind of solipsism or narcissism within the practice," she said, "and there are other times where it's absolutely never about you; it's about how you deal with your community and your family and the aspects of what it is to be human. So I try to find a really good balance between those."

Joan Jonas (b. 1936)

The pioneering video and performance artist lives and works in Manhattan, in the SoHo loft she has rented since 1974. Although she doesn't follow the exact same routine every day, Jonas generally gets up at about 7:30 a.m. and takes her miniature poodle, Ozu, out for a walk. Then she has coffee at a favorite café in the neighborhood and reads the newspaper. Returning to her loft, Jonas goes to work and pretty much continues all day, often with music on in the background. (Morton Feldman is a favorite.) Jonas tries to draw every day, and will often begin her workday by doing that—or if she's working on a script for a new video, she may do that first thing. If she has assistants coming in, they'll arrive at about 10:00 a.m. and stay until 6:00 p.m. (Jonas has three part-time assistants: one to help with video editing, one to lay out plans for museum and gallery exhibitions, and one who does various tasks, such as solving construction and installation problems.) Research is also a big part of her working process. "I'm always looking for stories," Jonas said in 2017. "I read for that reason; I'm doing research. One of my activities is going to the bookstore, getting books, reading books, looking through books for ideas."

While she's out, Jonas often carries a small notebook for writing down ideas, or if she doesn't have a notebook she'll use her iPhone. But coming up with new ideas is not her main concern. "I think I've been using the same ideas over and over again, in different ways," Jonas said. "It's a kind of language I've developed. So I'm not sure how many brand-new ideas I have, but I reinvent the ideas I've already worked with, or put them in a different context."

Jonas takes an hour-long break for lunch, and her day is

punctuated by trips outside with Ozu. "The dog gets walked a lot, several times a day," she said. "I like to walk around the neighborhood and say hello to a few people who are left here who I know, in the shops. Or go to galleries nearby. But usually I work all day." In the evenings she sees friends for dinner, and she will host a dinner party at her loft once a month or so. Afterward she reads or watches old films on cable TV or her computer. Bedtime is usually at about 11:00 p.m., but sometimes not until midnight or 1:00 a.m. "And I often can't sleep so I read during the night also," Jonas said. "Or look at movies during the night, on my computer."

Jonas doesn't ever feel creatively blocked, and she finds that inspiration comes easily and through everyday life—while walking in the park, spending time with friends, going to the Metropolitan Museum of Art, or visiting new places. "I think the way to become inspired is to empty your mind and let things come into your mind," she said. Inspiration is not, she thinks, something terribly precious or unusual. "I don't separate inspiration from doing research and becoming interested in something," Jonas said. "I don't separate those things into categories. It's all in the same experience of being curious about the world. That's what I find inspiring, the world—you know, the world around me."

DEADLY DETERMINATION

Marie-Thérèse Rodet Geoffrin (1699–1777)

Geoffrin was one of the major *salonniéres* of the French Enlightenment, who, along with Julie de Lespinasse and Suzanne Necker, transformed the Parisian salon from a leisurely social gathering into a center of serious intellectual and artistic enterprise. Geoffrin was born in Paris, orphaned young, and married off at fourteen to a wealthy manufacturer thirty-five years her senior; two years later she gave birth to the first of their two children. Denied a formal education, Geoffrin found a substitute in the salon of her neighbor Madame de Tencin, where many of the most important writers of the day gathered. By the time of Tencin's death in 1749, Geoffrin had established her own salon; there, as the historian Dena Goodman has written, she introduced two crucial innovations. "First, she made the one-o'clock dinner rather than the traditional late-night supper the sociable meal of the day, and thus opened up the whole afternoon for talk," Goodman writes. "Second, she regularized these dinners, fixing a specific day of the week for them (Monday for artists, Wednesday for men of letters)." The regularity and structured nature of Geoffrin's gatherings became a model for other Parisian women and helped make the salon a key institution of the Enlightenment. When an Italian economist who frequented Geoffrin's salons left Paris for Naples, he and his friends tried to establish a similar weekly gathering on Fridays, and discovered just how much skill it required. "Our Fridays are becoming Neopolitan Fridays," he wrote, "and

*An 1840 portrait of Madame Geoffrin
by Amélie Cordelier de la Noue*

are getting farther away from the character and tone of those of France, despite all [our] efforts. . . . There is no way to make Naples resemble Paris unless we find a woman to guide us, organize us, *Geoffrinise* us."

Geoffrin's own lifestyle was as carefully regulated as her salons. A letter she wrote to her daughter from Warsaw in 1766 gives a revealing glimpse of the daily routine she followed both at home and while traveling:

I live here as in Paris. I rise every day at five o'clock; I drink my two large glasses of hot water; I take my coffee; I write when I am alone, which is rare; I do my hair in company; I dine every day with the king, *chez lui,* or with him and *les seigneurs.* I make calls after dinner; I go to the theater; I return to my place at ten o'clock; I drink my hot water, and I go to bed. And in the morning I begin all over again. I eat so little at these great dinners that I am often obliged to drink a third glass of water to appease my hunger. I owe to the severity of this diet my good health. I will be faithful to it until I die.

Elizabeth Carter [1717–1806]

Carter was an English intellectual, poet, and translator who wrote for *The Gentleman's Quarterly* and Samuel Johnson's *Rambler,* published two books of poetry, and, in 1749, began a translation of the writings of Epictetus, published to great acclaim in 1758. A clergyman's daughter, she was taught Latin, Greek, and Hebrew as a child, and she went on to study French, German, Italian, Spanish, Portuguese, and Arabic—as well as astronomy, ancient geography, ancient and modern history, and music. Carter never married; as her nephew wrote in a memoir, "Very early in life Mrs. Carter seems to have formed a resolution, which she was enabled to keep, of devoting herself to study, and living a single life." She lived with her father until his death in 1774; by that time, the subscription sales for *All the Works of Epictetus, Which Are Now Extant* had earned Carter enough to buy herself a large house with a view of the sea. Although she lived her whole life in Deal, a fishing port on the Kent coast, she generally spent the winters in London, where she became a member of the Blue Stockings Society, a group of literary women who gathered around the wealthy patron Elizabeth Montagu.

Carter's achievements were due, in part, to her habit of waking early in the morning, which she claimed she could not do without assistance. "As you desire a full and true account of my whole life and conversation," she wrote in a 1746 letter, "it is necessary in the first place you should be made acquainted with the singular contrivance by which I am called in the morning."

> There is a bell placed at the head of my bed, and to this is fastened a packthread and a piece of lead, which . . . is conveyed through a crevasse of my window into a garden below, pertaining to the Sexton, who gets up between four and five, and pulls the said packthread with as much heart and good will as if he was ringing my knell. By this most curious invention I make a shift to get up, which I am too stupid to do without call-ing. Some evil-minded people of my acquaintance have most wickedly threatened to cut my bell-rope, which would be the utter undoing of me; for I should infallibly sleep out the whole summer.

This description was written when Carter was in her late twenties, but according to her nephew, her days followed a similar pattern for most of her life. After being roused by the sexton's bell ringing, Carter sat down to her "several lessons as regular as a school-boy, and lay in a stock of learning to make a figure with at breakfast." But before eating she would take up her walking stick and embark on a 6:00 a.m. walk, alone, with her sister, or with a neighbor whom Carter roused out of bed and dragged along, half asleep, on her rambles.

After breakfast, Carter retired to her quarters and divided her time among several activities:

My first care is to water the pinks and roses, which are stuck in about twenty different parts of my room; and when this task is finished, I sit down to a spinnet [a smaller type of harpsichord] . . . with as much importance as if I knew how to play. After having deafened myself for about half an hour with all manner of noises, I proceed to some other amusement, that employs me about the same time, for longer I seldom apply to any thing; and thus between reading, working, writing, twirling the globes, and running up and down stairs an hundred times to see where every body is, and how they do, which furnishes me with little intervals of talk, I seldom want either business or entertainment.

Carter continued this habit of working in thirty-minute bursts throughout her life; according to her nephew, she "hardly ever read or worked for more than half an hour at a time, and then she would visit for a few minutes any of her relations who were staying in her house, in their respective apartments, or go into her garden." Despite waking between 4:00 and 5:00 a.m., Carter would often work late into the night, and as a young student intent on mastering three ancient languages she got into the habit of taking snuff to help her stay alert. Over time she developed additional methods of warding off fatigue during her long work hours. "Besides the taking snuff, she owned that she used to bind a wet towel round her head, put a wet cloth to the pit of her stomach, and chew green tea and coffee," Carter's nephew wrote. "To oblige her father, she endeavoured to conquer the habit of taking snuff, and would not resume it without his consent. This he at length reluctantly gave, finding how much she suffered from the want of it."

Mary Wollstonecraft (1759–1797)

Wollstonecraft wrote her three-hundred-page treatise *A Vindication of the Rights of Woman* in six weeks. She always wrote fast, completing most of her works in a similar amount of time, sometimes to their detriment; in the words of her husband, William Godwin, *Vindication* was "undoubtedly a very unequal performance, and eminently deficient in method and arrangement." But the English author's audacity and indignation overcame any unevenness in her prose, and *Vindication*'s publication in 1792 made her one of the most famous and influential women in Europe. Wollstonecraft wasn't one to bask in success, however, and soon moved on to the next piece of writing. As she wrote in a letter, "Life is but a labour of patience: it is always rolling a great stone up a hill; for, before a person can find a resting-place, imagining it is lodged, down it comes again, and all the work is to be done over anew!"

Mary Shelley (1797–1851)

Shelley wrote her first and most famous novel, *Frankenstein,* in nine months, from June 1816 to March 1817—a remarkable feat for a first-time novelist, and even more so considering that the author was pregnant during the first several months of the process, giving birth in December 1816. She was aided in the writing by her husband, the Romantic poet Percy Bysshe Shelley, who proved an astute editor and was happy to engage in long discussions about the novel's plot and form. The resulting pages, Mary wrote in a preface to the 1831 edition, "speak of many a walk, many a drive, and many a conversation." But Percy's assistance did not extend to helping out with their baby, overseeing the household servants, or attending to houseguests—according to the biographer Charlotte Gordon, "not once did he offer to help with domestic obligations. As the resident genius, he wandered in and out of the house at any time of day or night." Mary, on the other hand, always stuck to a strict routine of writing in the morning, walking and performing chores or errands in the afternoon, and reading in the evening. Nevertheless, she seemed tolerant of Percy's self-centered aloofness; after his death by drowning in 1822, she looked back on their life together as a shared idyll. "And now, once again, I bid my hideous progeny go forth and prosper," she wrote in the 1831 preface to *Frankenstein*. "I have an affection for it, for it was the offspring of happy days."

Clara Schumann (1819–1896)

Schumann was a German piano prodigy who achieved celebrity first in her native Leipzig and then throughout Europe, where she was invited to perform for royalty and showered with adulation by the press and by the frenzied audiences that thronged her performances. The young virtuoso was undaunted by the pressures of success, but her marriage in

1840 to the composer Robert Schumann nearly derailed her career. Robert required silence to compose, and as a result Clara could not practice piano—or pursue her own ambitions as a composer—during the days or weeks that her husband was seized by inspiration. "My piano playing is falling behind," she complained during one such period in June 1841. "This always happens when Robert is composing. There is not even one little hour in the whole day for myself!" Eventually, she carved out a slice of time each day from 6:00 to 8:00 p.m., when Robert, according to the biographer Nancy B. Reich, "took his customary beer at a neighborhood tavern."

Robert was aware of the pain he was causing his wife, but he considered it an unfortunate necessity. He wrote, "Clara realizes that I must make full use of my powers, now that they are at their best, in the fulness of my youth. Well, so it must be when artists marry, and if two people love each other, it is right enough." He never thought to help out with the household, and although the married couple was able to hire servants, there was always much to be done: In 1841, Clara gave birth to the first of an eventual eight children. Nevertheless, despite the children's needs and Robert's demands for a quiet home life, Clara did manage to continue her performing career. During the fourteen years of their marriage she gave at least 139 public concerts, a testament to her discipline and tenacity. It helped that the performances were an important source of income for the family—but, for Clara, money was just a convenient excuse. She wrote, "Nothing surpasses creative activity, even if only for those hours of self-forgetfulness in which one breathes solely in the world of sound."

Charlotte Brontë (1816–1855)

Brontë's childhood was marked by the deaths of her mother and her two older sisters, and her young adulthood was marred by miserable stints as a teacher and a governess. ("I see now more clearly than I have ever done before that a private governess has no existence, is not considered as a living and rational being except as connected with the wearisome duties she has to fulfill," she wrote to her sister Emily.) But with the death of her aunt Elizabeth in 1842, Brontë and her two younger sisters received an inheritance that allowed them to write full-time—or at least all the time that they were not engaged in housework at the family home, Haworth Parsonage, where the sisters spent most of their lives and wrote their novels: Charlotte's *Jane Eyre, Shirley,* and *Villette;* Emily's *Wuthering Heights;* and Anne's *Agnes Grey* and *The Tenant of Wildfell Hall.*

Even after she was freed from having to earn a living, Charlotte did not—or could not—write every day. Her friend and biographer Elizabeth Gaskell writes:

> Sometimes weeks or even months elapsed before she felt that she had anything to add to that portion of her story which was already written. Then, some morning, she would waken up, and the progress of her tale lay clear and bright before her, in distinct vision. When this was the case, all her care was to discharge her household and filial duties, so as to obtain leisure to sit down and write out the incidents and consequent thoughts, which were, in fact, more present to her mind at such times than her actual life itself. Yet notwithstanding this "possession" (as it were), those who survive, of her daily and household companions, are clear in their

*An 1850 portrait of Charlotte Brontë
by George Richmond*

testimony, that never was the claim of any duty, never
was the call of another for help, neglected in an instant.

As for her writing hours, Gaskell reports that Brontë and
her sisters put away their literary work every evening at
9:00 p.m. At that hour they gathered to talk over their work
in progress, pacing up and down the sitting room as they
described their novels' plots and, once or twice a week, reading aloud what they had written for comments and advice.
"Charlotte told me," Gaskell writes, "that the remarks made

had seldom any effect in inducing her to alter her work, so possessed was she with the feeling that she had described reality; but the readings were of great and stirring interest to all, taking them out of the gnawing pressure of daily-recurring cares, and setting them in a free place."

Christina Rossetti (1830–1894)

According to her brother William, the English poet's writing was "entirely of the casual and spontaneous kind." Rossetti believed that good poetry arrived of its own accord, and that trying to force the process was more or less a waste of time. "I never had my verse-writing power so under command as to be able to count on its exercise," she wrote. After the release of her first poetry collection, Rossetti's publisher inquired about a second volume. Rossetti answered, "Write to order I really can*not*: not of course that I could not then produce somewhat in bulk; but if I have yet done aught worth doing, it has been by simply taking what came to me when it came. Indeed, if I may at all hope to be remembered, I would rather live as a single book writer than as an only-one-readable book writer."

Julia Ward Howe (1819–1910)

Howe is best known for writing the "Battle Hymn of the Republic," the 1862 poem that became a Civil War anthem and made its author famous and revered in her own time. But Howe also wrote several poetry collections and plays—many

Julia Ward Howe at her desk, 1906

of them while raising six children, and in defiance of her husband, who opposed her literary career—and she was a tireless campaigner for abolitionism, women's suffrage, and other social reforms. The year after Howe's death at ninety-one, her daughter Maud published a memoir of her later years that sought to explain how her mother had accomplished so much. "First, and last, and all the time, she worked, and worked, and worked, steadily as nature works, without rest, without haste," Maud writes. "She was never idle, she was never in a hurry." This approach was evident in Howe's daily routine, which struck a seemingly ideal balance of work and leisure. Howe rose at 7:00 a.m. and immediately took a cold bath (adjusted to a tepid bath in her later years). Then she had breakfast with the family, generally a boisterous affair, for Howe "came down in the morning with her spirits at their highest level," Maud writes. With breakfast, she drank a cup of tea, which along with a little wine at dinner was her only stimulant—"for her spirits were so buoyant," Maud notes, "her temperament so overflowing with the *joie de vivre,* that we called her the 'family champagne.'"

Immediately after breakfast, Howe read her letters and the newspapers. "Then came the morning walk, a bout of calisthenics, or a game of ball," Maud writes; "after this she settled to the real serious business of the day; ten o'clock saw her at her desk." To "tone up her mind," Howe started her day with the most challenging work, reading German philosophy and Greek drama, history, and philosophy (after teaching herself Greek at age fifty). Then she turned to whatever literary task she was engaged in, "put the iron on the anvil," and hammered away until lunch, which was preceded by a twenty-minute nap. At mealtimes, she always ate whatever she pleased, with no ill effects; according to Maud, "It was said, in the family, that she had the digestion of an ostrich."

After lunch, she returned to her desk to continue the morning's work, answer letters, and, finally, read something lighter, such as Italian poetry, a travel book, or a French novel. Howe never worked after dark; if she didn't have a meeting or another engagement to attend, she used the evening to spend time with her family, with dinner followed by "talk, whist, music, and reading aloud."

If Howe clearly enjoyed her old age, it was partly because an unhappy marriage had prevented her from enjoying much of her earlier adulthood. She married at twenty-four and quickly discovered that her husband's expectations of the union were vastly different from her own. Where she had assumed a relatively equal partnership with mutual support for each spouse's intellectual activities, her husband desired a large family and a wife who would oversee the domestic sphere while leaving him free to pursue his own writing. Howe was mortified; she spent the first years of marriage "in a state of somnambulism, occupied principally with digestion, sleep, and babies" that, she wrote, felt "like blindness, like death, like exile from all things beautiful and good." She pushed against these restrictions, at first timidly but with increasing boldness, eventually infuriating her husband by publishing a book of poetry (1853's *Passion-Flowers*) without his knowledge or consent, and then repeating the offense with more publications over the ensuing years. It was only after his death in 1876 that Howe was able to fully enjoy her by-then considerable prestige and celebrity—so it's no wonder that she filled her last decades with such evident relish. Near the end of her life, Howe's daughter asked her "for a statement of the ideal aim of life." The ninety-one-year-old paused a moment, then summed it up in a phrase: "To Learn, To Teach, To Serve, And To Enjoy!"

Harriet Beecher Stowe (1811–1896)

"If I am to write, I must have a room to myself, which shall be my room," Stowe wrote in a letter to her husband in 1841, anticipating Virginia Woolf's call for "a room of one's own" by almost a century. Stowe was then thirty years old and had been publishing stories in national magazines for several years, and she would soon publish her first book, a collection of short domestic fiction. By this time she was also the mother of four of an eventual seven children, and though her husband, a professor of theology, was enlightened by the standards of the day—he encouraged Stowe's writing and readily agreed to her request for a room of her own—he still expected his wife to take charge of running the house and raising their children. In an 1850 letter to her sister-in-law, Stowe described a typical day:

> Since I began this note I have been called off at least a dozen times—once for the fish-man, to buy a codfish— once to see a man who had brought me some baskets of apples—once to see a book man . . . then to nurse the baby—then into the kitchen to make a chowder for dinner and now I am at it again for nothing but deadly determination enables me to ever write—it is rowing against wind and tide.

Remarkably, Stowe was able to write for three hours each day despite the never-ending stream of domestic obligations. ("The nursery & the kitchen were the principal fields of my labor," she said later.) Her situation changed dramatically with the 1852 publication of *Uncle Tom's Cabin,* which sold three hundred thousand copies in the first year and made Stowe wealthy and world-famous almost overnight. This brought its own headaches: Within a few months of the novel's publication, Stowe was "already besieged with applications for pecuniary assistance," her sister wrote. But there was never again any question of Stowe's writing taking a backseat to household work. When Stowe embarked on a follow-up to *Uncle Tom's Cabin,* her husband wrote to her publishers that "we shall do every thing in our power to lighten her domestic cares."

Rosa Bonheur (1822–1899)

Bonheur was the most famous female artist of the nineteenth century, widely celebrated for her animal paintings, especially her epic 1853 canvas *The Horse Fair.* Unlike other women artists of the time, Bonheur insisted on faithfully representing every detail of her subjects' anatomy, earning praise for her "masculine" style. She was also notorious for wearing men's clothes, which was not only scandalous but illegal in nineteenth-century France; in the 1850s, Bonheur was one of twelve women granted a cross-dressing license by the Paris police. (George Sand was one of the others.) Bonheur secured the permit because she said that she needed to wear trousers for her work, which required visiting slaughterhouses to gain her detailed knowledge of animal anatomy. She said, "I strongly disapprove of women who refuse to wear normal clothes because they want to pass themselves off as men. . . . If you see me dressed this way, it's not the least to make myself stand out, as too many women have done, but only for my work. Don't forget I used to spend days and days in slaughterhouses. Oh! You've got to be devoted to art to live in pools of blood, surrounded by butchers."

In fact, it was an open secret that Bonheur frequently wore men's clothes in her home and studio as well—but she had good reason to downplay this fact. Flaunting her cross-dressing could have caused public opinion to turn against her,

An 1893 portrait of Rosa Bonheur

which would not only have hurt the sales of her paintings but might have invited unfriendly scrutiny of her domestic partnerships with women. The first was with Natalie Micas, the daughter of family friends; they met when Bonheur was fourteen and Micas was twelve, and became close companions and eventually lovers, living together until Micas's death in 1889. Soon afterward, Bonheur was visited by a young American painter named Anna Klumpke; eight years later, Klumpke asked if she could return to paint Bonheur's portrait. Bonheur agreed, and before the painting was done, she confessed her love, which Klumpke reciprocated. They lived together until Bonheur's death the following year.

By then Bonheur had lived for nearly forty years on the

estate she purchased at By, near Fontainebleau, which she and Micas nicknamed the Domain of Perfect Affection. When Klumpke arrived there in 1898 to paint Bonheur's portrait, she was quickly brought up to speed on the great artist's daily schedule. "I always go to bed with the sun and rise at five," Bonheur told her. "Between seven and nine my servant and I take the two dogs for a drive. Then I work until lunch, read the paper and take a nap. After two, I'm all yours." Bonheur used to work longer hours, she told Klumpke, but she no longer found it necessary. "Now I tend to dawdle, doing less but thinking more," she said.

Later, Klumpke learned of another key aspect of Bonheur's morning routine: The artist's bedroom was filled with birdcages, in which she kept more than sixty birds, "of all kinds and colors, who made a deafening din from morning until night," Klumpke wrote. Every morning after waking, Bonheur went from cage to cage, feeding her beloved creatures. But, Klumpke wondered, didn't they bother her when she was trying to sleep? "Not at all," Bonheur replied. "I never close the curtains, and the sun wakes me before my birds start warbling. I love to catch the morning's first ray of light. That's why I'm so happy every morning when the clouds haven't deprived me of my favorite wakeup call."

Birds were hardly the only animal in Bonheur's care—she also kept, Klumpke reported, "dogs, horses, donkeys, oxen, sheep, goats, red deer, roe deer, lizards, mouflons [a type of wild sheep], boars, monkeys, the sweetest and fiercest lions." One of the lions, named Fatima, was known to follow Bonheur around like a poodle, and the pet monkeys were given the run of the house. Of one monkey, named Ratata, Bonheur wrote: "In the evening she comes home and does up my hair. I think she takes me for an old male of her kind!"

But the real purpose of this extensive menagerie was to give Bonheur plenty of subjects for her paintings, and to allow her to work from her estate without having to make the rounds of farms, stockyards, animal markets, and horse fairs. To paint her animals out in the fields, Bonheur commissioned the construction of an unusual wagon that protected her from inclement weather, described by a friend as "a kind of cabin on four wheels" with one side "all in glass, behind which, protected from cold air, sat Rosa Bonheur." With her animals and her painting and the love of Micas and, later, Klumpke, Bonheur had everything she needed. "I am an old rat," the artist wrote in 1867, seven years after settling on her estate, "who after sniffing about over the hill and dale retires quite satisfied to his hole, yet in reality somewhat sad to have seen the world without taking part in it."

Eleanor Roosevelt (1884–1962)

Roosevelt may not have been an artist in the traditional sense, but she was certainly a creative force, an instigator of social change through a potent mix of optimism, pragmatism, stubbornness, and steady, ceaseless effort. As America's longest-serving First Lady, she went on monthly lecture tours, made weekly radio broadcasts, held regular press conferences for female journalists, and, starting in 1936, wrote a syndicated newspaper column, "My Day," which she filed six days a week for nearly twenty-six years, with virtually no interruptions. After her husband's death in 1945, Roosevelt became the country's first delegate to the newly formed United Nations, and the following year she became the first chairperson of the

UN Commission on Human Rights, where she was instrumental in drafting the 1948 Universal Declaration of Human Rights. At the same time she was active in countless other causes; she traversed the country for speaking engagements; she was a behind-the-scenes force in Democratic politics; and she wrote several books and stayed on top of a gargantuan correspondence—according to her autobiography, she received about a hundred letters a day, all of which got a reply. (Most of those answers were made by one of Roosevelt's three assistants, but she personally replied to ten to fifteen letters a day.)

In her book *You Learn by Living,* Roosevelt considered the problem of how to make the best use of one's time, a subject on which she had clearly had some expertise:

> There are three ways in which I have been able to solve that problem: first, by achieving an inner calm so that I can work undisturbed by what goes on around me; second, by concentrating on the thing in hand; third, by arranging a routine pattern for my days that allots certain activities to certain hours, planning in advance for everything that must be done, but at the same time remaining flexible enough to allow for the unexpected.

Roosevelt's daily routine was always packed with activity; "I don't normally have many quiet minutes in the day," she wrote. She generally woke at 7:30 in the morning and worked right up until her bedtime at about 1:00 a.m. Writing "My Day" was often one of the last things to get done, with Roosevelt frequently dictating the column from bed at 11:00 p.m. or later. According to a longtime friend, "She gets along perfectly on five or six hours' sleep a night and apparently does not know the meaning of the word 'fatigue.'"

Roosevelt's example is inspiring—but for her assistants, it could be a grueling job to keep up with her. According to her daughter, Anna, Roosevelt's work ethic was an almost fearsome thing:

> I used to just cringe sometimes when I'd hear Mother at eleven thirty at night say to [her longtime secretary Malvina "Tommy" Thompson], "I've still got a column to do." And this weary, weary woman would sit down at a typewriter and Mother would dictate to her. And both of them so tired. I remember one time when Tommy with asperity said, "You'll have to speak louder, I can't hear you." And Mother's response was, "If you will listen, you can hear *perfectly* well."

Dorothy Thompson (1893–1961)

Thompson was a famously opinionated and irreverent American journalist whose thrice-weekly news column, "On the Record," reached millions of people around the globe. According to the biographer Peter Kurth, she wrote the column

> by hand, in bed, where she lay most mornings until well after noon, reading newspapers, telephoning friends, answering mail, drinking black coffee, and chain-smoking Camel cigarettes. One of the secretaries was always in attendance to take down her dictation, but unless she had other writing to do—a speech or an article or one of her regular radio broadcasts—she

preferred to work on the column by herself, and only when she was happy with the way it sounded would she rise and read it aloud to anyone who might be in the room. When a column was finished, it was hastily typed and sent by messenger to the *Herald Tribune* office, where it was checked for libel and grammatical errors (but rarely edited otherwise) and then dispatched by airmail or telegraph to subscribing papers around the country. Dorothy was then free to rise, get dressed, and pace the apartment for the rest of the day, a yellow legal pad clutched tightly in her hand so she could easily jot down ideas as they came to her. Quantities of foolscap, as well as Parker pens and L. C. Smith typewriters, were scattered the length and breadth of the house because Dorothy never knew when she might "get curious" and need to write about something. She would keep on writing, annotating, telephoning, and talking things out until the cocktail hour, when her friends would begin to drop by for drinks.

Thompson's columns ran a thousand words apiece, and in 1938 alone she wrote 132 of them, as well as a dozen long magazine articles, more than fifty speeches and miscellaneous articles, countless radio broadcasts, and a book on the era's refugee crisis. She got it all done thanks, in part, to a steady supply of Dexedrine and other stimulants prescribed by her doctors—but Thompson believed the real motivating force was her bottomless well of frustration with humankind's chronic ineptitude. "I am living on quantities of adrenalin[e]," Thompson wrote, "self-distilled, from the fury I feel at every waking moment. The fury I feel for appeasers, for the listless, apathetic and stupid people who still exist in this sad world!"

VIBRATIONS OF CHANCE

....

Janet Frame (1924–2004)

Frame was the New Zealand author of twelve novels, four collections of short stories, one collection of poems, and a three-volume autobiography. She grew up one of five children in a working-class family on New Zealand's South Island, studied at the local college of education, and initially found work as a teacher, but after a suicide attempt she was committed to a mental institution and subsequently misdiagnosed as schizophrenic. Frame spent the better part of the next eight years in and out of various psychiatric facilities, where she underwent two hundred electroshock treatments. Nevertheless, she managed to write fiction with increasing dedication, and published her first book, *The Lagoon and Other Stories,* in 1951, while she was a patient at Seacliff Lunatic Asylum. There, she was scheduled to have a lobotomy, but when Frame's doctors learned that her book had won New Zealand's most prestigious literary prize, the procedure was called off. Instead, she was released.

From Seacliff, Frame went to stay with her sister, who took her to visit Frank Sargeson, a well-known local writer. Impressed by Frame's stories, Sargeson offered to let her stay in an army hut behind his cottage and helped arrange for her to receive state medical benefits. About a month after being released from Seacliff, Frame moved onto Sargeson's property and suddenly found herself a full-time writer. "I had an army hut containing a bed, a built-in desk with a kerosene lamp, a rush mat on the floor, a small wardrobe with an old curtain strung in front, and a small window by the head of the bed," she wrote in the second volume of her autobiography. "Mr Sargeson (I was not yet bold enough to call him Frank) had already arranged for a medical certificate and a benefit of three pounds a week which was also the amount of his income. I thus had everything I desired and needed as well as the regret of wondering why I had taken so many years to find it."

Frame quickly adapted herself to Sargeson's daily routine, although she couldn't break herself of the Seacliff habit of getting up very early and dressing immediately. "He did not get up until half-past seven, with breakfast at eight, and it seemed hours before I could pluck up courage to go up to the house with my chamberpot and my washing things, waiting until he was up and dressed," she wrote.

Usually I helped myself to my own breakfast of a yeast drink brewed overnight, home-made curds topped with honey, and bread and honey and tea. If Mr Sargeson had breakfast with me, sitting on his side of the counter, I was inclined to chatter. Within the first week of my stay he drew attention to this. "You babble at breakfast," he said.

I took note of what he said and in future I refrained from "babbling," but it was not until I had been writing regularly each day that I understood the importance to each of us of forming, holding, maintaining our inner world, and how it was renewed each day on waking, how it even remained during sleep, like an animal outside the door waiting to come in; and how its form and power were protected most by surrounding silence. My hurt at being called a "babbler" faded as I learned more of the life of a writer.

After breakfast, Frame returned to her hut to work on her first novel, *Owls Do Cry*. At 11:00 a.m., Sargeson would come out with a cup of tea and a rye wafer spread with honey; after tapping gently on the door, he would enter the hut and leave the tea things on Frame's writing table, respectfully "averting his gaze from the nakedness of my typed pages," she wrote. As soon as he was gone, she "seized" the tea and wafer, then continued working until 1:00 p.m., when Sargeson would again come tap on the door to let her know that lunch was ready. At lunch, the older writer would read aloud from a book, "and discuss the writing while I listened, accepting, believing everything he said, full of wonder at his cleverness," Frame wrote.

Frame did not settle in Sargeson's hut permanently—after sixteen months, she received a grant that allowed her to travel to Europe, where she lived and worked for the next several years—but the routine she established there served her well throughout her life, as did the habit she adopted of tracking her day's writing progress in an exercise book, in which she ruled columns for the date, the number of pages she hoped to write, the number of pages she actually wrote, and a column titled "Excuses." Later in her career, she eliminated the last column and instead tracked her "Wasted Days"—as, she wrote, "I did not need to identify the known excuses to myself."

Frame went on to win dozens of literary awards, but she did not become truly famous until the filmmaker Jane Campion adapted Frame's autobiographies into the 1990 film *An Angel at My Table*. After Frame's death, Campion wrote about visiting the writer in her New Zealand home in order to ask for the rights to her autobiographies. "Frame was not like anyone else I had met: she seemed freer, more energized, and absolutely sane," Campion wrote.

> I remember her house as being a bit of a mess: the kitchen was cluttered with dishes, and there was no door on the bathroom, just a curtain. She had a glamorous white Persian cat that we stroked and admired. Later she took me through the house and showed me how she worked. Each room and even parts of rooms were dedicated to a different book in progress. Here and there she had hung curtains to divide the rooms like they do in hospital wards to give the patients privacy. On the desk where she had last been working was a pair of earmuffs.

Frame told Campion that she couldn't "bear any sound"— hence the earmuffs, and also the extra layer of bricks Frame had put on the front wall of her bungalow, in a futile attempt at soundproofing. Campion later used the earmuffs in her film; in the final scene, Frame is shown writing in a trailer in her sister's backyard, donning earmuffs to block out the noise of her sister's children playing outside. It is a fitting image for the writer, who was never entirely comfortable in society but found meaning and direction in her writing. "I think it's all that matters to me," she once told Frank Sargeson. "I dread emerging from it each day."

Jane Campion (b. 1954)

For Campion, the long process of realizing a film almost always begins with writing; the New Zealand–born filmmaker has written or cowritten the screenplays for five of her seven feature films, as well as for her TV series *Top of the Lake.* In interviews, she has described this as a largely intuitive process. "It starts with a feeling that's quite unnameable," Campion said in 1993. "And a mood, you know? And then you try to write things that create the mood you are feeling or thinking of." If the process works, then ultimately "the film is the mood," she said.

When Campion was starting to write the screenplay for her 1993 film *The Piano,* she spent a week alone, wallowing in the mood of the story and the mind-set of her protagonist, occasionally bringing herself to tears in the process. "I have to spend a few days in it," she said, "and then once I've got it, I can . . . go out and work more sort of from a nine to five basis." But even then her writing process remains fragile and easily disrupted. "Sometimes I'm having a really inspired time, I'm really feeling like I'm penetrating some ideas, I'm working and working," she said in 1997. "Then I get hungry or tired, and I think, Fuck it, if only I could have gone on for another hour, I could have got somewhere!"

Agnès Varda (b. 1928)

Varda is often called the grandmother of New Wave cinema, a description that feels appropriate now that she is past ninety and has made twenty-one feature films and more than a dozen shorts; but when the label was first applied, Varda was barely thirty and hardly considered herself an Old Master of cinema. When she made her first film, 1954's *La Pointe Courte*, Varda later protested, she had seen only five movies in her entire life. *La Pointe Courte* was, in fact, originally intended to be a novel. "But I drew pictures by way of an outline and I showed these to a man who was an assistant film director," she said in 1970. "He suggested to me that cinema might be the ideal medium. And so I went ahead with some money that I had borrowed." In the same interview, Varda described her filmmaking motivations as "an underground river of instincts."

It took Varda seven years to make her next film, *Cleo from 5 to 7*, "not because I was a woman, but because I was writing the kind of films that are difficult to set up financially," she said. But Varda was also vocal about the difficulties facing women in the cinema, as in any male-dominated profession. "There are two problems—the problem of the promotion of women in all professions in equal number to men, and the problem of society: how can women who still want to have children be sure to be able to have them when they want, with whom they want, and how are we going to help them raise the children," Varda said in 1974. As for herself, she added, "there is only one solution and that is to be a kind of 'super-woman' and lead several lives at once. For me the biggest difficulty in my life was to do that—to lead several lives at once and to not give in and to not abandon any of them—to not give up children, to not give up the cinema, to not give up men if one likes men."

In 1974, German television gave Varda carte blanche to make a new film, with a one-year deadline—but a year earlier she had given birth to her second child, and she knew from experience how difficult it was to care for a small child while on a film set. So she resolved to make her next film without leaving home. "I told myself that I was a good example of women's creativity—always a bit stuck and suffocated by home and motherhood," she said in 1975.

> So I wondered what could come of these constraints. Could I manage to restart my creativity from within these limitations? . . . So I set out from this idea, from this fact that most women are stuck at home. And I attached myself to my hearth. I imagined a new umbilical cord. I had a special eighty-meter electric cable attached to the electric box in my house. I decided I would allow myself that much space to shoot [her next film]. I could go no further than the end of my cable. I would find everything I needed within that distance and never venture further.

The plan worked: Varda ended up filming the daily lives of the merchants in her neighborhood, for the documentary *Daguerréotypes*. This was fairly typical of her working process; she liked to work fast, "to film as soon as the idea comes to me," she said, while she was still "in the throes of imagination." (She wrote her 1965 film *Le Bonheur* in three days.) Nevertheless, Varda was dismissive of the idea of inspiration:

> You know artists used to talk about inspiration and the muse. The muse! That's amusing! But it's not your muse, it's your relationships with the creative forces that makes things appear when you need them. . . . So you have to work with free association and dreaminess, let yourself go with memories, chance encounters, objects. I try to achieve a balance between the rigorous discipline I've learned in my thirty years of making films

and these many unforeseen moments and the vibrations of chance.

One of the advantages of getting older, Varda said in 1988, was that she felt a growing tranquility about her career. She no longer got tense about the work she had yet to do; she enjoyed, she said, "the privilege of having something in me that no one can touch, which no one can destroy." And then, when the opportunity to make a new film came along, she would spring into action with tremendous energy. "I tend to wear out the people on my team with the extreme speed at which I do things and also by my demands on them," she said. "I get up at five a.m. to write my dialogs. I get to the set an hour before anyone else to check things out. I may have last minute ideas and want to set them in motion right away. I make incredible demands without any doubts about whether they'll work."

Françoise Sagan (1935–2004)

The French novelist, playwright, and screenwriter was best known for her first book, *Bonjour Tristesse,* published in 1954 when she was eighteen years old. Sagan wrote the book, she said, in "two or three months, working two or three hours a day," without much forethought or advance planning. "I simply started it," she said. "I had a strong desire to write and some free time." She wasn't sure she could write an entire book, but once she began the attempt she "wanted passionately to finish it." Afterward, Sagan thought publication unlikely but dropped it off at a Paris publisher anyway; the

Françoise Sagan, Paris, 1955

publisher offered her a lucrative contract and brought out the book a few months later.

Bonjour Tristesse was an immediate best seller and made its teenage author a celebrity, dubbed "an 18-year-old Colette" by *Paris Match*. The book's profits allowed her to live an extended adolescent fantasy, spending freely, drinking immoderately, and eschewing bourgeois values and comforts. "I don't like falling into habits, living in the same old setting, living through the same old things," Sagan said in 1974, twenty years after her literary debut. "I'm always moving house—it's quite manic. The material problems of day-to-day living bore me silly. As soon as someone asks me what we should have for dinner I become flustered and then sink into gloom."

Needless to say, Sagan never followed any particular writing routine. "Sometimes I write in bursts of ten days or a fortnight at a time," she said. "In between, I think about the story, day-dream and talk about it. I ask people for their opinions. Their opinions matter a lot." She always started with a rough draft, which she wrote quickly, sometimes completing ten pages in an hour or two. "There's never any plan because I like improvising," she said. "I like to feel that I'm pulling the strings of the story and that I can pull them whichever way I like." But after the draft was done she revised carefully, paying special attention to the rhythm and balance of her sentences: "There mustn't be a syllable or a beat missing." When the writing didn't meet her standards, Sagan found the process "humiliating," she said. "It's rather like dying; you feel so ashamed of yourself, ashamed of what you've written. You feel pathetic. But when it's going well, you feel like a well-oiled machine that's working perfectly. It's like watching someone run a hundred yards in ten seconds. It's a miracle."

Gloria Naylor (1950–2016)

Naylor wrote her debut novel, *The Women of Brewster Place,* while she was an undergraduate at Brooklyn College, and while also working as a switchboard operator at a hotel and going through a divorce. "I didn't realize then that mine was an impossible schedule," she recalled later. She wrote whenever she could fit it in, on her days off, between work and classes, and during night shifts at the hotel. "I was working alone because you know one operator can handle a hotel at night," she said in a 1988 interview. "And after about 2:30 or 3:00, I would sit there and edit what I had written during the day. I had to do it like that." Although this suggests formidable willpower, Naylor insisted that she was "not an overly disciplined person. It was something I wanted to do. It was something that was starting to flow out of me. It was helping me to achieve order because my personal life had been in total chaos."

She finished the novel the same month she graduated from college, and initially she intended to go on to earn a doctorate and become a professor. But the immediate critical and commercial success of *Brewster Place*—which won the 1983 National Book Award for a first novel—changed her plans; Naylor quit graduate school after earning her master's and set out to become a professional writer, supporting herself through fellowships, teaching jobs, and, eventually, a position on the executive board of the Book of the Month Club. Her working schedule varied, depending on the project at hand and her other commitments, but when she could she preferred to start in the early morning and work until noon or 1:00 p.m., then spend the afternoon on nonliterary chores. She was never picky about her writing conditions. "My needs are simple," she said. "Bottom line: I need a warm and quiet place to work."

She was similarly matter-of-fact about the writing process, describing herself as "a transcriber of stories" that arrived pretty much of their own accord. "The process starts with images that I am haunted by and I will not know why," she said. "People will say, 'How do you know that's to be a story or a book?' I say, 'Because it won't go away.' You just feel a dis-ease until somehow you go into the whole, complicated, painful process of writing and find out what the image means. And often, when I've gotten into a work, I have been sorry to find out what the image meant. But the die is cast."

Alice Neel (1900–1984)

Neel was one of the great portrait artists of the twentieth century, although she didn't begin to be recognized until she was in her sixties and had been working in near obscurity for decades. Despite poverty, critical and commercial neglect, and the responsibility of raising her two sons alone, Neel managed to paint pretty much every day, getting by on various forms of government assistance—initially drawing a salary as a Works Progress Administration artist, and then, when that program ended, collecting welfare. (According to her family, she was also a lifelong shoplifter.) When an interviewer asked how she painted with two young kids in the house, Neel said that, at first, she worked at night while they were sleeping; later, when they got older, she worked during the day while they were at school. She never seriously considered taking time off from her art. "If you decide you are going to have children and give up painting during the time you have them, you give it up forever," she said. "Or if you don't, you just become a dilettante. It must be a continuous thing. Oh, you may stop for a few months, but I don't think you can decide to stop for years and do a different thing. You get divorced from your art." In this and everything else,

Alice Neel, New York, 1961

Neel refused to compromise; it was the artist's prerogative to be selfish, she thought, and she would not feel guilty about it, especially when male artists were granted these privileges without question. She told students in a 1972 lecture, "I felt women represented a dreary way of life, always helping a man and never performing themselves, whereas I wanted to be an artist myself! I could certainly have accomplished more with a good wife. That is quite male chauvinist, but this was the world with which I was confronted."

Shirley Jackson (1916–1965)

"You were encouraged to write by your family?" a reporter from the *New York Post* asked Jackson in September 1962.

"They couldn't stop me," she replied. Jackson wrote six novels and dozens of short stories—including, most famously, "The Lottery," her 1948 tale of ritual stoning in a sleepy New England village—while also managing a bustling family life, with four children, a menagerie of pets, and a husband who took the hands-off approach to parenting typical of midcentury American fathers. While he worked as a literary critic, a magazine editor, and a professor, Jackson ran the household and squeezed in her writing around childcare and housekeeping duties. She said in a 1949 interview, "50 per cent of my life is spent washing and dressing the children, cooking, washing dishes and clothes, and mending. After I get it all to bed, I turn around to my typewriter and try to—well, to create concrete things again."

Though Jackson sometimes complained about the difficulty of reconciling the two roles, she also—as Ruth Franklin argues in her biography *Shirley Jackson: A Rather Haunted Life*—"seems to have derived imaginative energy from the constraints." Franklin continues:

Writing in the interstices—the hours between morning kindergarten and lunch, while a baby napped, or after the children had gone to bed—demanded a discipline that suited her. She was constantly thinking of stories while cooking, cleaning, or doing just about anything else. "All the time that I am making beds and doing dishes and driving to town for dancing shoes, I am telling myself stories," she said in one of her lectures. Even later, when the children were older and she had more time, Jackson would never be the kind of writer who sat at the typewriter all day. Her writing did not begin when she sat down at her desk, any more than it ended when she got up: "A writer is always writing, seeing everything through a thin mist of words, fitting swift little descriptions to everything he sees, always noticing."

And, compared to housekeeping, writing was fun. "My husband fights writing," Jackson said in 1949; "it is work for him, at least he calls it work. I find it relaxing. For one thing, it's the only way I can get to sit down. There is delight in seeing a story grow; it's so deeply satisfying—like having a winning streak in poker."

Alma Thomas [1891–1978]

The first African American woman to have a solo exhibition at the Whitney Museum of American Art, Thomas taught art to public-school students in Washington, D.C., for twenty-five years while pursuing her own practice on the side. She didn't become a full-time artist until she retired from teaching in 1960, at age sixty-eight, and she didn't receive widespread recognition for another decade. (The Whitney Museum exhibition opened in 1972, when Thomas was eighty.) Asked why she didn't try to become a professional artist right after college, where she had studied painting and sculpture, Thomas said that it wasn't that simple; she told a friend that "for educated young black people there were so many expectations then, so many pressures to conform." But, she added, "I never lost this need to create something original, something all my own."

Throughout her years of teaching, Thomas was always seeking out ways to continue developing as an artist. Starting

Alma Thomas, 1976

in 1930, she spent three summers at Columbia University, in New York, earning a master's in art education; while in the city, she began devotedly attending its museums and contemporary-art galleries. And in 1950, at age fifty-nine, Thomas enrolled at American University, to continue her studies in painting and art history. She never married or had children, believing it would have been too much of a distraction; she said, "a woman simply can't do justice both to a family and to art. She has to choose which she wants."

After she finally retired from teaching, Thomas threw herself into painting full-time, embracing watercolors as her primary medium. She worked in the kitchen or living room of her small house in Washington, propping canvases on her lap or balancing them on the sofa. She claimed to have no regrets about her late start. "I don't know how it happened, but it seems to me that I've conducted my life so that every time I came to a crossroads I took the right turn," she told a visiting critic in 1977.

> I never married, for one thing. That was a place I know I made the right choice. The young men I knew cared nothing about art, nothing at all. And art was the only thing I enjoyed. So I have remained free. I paint when I feel like it. I didn't have to come home. Or I could come home late and there was nobody to interfere with what I wanted, to stop and discuss what they wanted. It was what I wanted, and no argument. That is what allowed me to develop.

If Thomas did have one regret, it was that not long after becoming a full-time painter she developed chronic arthritis that made her increasingly frail. "Do you have any idea what it's like to be caged in a seventy-eight-year-old body and to have the mind and energy of a twenty-five-year-old?" she asked. "If I could only turn the clock back about sixty years, I'd show them."

Lee Krasner (1908–1984)

Krasner was once asked to name the greatest sacrifice she had made for her art. "I sacrificed nothing," she replied. Many observers had a hard time believing her. Krasner began studying painting in high school, became a full-time artist in her mid-twenties, and by the end of her life had received widespread recognition as a pioneer of Abstract Expressionism. But for fourteen years she was also married to Jackson Pollock, and his achievements as a painter—and his notorious self-destructiveness, which culminated in his death in a drunken car accident in 1956—always overshadowed Krasner's own career. Nevertheless, she insisted that her and Pollock's partnership was an equal one, and that he was always "very supportive" of her work. "Since Pollock was a turbulent man, life with him was never very calm," Krasner said. "But the question—should I paint, shouldn't I paint—never arose. I didn't hide my paintings in a closet; they hung on the wall next to his."

It was Krasner who pushed for their move out of New York City, where they had met and become a couple, hectoring Pollock's gallerist and patron, Peggy Guggenheim, for a $2,000 loan to help them buy an old, unheated farmhouse in Springs, a fishing village on eastern Long Island. They moved in the fall of 1945, and Pollock converted a barn on the property into his studio; Krasner took a small upstairs bedroom in the farmhouse as hers. In Springs, Pollock would sleep until 11:00 a.m. or noon and then goof off until the late afternoon, when he would head into the barn to begin painting. Meanwhile, Krasner would get up at 9:00 or 10:00 a.m. and work upstairs. "He always slept very late," Krasner recalled.

> Morning was my best time for work, so I would be in my studio when I heard him stirring around. I would go back [downstairs], and while he had his breakfast I had my lunch. . . . We had an agreement that neither of us would go into the other's studio without being

asked. Occasionally, it was something like once a week, he would say, "I have something to show you." . . . He would ask, "Does it work?" Or in looking at mine, he would comment, "It works" or "It doesn't work."

Life in the country was good for them, at least at first. They divided up the chores more or less evenly, with Krasner doing the cooking but Pollock in charge of baking (he made "marvelous bread and pies," she said), and with the spouses sharing the gardening and lawn work. Without his New York pals to go out with, Pollock initially drank less, and it was during these years that he developed the drip-painting technique that characterized his mature style. Krasner had her own creative breakthrough; after years of feeling miserably stuck, working her canvases over and over until they became "pasty crusts of grey," in the words of one critic, she arrived at her Little Image series—intimate canvases layered with abstract symbols, some achieved with her own version of drip painting—which became among her most successful paintings, although their importance was not recognized until the 1970s.

Eventually, as Pollock resumed drinking and his binges grew worse, Krasner moved from the upstairs bedroom to her own separate studio building, a former smokehouse on an adjoining acre of land that they were able to purchase. After Pollock's death, Krasner divided her time between Long Island and Manhattan, where she took an apartment in a doorman building on the Upper East Side. She turned the master bedroom into her studio and slept in the smaller guest bedroom, which made it easy for her to get up in the night and paint during her periodic bouts of insomnia. In 1974, Krasner described her work schedule as "a very neurotic rhythm of painting. I have a high discipline of keeping my time open to work. If I'm in a real work cycle, I'll pretty much isolate myself and paint straight through, avoiding social engagements." The times in between these concentrated work spells were difficult; she was always eager to get back to painting, but she didn't believe in forcing the process. "I believe in listening to cycles," she said in 1977. "I listen by not forcing. If I am in a dead working period, I wait, though those periods are hard to deal with. For the future, I'll see what happens. I'll be content to get started again. If I feel that alive again. If I find myself working with the old intensity again."

Grace Hartigan (1922–2008)

Hartigan was one of the foremost painters of the second-generation Abstract Expressionists, those mostly New York artists who followed in the footsteps of Willem de Kooning and Jackson Pollock to expand the bounds of visual abstraction. Hartigan's journals from the early 1950s, published in 2009, vividly chart her creative process. In this July 1955 entry, Hartigan describes her lifestyle as a young painter on New York's Lower East Side:

Now my days alone have a certain shape to them—I wake about nine, turn on the symphony and have juice, fruit and a pot of black coffee. Read a bit (still Gide's Journal), talk on the phone . . . Then three or four, sometimes five hours on this canvas—it hasn't begun to come yet, but I keep thinking of things to do.

Then a few domestic chores for myself, a cold shower, a cold hard boiled egg and one or two rums

Grace Hartigan, New York, 1950s

with Rose's lime, more reading, some records. To-night I meet Frank [the poet Frank O'Hara] at the Cedar for dinner, then to the late showing of "East of Eden." I feel sharp, my reading is concentrated and not "escape." I have thoughts, ideas. And the news of Tom Hess' coming article on the younger painters, profuse reproductions of "everyone," but me, does not fill me with paranoia and depression, I am interested, but not upset.

The article Hartigan mentions was one of the last times she would be left out of this kind of survey. But she was not always so sanguine about her career prospects, or so straightforwardly productive. Rather, Hartigan vacillated between periods of confident progress and painful inactivity. Months earlier, she had written:

> I am in one of those terrible times when I feel "painted out." I alternate between ennui and restlessness—an ennui that stupefies me, keeps me curled in my chair for hours and hours, reading anything—movie books, detective stories, "literature," old journals. Or the restlessness that makes me walk the floor, staring out one window and then another, or sends me dashing into the street to stare into people's faces or dash from one gallery to another, or pace frantically through museums looking for what, some clue, some hint, anything in life or art that will get me out of this pit.

Eventually, the working spirit would come back of its own accord, sometimes after a few days, sometimes not for weeks. "Art cannot be seized head on, it must be stalked, it is elusive," Hartigan wrote in her journal. "And the only way it can be ever found is not knowing it except through occasional flashes of insight and revelation." And this required constant vigilance and determination. As Hartigan wrote in another journal entry, "One must be fierce."

Toni Cade Bambara (1939–1995)

Bambara began her career as a short-story writer, publishing two collections—*Gorilla, My Love* and *The Sea Birds Are Still Alive*—in the 1970s. She never followed a strict writing schedule, using spare bits of time while raising her daughter, teaching and lecturing at universities, and working as a civil-rights activist. "There's no particular routine to my writing," Bambara told an interviewer, "nor have any two stories come to me the same way."

> I'm usually working on five or six things at a time; that is, I scribble a lot in bits and pieces and generally pin them together with a working title. The actual sit-down work is still weird to me. I babble along, heading I think in one direction, only to discover myself tugged in another, or sometimes I'm absolutely snatched into an alley. I write in longhand or what kin and friends call deranged hieroglyphics. I begin on long, yellow paper with a juicy ballpoint if it's one of those 6/8 bop pieces. For slow, steady, watch-the-voice-kid, don't-let-the-mask-slip-type pieces, I prefer short, fat-lined white paper and an ink pen. I usually work it over and beat it up and sling it around the room a lot before I get to the typing stage. I hate to type—hate, hate—so things get cut mercilessly at that stage. I stick the thing in a drawer or pin it on a board for a while, maybe read it to someone or a group, get some feedback, mull it over, and put it aside. Then, when an editor calls me to say, "Got anything?" or I find the desk cluttered, or some reader sends a letter asking, "You still breathing?" or I need some dough, I'll very studiously sit down, edit, type, and send the damn thing out before it drives me crazy.

But Bambara's switch from short stories to the novel—she published her debut novel, *The Salt Eaters,* in 1980—also meant adjusting her approach to writing. She wrote in a 1979 essay:

I'd never fully appreciated before the concern that so many people express over women writers' work habits—how do you juggle the demands of motherhood, etc.? Do you find that friends, especially intimates, resent your need for privacy, etc.? Is it possible to wrench yourself away from active involvement for the lonely business of writing? Writing had never been so central an activity in my life before. Besides, a short story is fairly portable. I could narrate the basic outline while driving to the farmer's market, work out the dialogue while waiting for the airlines to answer the phone, draft a rough sketch of the central scene while overseeing my daughter's carrot cake, write the first version in the middle of the night, edit while the laundry takes a spin, and make copies while running off some rally flyers. But the novel has taken me out of action for frequent and lengthy periods. Other than readings and an occasional lecture, I seem unfit for any other kind of work. I cannot knock out a terse and pithy office memo any more. And my relationships, I'm sure, have suffered because I am so distracted, preoccupied, and distant. The short story is a piece of work. The novel is a way of life.

Margaret Walker (1915–1998)

"To choose the life of a writer," Walker wrote in the early 1980s, "a black female must arm herself with a fool's courage, foolhardiness, and serious purpose and dedication to the art of writing, strength of will and integrity, because the odds are always against her. The cards are stacked. Once the die is cast, however, there is no turning back." Walker knew all about dedication, and long odds: She began her first novel, *Jubilee,* in the fall of 1934, when she was a nineteen-year-old senior at Northwestern University, and finished the first draft in April 1965, more than three decades after its inception. In the intervening years she earned a master's degree, published a celebrated book of poetry—1942's *For My People*— embarked on a university teaching career, got married, and raised four children. But the novel was always in the back of her mind. Whenever she could, Walker tried to find time to continue the research and writing, but she often failed to fit it in; for a seven-year stretch, between 1955 and 1962, she didn't write a single word. "People ask me how I find time to write with a family and a teaching job," she wrote years later.

I don't. That is one reason I was so long with *Jubilee.* A writer needs time to write a certain number of hours every day. This is particularly true with prose fiction and absolutely necessary with the novel. Writing poetry may be different, but the novel demands long hours every day at a steady pace until the thing is done. It is humanly impossible for a woman who is a wife and mother to work on a regular teaching job and write. Weekends and nights and vacations are all right for reading but not enough for writing.

Indeed, Walker was able to finish the book only by going back to graduate school at the University of Iowa—leaving her husband and children behind, temporarily—and working out an arrangement whereby her novel would serve as her dissertation. Even so, she had to spend two years attending to other graduate-school requirements before she could give the novel her full attention. In the fall of 1964 she was finally able to get back to *Jubilee,* and then she worked fast, writing longer and longer hours as she neared the end. In the following spring, Walker "worked from seven in the morning until eleven and stopped for lunch," she later recalled. Then she "went back to the typewriter and worked in the afternoon until supper or tea at four and then after supper until eleven o'clock. I pushed myself beyond all physical endurance, and in two months, I was happy to lose twenty pounds."

She was happier to have finished the book—although she later admitted that *Jubilee*'s long gestation process was in many ways essential to its success. Asked what it was like to live with the book for so long, Walker said:

> You just become part of it, and it becomes part of you. Working, raising a family, all of that becomes part of it. Even though I was preoccupied with everyday things, I used to think about what I wanted to do with *Jubilee.* Part of the problem with the book was the terrible feeling that I wasn't going to be able to get it finished. . . . And even if I had the time to work at it, I wasn't sure I would be able to do it the way I wanted. Living with the book over a long period of time was agonizing. Despite all of that, *Jubilee* is the product of a mature person. When I started out with the book, I didn't know half of what I now know about life. That I learned during those thirty years. . . . There's a difference between writing about something and living through it. I did both.

A PRIVILEGED SPACE

Tamara de Lempicka (1898–1980)

Lempicka arrived in Paris in the summer of 1918, a Polish-Russian aristocrat forced by the Bolshevik Revolution to flee St. Petersburg with her husband, Tadeusz, and their young daughter, Kizette. It was a shocking drop in station: In Russia, the young couple had lived in comfortable style funded by their parents' wealth; in Paris, by contrast, the family initially shared a small hotel room with little more than a bed, a cot, and a washbasin. "The poor baby, our food, everything [was] washed in that one bowl," Lempicka later recalled. Tadeusz reacted with anger and resentment, refusing to accept a lowly post as a bank clerk, drinking too much, and picking fights with his wife that frequently ended in physical violence. Lempicka's response was the opposite: After a brief period of depression, she determined not only to improve her family's circumstances but to conquer Paris on her own terms.

Lempicka had already shown early promise as an artist, studying painting in Russia and abroad, and she soon resolved to resume her studies. By the end of 1919, she had enrolled in a private art academy, where she began spending most of her days; when classes were finished, she went to the Louvre to sketch the masterpieces there. She arranged her schedule so that she could have breakfast with her daughter in the morning and put her to bed at night; otherwise, she placed Kizette in the care of her husband or her mother, who was living nearby. "By the fall of 1922," the biographer

Tamara de Lempicka, 1940

Laura Claridge writes, "Tamara was trying to live the life of student, painter, wife, mother, breadwinner, and debauchee at the same time." Within a few years of completing her studies, Lempicka was already showing and selling her work, for increasingly large sums. She developed a style of painting that was perfectly matched to her era, a combination of "soft Cubism" and neoclassical portraiture that embodied Art Deco elegance, and that was particularly well suited to glamorous nudes.

As for the debauchery Claridge mentions, that took place after Lempicka had put her daughter to bed, when she would often head back out to a cabaret or the opera. Afterward, she would go exploring the seedier side of Parisian nightlife, frequenting the city's decadent gay bars in particular, where dancing, drink, and drugs were plentiful. Lempicka preferred pellets of hashish dissolved in sloe-gin fizzes or, her very favorite, hits of cocaine sniffed from a miniature silver teaspoon. Many nights ended in a Left Bank district notorious for its ramshackle bars filled with sailors, students, and others seeking anonymous sexual encounters, which Lempicka found to be an even more seductive high. (She claimed, "It is an artist's duty to try everything.") Returning home, her mind abuzz from the sexual and chemical stimulation, Lempicka got to work, painting nonstop for hours. Finally, to calm her nerves for sleep, she turned to the herbal supplement valerian. No matter what, she made sure to be up in time to have breakfast with Kizette the next morning, often getting only a few hours' sleep. It was around this time that she developed her motto: "There are no miracles," she said. "There is only what you make."

Romaine Brooks (1874–1970)

Born in Rome and raised by a cruel, mentally unhinged mother, Brooks studied painting in Italy and initially set up her studio on the isle of Capri. In 1902, her mother died and the twenty-eight-year-old painter inherited a considerable fortune, which enabled her to move to Paris and live a life of unusual independence for a woman at the time. (According

Self-Portrait *by Romaine Brooks, 1923*

to the biographer Diana Souhami, "She had an English chauffeur, a French maid, a Spanish concierge, and a Belgian chef, and she dressed in ermine, velvet and pearls.") Not having to worry about the sales of her paintings, Brooks pursued her idiosyncratic vision with single-minded intensity, ignoring the artistic movements of the era in favor of an almost monochromatic palette dominated by myriad shades of gray. In the words of one curator, Brooks "really painted as though Picasso and Matisse didn't exist."

In 1915, Brooks met Natalie Clifford Barney, an American writer who ran a lively salon in Paris frequented by Colette, Radclyffe Hall, Djuna Barnes, Thelma Wood, Dolly Wilde, Gertrude Stein, Alice B. Toklas, and other "ladies with high collars and monocles," as the bookseller Sylvia Beach put it. Brooks and Barney soon began a relationship that would last for more than fifty years, although each took lovers on the side and they only occasionally shared the same roof. For Brooks, it was an ideal arrangement. "I shut myself up for months without seeing a soul," she wrote of her creative process, "and give shape in my paintings to my visions of sad and gray shadows." Fortunately, Barney shared much the same view of cohabitation. "For me, to live alone as my own master is essential," she wrote in her book *Souvenirs Indiscrets,* "not for egotistical reasons or any lack of love, but in order to better give myself. To bathe in passionate intimacy on a daily basis, while living together in the same house and often in the same bedroom with the loved one, has always seemed to me the most certain way to lose somebody."

Nevertheless, in 1930, Brooks and Barney attempted a kind of negotiated cohabitation by building a house together in the south of France, near Saint-Tropez. They called it the Villa Trait d'Union—the Hyphenated Villa—and there they hoped to achieve an ideal balance of independence and togetherness. Indeed, the villa was really more like two connected residences: There was a shared living room and galleried loggia, but Brooks and Barney each had their own separate entrances, workrooms, and bedrooms (and they each kept their own servants as well).

Even with all this separation, however, Brooks grew annoyed with Barney's regular stream of visitors. Having her own workroom and bedroom wasn't enough—she needed true solitude to paint. As she once wrote, "I suppose an artist must live alone and feel free otherwise all individuality goes. I can think of my painting only when I am alone, even less do any actual work."

Eudora Welty (1909–2001)

"I've found it possible to write almost anywhere I've happened to try," the American short-story writer and novelist said in 1972. But Welty preferred to write at home, "because it's much more convenient for an early riser, which I am," she said. "And it's the only place where you can really promise yourself time and keep out interruptions." She liked to write the first draft of a short story in one sitting, work on revisions for as long as required, and then write the final version in one go, "so that in the end the whole thing amounts to one long sustained effort."

Welty began work in the morning while still in her nightgown, and she often didn't get dressed until she had reached a good stopping point in a story. She wrote in the upstairs bedroom of her house in Jackson, Mississippi, which her father built when she was sixteen and where she lived for the rest of her life. She wrote first drafts on a typewriter—"It gives me the feeling of making my work objective," she said—and she revised by cutting out passages and pinning them to the bed using dressmakers' pins, rearranging the pieces until she had figured out the right structure for her narrative. (Sometimes this meant moving what she thought was the beginning to the very end, or vice versa.)

In 1988, an interviewer asked Welty to describe in as

Eudora Welty outside her home
in Jackson, Mississippi, 1988

much detail as possible her ideal writing day. "Oh, boy," she replied. "Nobody's ever given me this chance before."

Okay. Wake up early. I'm one of the people who think best in the morning. I like to wake up ready to go, and to know that during that whole day the phone wouldn't ring, the doorbell wouldn't ring—even with good news—and that nobody would drop in. This all sounds so rude. But you know, things that just make a normally nice day are not what I want. I don't care where I am or what room I'm in. I'd just get up and get my coffee and an ordinary breakfast and get to work. And just have that whole day! And at the end of the day, about five or six o'clock, I'd stop for good that day. And I'd have a drink, a bourbon and water, watch the evening news—"MacNeil-Lehrer News Hour"—and then I could do anything I wanted to.

For lunch, Welty said, she would just stop for a minute and make something easy—a sandwich and a Coke, perhaps. In the evening, she would see a friend for dinner or attend another social engagement. But the real key to this perfect writing day, she said, was to know that the following day would be exactly the same. Although this was increasingly impossible for Welty to attain as she became an internationally celebrated writer, the ideal would be to have each day as wide open and free of interruption or obligation as possible. Then even if one day's writing was not very good, it wouldn't matter, because it was part of a larger process that continued from day to day, the "one long sustained effort" that led to her best writing. "It's the act of being totally absorbed, I think, which seems to give you direction," Welty said. "The work teaches you about the work ahead, and that teaches you what's ahead, and so on. That's the reason you don't want to drop the thread of it. It is a lovely way to be."

Elena Ferrante (b. 1943)

"I don't have a routine," the pseudonymous Italian novelist wrote in 2014, in reply to an interviewer's question about her writing habits.

> I write when I want to. Telling stories requires a lot of effort—what happens to the characters also happens to me, their good and their evil feelings belong to me. This is how it has to be, or else I don't write. When I feel exhausted, I do the most obvious thing: I stop writing and busy myself with the thousands of urgent matters that I've ignored and without which life no longer functions.

When she is writing, Ferrante follows no fixed schedule. "I write continuously and everywhere and at every hour of the day and night," she has said. Her only requirements are "a little corner somewhere," "a very small space" in which to work—and, more important, a sense of urgency about the project at hand. "If I don't feel the urgency to write, there is no proprietary rite that can help me," she has said. "I prefer to do something else—there is always something better to do."

Joan Didion (b. 1934)

In 1978, *The Paris Review* asked Didion if she had any writing rituals. "The most important is that I need an hour alone before dinner, with a drink, to go over what I've done that day," she said.

I can't do it late in the afternoon because I'm too close to it. Also, the drink helps. It removes me from the pages. So I spend this hour taking things out and putting other things in. Then I start the next day by redoing all of what I did the day before, following these evening notes. When I'm really working I don't like to go out or have anybody to dinner, because then I lose the hour. If I don't have the hour, and start the next day with just some bad pages and nowhere to go, I'm in low spirits. Another thing I need to do, when I'm near the end of the book, is sleep in the same room with it. That's one reason I go home to Sacramento to finish things. Somehow the book doesn't leave you when you're asleep right next to it. In Sacramento nobody cares if I appear or not. I can just get up and start typing.

In 2005, Didion told an interviewer that she typically spends "most of the day working on a piece not actually putting anything on paper, just sitting there, trying to form a coherent idea and then maybe something will come to me about five in the afternoon and then I'll work for a couple of hours and get three or four sentences, maybe a paragraph." The slowness of the writing process stems, Didion has said, from the sheer difficulty of thinking clearly. "Writing," she said in 2011, "forces you to think."

It forces you to work the thing through. Nothing comes to us out of the blue, very easily, you know. So if you want to understand what you're thinking, you kind of have to work it through and write it. And the only way to work it through, for me, is to write it.

When she's in between writing projects, Didion isn't necessarily able to relax. "It feels very different," she said in 2011. "I don't like it."

Sheila Heti (b. 1976)

"For a long time I thought that I didn't have a daily ritual, that I was failing because my life didn't resemble the lives of so many writers I had read about in *The Paris Review*—with their perfect schedules, their impossible lives, their 'discipline,'" the Canadian novelist and short-story writer said in 2016. "I knew you needed discipline to be a writer, but I am not the sort of person who can stick to anything for very long—an exercise routine, an eating programme, anything. I lose my enthusiasm very quickly." Over time, however, Heti has come to embrace her less-regimented approach:

> More and more as I get older, I want my writing and my life to interweave. I don't want my books or writing itself to be something separate from what I would do anyway, or to be about something apart from what I am thinking anyway—my writing should be no different from my thoughts going through the day. I don't know if I have come to this because I can't seem to separate out a privileged space for writing, in which I imagine other worlds, or if it's the reverse, but it's important for writing and life to be fairly seamless; to be the same thing. So that I can come to the computer at any time—night or day, for ten minutes or two hours, and begin writing from where I am—from what I am thinking

about. I want writing and living to be one thing, so that writing is just me living, but on the page—an extension of the living I was doing before I sat down to write.

Heti works at home, in the Toronto apartment she shares with her boyfriend. They don't follow a strict schedule, getting up at 7:00, 8:00, or 9:00 a.m. and going to bed between 10:00 p.m. and midnight. Once she's up, Heti immediately drinks one or two cups of coffee; then, depending on what time her boyfriend is leaving for work that day, she will spend some time with him or else open the computer and start working. "I try not to check my email till midday but I fail at this nearly every day," she said. She writes from bed or the couch—"I have a desk but never use it"—and she starts a new document for each day, or at least for each day that she writes. Sometimes she will hardly write at all for weeks or months, and then a month will arrive when she writes "thousands and thousands" of words a day. "I guess there is some kind of rhythm to it, but I haven't been able to see what it is," she said. "I know I write more when I'm in the luteal phase of my menstrual cycle—that is, the two weeks before my period, because I'm more emotional then, and need to write to sort things out, to calm myself down, to sort of untangle threads."

Heti's writing tends to fall into one of two categories: those bursts of imaginative writing that take hold occasionally, and the more quotidian writing she does the rest of the time. Much of the latter takes the form of journals, and most of this material never makes it to publication. But at some point Heti will realize that she's stopped writing one book and started writing the next one, and that's when she begins the formidable task of editing the book she's just finished. "I spend a ton of time editing, rearranging, because I write my books out of order, so the most difficult part of writing a book for me is figuring out the order of things, and what to leave in and what to take out," she said. "I write maybe twenty-five or fifty pages for every page that I end up publishing." She never rewrites scenes—if a scene is not good the first time, it doesn't go into the book—but she spends a lot of time editing individual sentences, both on the computer and on paper. At various points in this process she will send the computer file to a local print shop and have them spiral-bind the document, which she'll carry around and read in different locations for further edits. But often she'll end up returning to the original version, which, she said, she invariably prefers.

Miranda July (b. 1974)

July is a filmmaker, a performance artist, and a writer—of screenplays, short stories, and a novel—and she has succeeded in all of these mediums thanks to formidable self-discipline, although she does not see this as an entirely positive character trait. July is forever making rules for herself, and she works by heaping varying degrees of guilt, abuse, and deception onto her work life. One of her cherished mental tricks, for instance, is to avoid working on her "front-burner project" by tinkering with another, less-pressing project, beating herself up about procrastinating even though at some level she knows that it's by working in multiple disciplines that she creates her best work.

Having a child in 2012 only raised the stakes. "Once you have a kid it's sort of like the Olympics of self-discipline," July said in 2016. "It's like, 'Ah, now I can really flex my

muscles! Let's see if I can write a novel in just forty-five minutes a day!' " In fact, July wrote her debut novel, *The First
Bad Man,* over the course of her pregnancy and the first couple years of her son's life, finishing it after about three years
total. "At the beginning, it was simply, like, handing the baby
to the nanny for 30 minutes and going in my room and writing anything," July said. "But now I realize that was sort of
important."

July lives in Los Angeles and works in her former residence,
"a squalid little cave" that she kept as an office space after
moving in with her now husband, the filmmaker Mike Mills.
Most days she gets up at about 6:30 a.m. and does "mother-
ing things" for as long as that takes; then she drops off her son
at school and heads to her office, arriving at about 9:00 a.m.
Although she generally spends the workday alone, she puts
great care into getting dressed each morning. "I like clothes,
and I think I see it as a bit of an antidepressant," July said. "I
just like looking down and seeing the material and having the
sense that I'm fit for the world, even if I'm not in the world."

July works in too many mediums to follow one set work
routine, but very often writing is the primary goal of her
day. She prepares for it while still at home, by doing a quick
review of her emails to see if there are any fires that need
putting out before she gets to the office. Once she's there, she
enables Internet-blocking software on her computer for anywhere from three to six hours, and sets to work. Walking is a
key part of her writing process. "Often I feel like I'm playing
hooky," July said, "but I find there's only so many good ideas
you can have sitting in a chair. Of course the work has to be
done there; you have to write. But there's a way that I can get
really kind of frozen—where I'm literally not doing anything
and yet I forget to remember that I can get up and walk or
look at a book or do something else." Once she breaks this

chair-lock, July will set off on a walk around her neighbor-hood, and as she has ideas she'll record voice notes on her smartphone. Through long experience, July knows precisely "the amount of pressure to apply to my brain on a writing walk," she said. "It's not too much. You know, you kind of want to trick yourself that you're just enjoying being outside and maybe plant the seed of, like, 'How does this character do this?' And then let it go." For each writing project she ends up with hundreds of voice notes, which she'll consult while writing the first draft—"like a little bible," she said.

Before having her son, July would normally work until 7:00 p.m., but nowadays she stops at about 3:45, and a late night at the office means continuing until 5:30. As a result of this shorter work day, July sometimes gets stuck dealing with emails and other work tasks after her son is asleep, but generally she tries to avoid working in the evening, instead catching up with her husband before going to bed at about 10:00 p.m.

Patti Smith (b. 1946)

"I get up and if I feel out of sorts I'll do some exercises," the punk singer, visual artist, and poet said in 2015. "I'll feed my cat, then I go get my coffee, take a notebook, and write for a couple of hours. Then I just roam around. I try to take long walks and things like that, but I just kill time until something good is on TV." Smith writes at home, usually in bed—"I have a fine desk but I prefer to work from my bed," she has written, "as if I'm a convalescent in a Robert Louis Steven-son poem"—or else at a café near her Manhattan apartment. As for television, she is a devoted follower of crime shows, especially the darker varieties, and she sees parallels between their moody, obsessed detectives and the writing life. "Yesterday's poets are today's detectives," Smith wrote in her 2015 memoir *M Train*. "They spend a lifetime sniffing out the hundredth line, wrapping up a case, and limping exhausted into the sunset. They entertain and sustain me."

Ntozake Shange (1948–2018)

"I write whenever I get up," the American playwright and poet said in a 1983 interview.

> I also like to go to one of the cafés that I frequent and write during off-hours between 2 and 4:30 in the afternoon and between 6:30 and 8:00 in the evening. I'll have a glass of wine and Perrier water, and I just sit and write in my journal for an hour-and-a-half or two hours. That's very good for me to do because that environment is very protected. I'm not here at home by myself; so whatever my demons are, they're not going to be able to overwhelm me because I'm alone and vulnerable. If I have a real scary piece to write, I might go outside and do it . . . if I go outside and I know I'm around people, I feel very secure. Then I can write about all kinds of weird or scary things. The demons must control themselves.

But, for Shange, the writing process also meant letting go of control, at least part of the time. "I do feel myself as a medium sometimes," she said in 1991. "I think that the unconscious—which sometimes expresses itself through artists—is a medium of other spirits—of other deities: to let us have things that we can't have rationally."

Cindy Sherman (b. 1954)

Widely recognized as one of America's most important living artists, Sherman has built an astonishing career out of self-transformation, using makeup, wigs, costumes, and evocative backdrops (both real and virtual) to fashion herself into the subject of photographs that investigate issues of self-presentation, vulnerability, aging, and loneliness—not to mention their engagement with art history, celebrity culture, and societal standards of beauty. She has always worked alone; the few times she tried to utilize friends or family as models, she has said, left her feeling too attentive to their needs, and too self-conscious about her own process. "Even having an assistant around," Sherman said in 2012, "I'd feel self-conscious at times, like I'd better look busy now, rather than just spacing out, looking at images online or in magazines, or whatever I might do." Plus, when she tried working with others, Sherman got the sensation that they were having fun—"thinking this was like Halloween, or playing dress-up"—and that is emphatically not what she's after. She said in a 2003 interview:

> The levels I try to get to are not about the having-fun part. . . . I myself don't know exactly what I want from a picture, so it's hard to articulate that to somebody else—anybody else. When I'm doing it myself, I'm really just using the mirror to summon something I don't even know until I see it.

In the studio, Sherman positions a mirror next to the camera, and as she looks into the mirror she thinks "of *becoming* a different person . . . it's trance-like," she said in 1985. This does not happen on any kind of schedule—"I'm not a nine-to-five kind of artist," she has said—and Sherman can never predict how much time she'll need to create a new photo. "I guess it's a crapshoot," she once explained, speaking about her 1988–90 *History Portraits,* a series of off-kilter homages to Old Master paintings. "With some of those history portraits, I feel like I just whipped one out in a couple hours. Then there are others where I think I know what it is I want and I'll work at the same thing for days, and maybe never really feel satisfied. It's always different."

As for when she knows a series is complete, it is, again, mostly a matter of intuition. "There is usually a moment where I say, 'I've had enough of this, I'm sick of it,' or I feel like I've started to repeat myself within a series," Sherman explained in 2012.

> Then I go into production for the series—there's usually a deadline involved, so I'm focusing on that and doing whatever needs to be done for a show. Then I'm sort of drained or distanced from working, so I clean up my studio and put things away. Even though I might have other ideas on a back burner, a couple of years might go by before I get back into the studio again.

Indeed, one constant in her career has been long breaks, usually years long, in between photo series. During this time Sherman will feel that she never wants to take another photo—but so far, eventually, something has always brought her back for another attempt.

Renee Cox (b. 1960)

Cox is a Jamaican-born, New York–based artist known for her photographic series centered on the black female body—often her own—through which she has provocatively explored racial and gender politics since the 1990s. She does not follow a strict daily schedule, she said in 2017, "because that would be adhering to clock time, which is man-made. I don't really function like that." But Cox does wake up at the same time every day—6:00 a.m.—to meditate for forty-five minutes. "And I go back to sleep right after I do it," she said, laughing. She sleeps until about 9:30, and then three days a week she has a physical therapy session at 11:00 a.m. At about midday, she heads to her studio in the Bronx, driving the ten minutes from her home in Harlem. "I'm one of those unusual people in New York who drives everywhere," she said. "That's just the way I like it." In the studio, Cox is sometimes joined by assistants or interns; other times, she's alone. "I can be working there from 2:30 until midnight, or even later than that," she said. "Or I can be home by 7:00. It depends on what I'm doing." The one constant in her creative life is the absence of ego, or at least an aspiration toward that state. Her creative process really comes from a place of "no thought," she said. "It's a place where you don't have all of these distractions and all of this egoic thinking happening." Above all, she banishes negative thoughts, which means that she does not try to push herself or force things to happen in her work. "I'm not there to beat myself up," she said.

Petah Coyne (b. 1953)

Coyne is an Oklahoma-born, New York–based sculptor and installation artist who has been called "the queen of mixed media." She is known for her intricate, larger-than-life sculptural environments assembled from unusual sources; a partial list of the artist's materials on her website includes "dead fish, mud, sticks, hay, black sand, specially formulated and patented wax, satin ribbons, velvet, silk flowers, and more recently, taxidermy and cast-wax statues."

Coyne lives in Manhattan and commutes six days a week to her studio in the New York area. (She prefers to keep the exact location secret.) She is always trying to find the most efficient work schedule, both because her sculptures are phenomenally labor-intensive and as a result, she says, of her highly disciplined upbringing. "I come from a military background and a Catholic background; it's a double whammy," Coyne said in 2017. "But coming from such a rigid background I saw efficiency at its best, and I realized that if you were really organized you could accomplish a lot."

Coyne gets up at 4:30 a.m. and spends thirty minutes on emails; then, at 5:00, she starts to get ready for work while listening to an audiobook—she loves to listen to books, and will continue to do so throughout much of her workday, typically going through two or three audiobooks a week. She's out the door by 6:00 a.m., driving from her SoHo apartment to her studio, arriving in time to eat breakfast as the sun rises over the city; then, at 7:00 a.m., she goes through the door to her private portion of the studio and sets to work. "When I'm in the studio, I put my Bose headphones on, so I block out the noise, I select a good book, and I just go," she said. She keeps two works-in-progress in her studio at a time, and moves back and forth between them over the course of the morning. "I have these two pieces in my studio, constantly switching to and from, listening to great literature, and I'm just *moving*," she said. "It's like I'm dancing with the piece." When Coyne reaches a stopping point on one piece, she'll move it out of the studio and bring in another from storage. (Her twenty-thousand-square-foot studio includes her own private studio, workspace for her studio assistants, an office, storage for her work, and additional storage spaces that she rents to fellow artists at a friendly rate.) Sometimes unfinished works will stay in storage for as long as five years until, as she said, "I hear them talking to me," and they're brought back for completion.

Meanwhile, three days a week, at 8:00 a.m., Coyne's crew arrives—three studio assistants and three or four office assistants, who know not to intrude on the artist while she's working. When Coyne emerges from her studio at 1:00 p.m., everyone will have eaten lunch (Coyne eats alone in her private studio), and then the next phase of Coyne's workday begins. First she checks on her studio assistants and gives them their assignments for the following day; then she works in the office for the remainder of the afternoon. She wraps up between 6:30 and 7:30 p.m. and is home by 8:00, in time to eat dinner and spend a brief window of time with her husband before going to bed at 9:00 p.m.

Coyne's weekday meals are unvarying: oatmeal and berries for breakfast, salad for lunch, miso soup for dinner. "Food isn't that big for me," Coyne said. Her wardrobe is similarly limited. "I don't want to waste time, so I have the same awful outfit," she said. "I order the same five turtlenecks every year, the same five pairs of black pants, black socks, I'm ready to roll. I don't even think about it."

Coyne follows the above routine Monday through Friday. On Saturdays she has breakfast with her husband, works a half-day in the studio, and goes to a museum or to galleries. Or, if she's doing a collaborative project with another artist, that will happen on Saturdays instead. Saturday nights she has a proper dinner with her husband and they watch a movie. Sundays are completely free. "Sundays I don't do dog," Coyne said. "Read *The New York Times,* two movies with my husband. It's the day where you don't get out of your jammies."

Coyne's daily routine does shift periodically, as she is always trying to figure out the most efficient arrangement of her time. Remarkably, her current working habits are mellow compared to what she endured as a young artist trying to establish herself in New York. At the time, she was working in advertising during the day and making her sculptures in the evening. Twice a week she would pull all-nighters, toiling in her studio from the evening until the next morning, and then go back to her day job without having slept. The other weekday nights she would do three hours after work and get a normal night's sleep. She kept this up for almost a decade, until a string of well-received exhibitions allowed her to apply for grants and start piecing together an income as a full-time artist. "That was the hardest time in my life, to work that hard," Coyne said. To stick with it, she would think of herself as the commander of an army, and her body as a battalion of soldiers. "I would say, 'We are going to do this! Half of you go to bed, the other half stay up!' That's how I motivated myself. And I drank so much coffee. When I would show up in the morning [at work], I would be *dead.* But I would say to myself, 'We are going to do *this,* and we are going to do *this.*' You can talk yourself into anything."

FROM RAGE TO DESPAIR
AND BACK AGAIN

Djuna Barnes [1892–1982]

Born in a log cabin overlooking the Hudson River, Barnes briefly studied art in New York before leaving school to work as a newspaper reporter, specializing in impressionistic observational pieces and what would now be called stunt journalism. (For one article, she allowed herself to be force-fed by doctors and reported on the experience, then in the news because of hunger-striking suffragettes.) In 1920, *McCall's* sent Barnes on assignment to Paris, and she stayed there for the better part of the next two decades, turning from journalism to fiction and becoming one of the wittiest and most stylish members of the city's expatriate community of writers and artists. In Paris, she also fell in love with the sculptor and silverpoint artist Thelma Wood; the breakup of their relationship after eight years inspired the writing of Barnes's masterpiece, *Nightwood,* published in 1936.

Barnes wrote and revised much of the novel in the summers of 1932 and 1933 at Hayford Hall, an English country manor rented by the American heiress Peggy Guggenheim, who would become Barnes's most important benefactor, giving her a monthly stipend for decades. Guggenheim rented Hayford at the suggestion of her lover John Ferrar Holms, a dashing but alcoholic Englishman who loved to stay up all night drinking and holding forth on fifteenth-century poetry and other objects of his considerable erudition. He, Guggenheim, and Barnes were joined at Hayford by the writers

Djuna Barnes, Paris, 1920s

Emily Coleman and Antonia White, as well as by Guggenheim's two children from her previous marriage and White's
son—but the children stayed in a separate wing so that the
adults wouldn't be disturbed in the morning, an important
consideration given their marathon late-night drinking sessions filled with boisterous literary discussion and sometimes
contentious games of Truth.

For Barnes, the atmosphere was pretty near to ideal for her
writing. The endless literary talk was intellectually stimulat-
ing, and she could hole up in her bedroom for most of the

day working. According to the biographer Phillip Herring, Barnes's routine at Hayford was "to write in bed until lunch, read, then take a walk on the moor or hit a few tennis balls." The walks were somewhat fraught; Barnes later recalled that "the moors of Hayford Hall terrified me, because of the dead bones, horse skulls, and because the dog would dart at a rabbit & bring it (still warm & jerking) up to me or John or Peggy—finally I would *not go out at all* on the moor, because I simply could *not* endure it."

Otherwise, however, she couldn't complain. In the evenings, she would read aloud from her progress on the novel, and she would occasionally give pages to Holms for his editorial suggestions. Barnes would never be this productive again; she didn't publish her next work—a verse play called *The Antiphon*—until 1958, twenty-two years after *Nightwood*. Apparently, it wasn't for lack of trying. In an attempt to encourage Antonia White with her own literary efforts, Barnes once wrote:

It's getting the awful rust off the spirit that is almost insurmountable. It's why working every day is important—one may write the most lamentable balls but in the end one has a page or two that might not otherwise have been done. Keep on writing. It's a woman's only hope, except for lace making.

Käthe Kollwitz (1867–1945)

Kollwitz studied art in her native Königsberg, Germany, and later in Berlin and Munich. Her engagement in 1889 to a medical student was a minor scandal among her fellow students at the Women's School of Art in Munich, where it was assumed that art and marriage were incompatible. But Kollwitz thought she could reconcile the roles of artist and wife, or at least she hoped to. "There were grave contradictions in my own feelings," she admitted in her diary. "In the end I acted on this impulse: jump in—you'll manage to swim."

Soon after their marriage, the couple moved to a working-class district of Berlin, where Kollwitz's husband set up his medical practice on the second floor of a corner tenement; Kollwitz's studio was next door. Knowing that they would be unable to afford an apartment with a proper painting studio, Kollwitz abandoned her longtime dream of becoming a painter and stuck with the smaller-scale drawings and etchings that had been her focus up until that point. She soon became pregnant, apparently unintentionally, and gave birth to the first of two sons. As soon as they could afford it, the family hired a live-in maid to manage most of the housekeeping and child-rearing duties—then a common arrangement among middle-class German families. It was a crucial intervention for Kollwitz, who was able to continue working steadily despite her growing family. According to the biographer Martha Kearns,

> She followed a rigorous discipline she had practiced as a student, beginning work early in the morning, and stopping in mid- or late afternoon. She continued with her drawing and attempted to improve her etching. Requir-

ing quiet for concentration, she demanded absolute silence from her family when she was working, and was therefore sometimes called a tyrant.

But quiet was elusive, for most of [her husband's] clientele, waiting next door, were babies, children, and mothers of the working class—in Käthe's estimation, the most beautiful subjects to draw. When she did not have quiet, which was so often the case, she went next door and drew poor women as they waited to visit her husband.

By the late 1890s, Kollwitz's powerfully expressive drawings of working-class women and their children had made her one of the foremost artists in Germany, with her work shown in major exhibitions in Berlin and Dresden. Even so, according to her son Hans, "She constantly swung between long periods of depression and inability to work and the much shorter periods when she felt that she was making progress in her work and mastering her task. She suffered terribly during these spells of emptiness. Several times in her diaries she attempted to graph these periods and determine their course in advance. But this did not help her; she had to wait for the new surge of strength." Getting older seemed to help, or at least it reduced the length of her unproductive periods. "At no other time does Death seem so close or unwanted as when I am working on something that is important to me," Kollwitz wrote to an old art-school friend as she neared her sixtieth birthday. "Then I am very economical with my time. But when I can't work, I am lazy in every way and waste my time. So wish me a long life, so I can finish!"

Lorraine Hansberry (1930–1965)

Hansberry finished her landmark play *A Raisin in the Sun* in 1957, when she was twenty-seven years old; when it opened two years later, *Raisin* was the first play by an African American woman to be produced on Broadway, and Hansberry became the youngest playwright to win the New York Drama Critics' Circle Award. The Chicago-born writer enjoyed the acclaim, but she had trouble repeating the success of her first play, and by the early 1960s she was suffering frequent bouts of writer's block. "The days pass and pass and I do nothing," she wrote in her journal in July 1961. "Such times have been before. I just sit all day or traverse the streets in pointless rounds—and then sit at this desk and smoke cigarettes. Would like to be working but am in awful trouble with it." A few months later Hansberry noted that the "Blobby-globby days" were back again, and that she felt "that awful jackass feeling that I suppose is inextricable from being a writer."

Things improved the next year, after Hansberry and her husband bought a house in Croton-on-Hudson, about forty miles north of their apartment in Greenwich Village. In the fall of 1962, Hansberry went there alone, planning to "work or perish." She had never followed a regular writing schedule, and she didn't try to adopt one at her new residence. "They say that one should set a schedule and keep to it no matter what: 'write' no matter what," she wrote in her journal. "I can't help it—I think that's awfully silly, this sitting down and 'writing' like a duty. People celebrate it so much because it makes them feel that the writer isn't quite so precarious a creature." Hansberry did, however, believe in creating the proper surroundings for work. About five weeks after settling in "Chitterling Heights," as she jokingly called her country house, she described her new home office in her journal:

Lorraine Hansberry, Greenwich Village, 1959

I have rearranged the work space after the advice of Leonardo; large airy house (not too large) with small, compact, rather crowded even, work area: desk, machine, drawing board hem me in. I love it. It is as I wish it.

On the wall before me, my photo of Paul Robeson—and Michelangelo's David. At my shoulder the bust of Einstein. At the top of the stairs—[the Irish playwright Sean] O'Casey. The company I keep! But—just to keep things in perspective—I have made me a rather large reminder which is now tacked in the most prominent place of all. It reads:

"BUT"—THE CHILD SAID—"THE EMPEROR
ISN'T WEARING ANY CLOTHES...."

The new setup seemed to help—ten days later, Hansberry
was writing again. "The magic has come: about an hour
ago!" she wrote in her journal. "A torrent of what I have
been trying to write all along.... It will be all right now—a
lot of work. But I know *what* I am writing now. It came all
at once while I was in the kitchen and I wrote fourteen pages
in an hour that will hardly need revision I think. Thank God,
thank God! I could not have stood much more."

Natalia Ginzburg (1916–1991)

Ginzburg was an Italian novelist, essayist, translator, and
playwright, often considered the most important female
writer of postwar Italy. In the preface to a collection of interviews with Ginzburg, her granddaughter Lisa recalled watching the author go about her day:

There was a silence in her, a deep and intimate
silence.... In the noise of her very active days you
could hear the echo of the solitary hours at dawn
spent writing, stealing time from sleep to obey what
she herself called her "master": the vital, unquestion-
able, absolute need to give time to her writing. It was
an internal silence that you could read in her face, in the
way she would half-shut her eyes, absorbed in the effort
of listening carefully to what was going on around her,
listening so that later she could "chew it over." The

"ruminating" of thoughts was an idea of which she was particularly fond, the same one she used to defend her periods of sheer idleness. The idleness is useful, she would say, because only when we are idle does the mind "ruminate."

Although her granddaughter recalls Ginzburg writing in the early morning, this was not always her habit. In 1940, Ginzburg's husband, the anti-Fascist activist and journalist Leone Ginzburg, was exiled by the Fascists to a remote, impoverished village in the Abruzzi, in central Italy, and Ginzburg and their two young children joined him there. Over the previous couple of years, Ginzburg had been too overwhelmed by motherhood to continue the fiction writing that had been her passion since childhood. "I could not understand how anyone could sit herself down to write if she had children," she later wrote. But in the village Ginzburg was inspired to try writing again; she felt that she was able to "control" the feeling that she had for her children and separate herself from them enough to again create a fictional world. She found a girl in the village who would look after the children in the afternoons, allowing Ginzburg to write from 3:00 to 7:00 p.m., hours when she worked "greedily and joyfully" on the story that would become her first novel, *The Road to the City,* published in 1942.

Despite the family's political exile, Ginzburg said that the novel was written from a place of great happiness. Her next novel, by contrast, was written in a state of "profound melancholy," after the murder of her husband by the Italian police. (The fall of Mussolini had allowed him to return to Rome, only to be captured and tortured in the Regina Coeli prison; he was thirty-four.) One of Ginzburg's best-known essays,

"My Vocation," reckons with the difference between writing out of happiness and out of misery—both states of mind that, Ginzburg argued, set traps for literary creation. In periods of happiness, she wrote, it is easy to exercise the imagination and invent characters and situations outside one's own experience—but those characters may not be invested with the compassion necessary for great literature, and the fictional world may lack "secrets and shadows." By contrast, works written from unhappiness can be weighed down by the author's intense sympathy for the characters, which are often too close to his or her own situation and are a transparent attempt to process personal grief. Ginzburg thought that it was impossible to console oneself through writing. "You cannot deceive yourself by hoping for caresses and lullabies from your vocation," she wrote.

But looking back on that essay many years later, Ginzburg said that her thinking had changed slightly over the ensuing decades: "I have to say that as life went on I understood that when you are more adult, a state of mind is less important to writing, in that at a certain stage in your life you have so many losses that there is always an underlying unhappiness. And therefore it influences less. You learn to write in any state of mind, and you feel more . . . I wouldn't say distant from your own life but a bit readier to dominate it."

Gwendolyn Brooks [1917–2000]

Brooks started submitting poems to literary magazines as a teenager, but she didn't succeed in selling one to a well-known magazine until she was twenty-eight. "This should encourage youngsters who feel discouraged at not getting anything published," she said much later. "All you have to do is stick it out for fourteen years."

Brooks continued to stick it out even as, to all appearances, she was "primarily a housewife, which is the last thing I'm really interested in being," she said. The year after her first child was born, she "scarcely put pen to paper," she said. But apart from that she "managed to keep at it." In 1945, when her son was five years old, she published her first book of poetry. Four years later, she published her second book, and the following year it was awarded the Pulitzer Prize, making Brooks the first African American to receive the award for poetry.

In 1973, an interviewer asked Brooks if poems arrived to her complete. "A poem rarely comes whole and completely dressed," she replied.

> As a rule, it comes in bits and pieces. You get an impression of something—you feel something, you anticipate something, and you begin, feebly, to put these impressions and feelings and anticipation or rememberings into those things which seem so common and handleable—words.
>
> And you flail and you falter and you shift and you shake, and finally, you come forth with the first draft. Then, if you're myself and if you're like many of the other poets that I know, you revise, and you revise. And often the finished product is nothing like your first draft. Sometimes it is.

For Brooks, the amount of time that passed between the initial idea and a finished poem was totally unpredictable. Sometimes it took fifteen minutes, she said; sometimes, fifteen months. "It is hard work," she said. "It gets harder all the time."

Jean Rhys (1890–1979)

In 1957, the BBC was preparing a radio adaptation of Rhys's 1939 novel *Good Morning, Midnight,* and it placed an advertisement asking for anyone with knowledge of the author's whereabouts to get in touch. At the time, Rhys hadn't published anything in almost two decades, and many of her acquaintances had lost track of her and assumed that she had died of suicide or alcoholism—believable ends for the Dominica-born author, who seemed to have a gift for self-destructive behavior, and who had spent much of her twenties and thirties destitute and depressed, reeling from one doomed relationship to the next, self-medicating with alcohol. But the BBC advertisement did turn up news—Rhys herself wrote back. She was living with her third husband in Cornwall, and not only was she alive, she was working on a new novel. She soon signed a contract for the book, telling her editors that she expected to be done with it in six to nine months.

In fact, it took Rhys nine years to finish the book, *Wide Sargasso Sea,* now widely considered her masterpiece and one of the best novels of the twentieth century. The writing took so long, in part, because Rhys was a perfectionist who reworked the novel over and over until it met her exacting standards—and also because she was spectacularly inept at managing her day-to-day life and was almost continually derailed from the project. As one of her editors, Diana Athill, wrote, "Her inability to cope with life's practicalities went beyond anything I ever saw in anyone generally taken to be sane."

A few years into the new book, in 1960, the seventy-year-old Rhys and her husband relocated from Cornwall to a primitive cottage deep in the Devon countryside, where Rhys would live for the rest of her life. The move was her brother's idea; after visiting the couple in Cornwall and being shocked by their squalid living conditions, he felt compelled to intervene, taking it upon himself to find and purchase a new house for them. He chose the remote location, it seems, because he figured Rhys couldn't get into too much trouble there. Just to be on the safe side, he went to the village rector with a warning. "I've brought trouble into your parish," he began.

It wasn't long before Rhys justified her brother's concern. Although she was thrilled by the idea of the new cottage, she quickly soured on the location. "This place, which I imagined would be a refuge, is a foretaste of hell at present," she wrote soon after arriving. She disliked the constant rain, the suspicious-seeming villagers, the lack of libraries or bookshops, even the local animals—the cows "moo at me in a very disapproving way," she wrote to her daughter. This wasn't a joke, or at least not for long; Rhys grew increasingly disturbed that a neighboring farmer's cows kept coming too close to her house, and she complained vociferously. The farmer put up a barbed-wire fence to keep the cows away—but Rhys took this gesture of kindness as some kind of affront, got roaring drunk, and made a scene, screaming at the neighbor and throwing milk bottles at the fence, while the rest of the village looked on in horror.

From then on, Rhys was an object of gossip and derision in the village; many of the locals wouldn't speak to her, and one of Rhys's neighbors accused her of being a witch. (Rhys chased her into the road with a pair of scissors, earning herself a weeklong stay in a mental hospital.) But in a stroke of luck, the village rector turned out to be one of her most important allies—a lover of classical literature, he took a look at Rhys's novel-in-progress and was astute enough to recognize her talent. Thereafter, he visited regularly, doing whatever he could to insulate the sensitive author from her worries and keep her on track with the book. "She needs endless supplies of whisky, and endless praise," he told his wife, "so that is what she must have." He brought her a bed table so that she could write in bed—a longtime habit of hers—and he persuaded her to allow a doctor in for a checkup, which resulted in Rhys getting a store of "pep pills" that she took with mixed results. (She wrote in a 1961 letter, "I've some wonderful pep pills—they may do the trick though I feel very rum, *extraordinary* next day if I take more than two. Drink *much* safer in my opinion.")

Even with the rector's assistance, Rhys's novel progressed slowly. She wrote in March 1962, "I feel I have been here for years, toiling away at my book—it's like pulling a cart up a very steep hill." A year later, she sounded much the same note in a letter to Athill: "I do feel that I am exhausting everybody. The only thing is that I've exhausted myself too—from rage to despair and back again." In 1957, Rhys's husband had suffered a stroke, and he was in and out of the hospital throughout the subsequent years. When he was home, Rhys was too occupied with his care to do much writing; when he was in the hospital, she was worried and lonely, although she was able to seize on these periods to work on the novel. She wrote to Athill in September 1964, a year and a half before the book was finally finished, "When I remember how light heartedly I began this book!—I thought it would be easy—my God! Quite apart from illness, moves, catastrophes and ructions galore there's the effort to make an unlikely story seem possible and inevitable and right."

The publication of *Wide Sargasso Sea* in 1966—and the death of Rhys's husband that same year—ushered in a period of relative calm for the author. She was freed of the burden of caring for her husband, and she had a measure of financial security and literary prestige that she had never enjoyed before. A letter to her daughter from late 1965 describes the routine she would follow more or less for the remainder of her life:

> Such a funny existence here. I go to bed at *eight* p.m. Can you imagine it? But by that time it's been dark for *hours*. So I take a shot of whisky (which is too expensive really) and pretend it's bedtime. Then at three or four a.m. I'm broad awake. So I toss and turn a bit, then get up, still in the dark, and go into the kitchen for tea. It is, funnily enough, the best part of the day. I drink cup after cup, and smoke one cigarette after another, and watch the light, if any, appear at last.

Once she was up, Rhys spent almost her entire day in the kitchen, "the one place where I could stop feeling anxious or depressed, where the silence was bearable," she wrote. "I can see the sun rise from one corner, the sun set from another." (The kitchen was also, for many years, the only room in the house Rhys could afford to heat.) After a while, the newspapers and the mail would arrive, and Rhys would read and write—replying to letters, working on her last book, the autobiography *Smile Please*. Eventually, if she was hungry, she would plan an elaborate meal, her first of the day. If she wasn't hungry, she would dine on bread, cheese, and a glass of wine. It was a solitary existence, but after the turmoil and anxiety that had characterized so much of her life, not an unhappy one. As Rhys wrote, "Isn't the sadness of being alone much stressed and the compensations left out?"

Isabel Bishop (1902–1988)

Bishop came to New York from Detroit at sixteen, a high school graduate intending to study commercial art and become an illustrator. "Then something happened to me," she said many years later. What happened was that Bishop discovered the modern art movement, and with the aid of a monthly stipend from a wealthy relative, she switched from illustration to painting, enrolling in the Art Students League in 1920. After six years of studies there, she rented a studio on 14th Street overlooking Union Square, then "a rather shabby business region of New York," with a constant churn of office workers, department-store shoppers, soap-box sermonizers, unemployed loiterers, and fellow artists. For the next six decades, Bishop drew on the life of Union Square for her "romantic realist" paintings, often sitting on a bench to sketch people as they made their daily rounds, paying special attention to the dress and gestures of the emerging class of career girls then filling the city's offices. But she endured years of dissatisfaction and self-doubt before she found an effective method of capturing that life on canvas. "I was trying everything very hard," she remembered later. "I was very miserable. Frustrated. One tries, and it doesn't [work]—one 'blows in' one way and it comes out another way. In the end it isn't at all what one wanted. And yet, whatever validity can be found in one's work has to be found there, in what one didn't consciously or deliberately intend."

Over time, Bishop developed a painstaking process for realizing her paintings. She began with a rough sketch, then made a series of more developed drawings. Next she made an etching—and after that an aquatint (a type of etching in which the plate is exposed to acid to create a surface that

Isabel Bishop in her studio, 1959

will hold ink, allowing for watercolor-like prints). Only then would she begin the actual painting, and here again she used an extremely laborious process, borrowed from the Flemish Baroque artist Rubens. "I do use a very complex technique I'm sorry to say," Bishop said. "Not because I wanted to be complex, but in an effort to make the painting speak back to me. I'd do anything to get that result." Often, it took her a year to complete a single painting. She positioned her easel so that she could look out the window at Union Square while she worked, in order to "verify what I was doing," she said. The question she would ask herself at these moments was "Is it so?"—i.e., was the painting doing justice to the real-life scene below? "It was like eating, like nourishment," she said, "to look out and see people, going in all directions, a kind of ballet, very ornate."

In her early twenties Bishop suffered an unhappy love affair and made three suicide attempts. But she recovered and, in 1934, married a brilliant young neurologist, Harold George Wolff, and moved into his house in Riverdale, a wealthy suburban enclave in the Bronx. Wolff was a rigid man—one neighbor recalled arriving for dinner parties and being handed a three-by-five-inch card with a neatly typed agenda listing the exact time for each portion of the evening, including when guests were expected to leave—but he strongly supported Bishop's art career. "It was very important that he took that attitude and it was very unusual for that time," Bishop said. "We left the house together every morning; he went to his work and I went to my studio. There was never any question about it." They worked from 9:00 a.m. to 5:00 p.m., taking the train together from Riverdale to Grand Central Terminal, where Bishop would catch the subway to Union Square; and then they would follow the reverse commute home. After their only child, a son, was born in 1940, Bishop quickly resumed the routine; her mother-in-law lived in their house and handled the childcare duties while Bishop and her husband worked. (This arrangement was not entirely tension-free. "It was helpful," Bishop said later. "And it was difficult.") Apparently, their work encompassed weekends as well—in a 1970s interview, Bishop said that as long as her son was at home, she went to her studio six days a week and took off Sundays to spend time with the family; once her son left the house, she resumed her seven-day-a-week work schedule.

On the wall of her studio, Bishop hung a quote from Henry James's story "The Middle Years": "We work in the dark—we do what we can—we give what we have. Our doubt is our passion, and our passion is our task. The rest is the madness of art." Asked about the quote in a 1977 interview, and about how she arrived at her lifelong commitment to "the madness of art," Bishop said: "I've thought about it a great deal. In my case, it just happened gradually, anything but deliberately. One simply found oneself in a state of commitment. And after that, there wasn't any choice except jumping off a roof."

Doris Lessing (1919–2013)

In 1949, Lessing arrived in London with her six-year-old son, Peter, and the finished manuscript of her first novel, *The Grass Is Singing*. She was traveling from Southern Rhodesia (now Zimbabwe), where she had grown up the child of British parents, and where, before the age of thirty, she had married twice, divorced twice, and had three children. When she left for London, the first two children, ages ten and eight, stayed behind with her first husband, and Lessing would see them only occasionally during the remainder of their childhoods—facts that, once she became a famous author, would be forever dredged up by journalists, to Lessing's dismay and irritation. Repeatedly confronted with this act of abandonment, Lessing always said that she had no real choice in the matter. She had married her first husband at age nineteen, already pregnant with their first child, and within a couple years had found herself an unsatisfied housewife in a cultural backwater, with no energy or time for the writing she was determined to make her life's work. So she left

Doris Lessing, London, circa 1950

her husband and two young children to pursue the life she wanted, finding a job and an apartment of her own, writing and getting involved in left-wing politics (and later remarrying and having a third child); her eventual move to London was just an extension of that first break. She never pretended that she had behaved admirably. "This was a terrible thing to do," Lessing said in 1997, "but I had to do it because I have no doubt whatsoever if I had not done it, I would have become an alcoholic or ended in the loony bin. I couldn't stand that life. I just couldn't bear it." In her more exasperated moments she gave less nuanced replies. "No one can write with a child around," she said once. "It's no good. You just get cross."

But of course Lessing did write with her son Peter around. Indeed, she later said that having a child to take care of upon her arrival in London had saved her; otherwise, she would have been seduced by 1950s Soho. ("There was a constellation of talents, but mostly they drank and talked their gifts away," she wrote.) Instead, Lessing arranged their lives so that Peter was looked after and she had time for her writing. At first she found secretarial work to pay their expenses, but then a modest advance for her next book allowed Lessing to quit that job and write full-time. In the second volume of her autobiography, Lessing described her routine during those early days in London:

> I woke at five, when the child did. He came into my bed, and I told or read stories or rhymes. We got dressed, he ate, and then I took him to the school up the street. . . . I shopped a little, and then my real day began. The feverish need to get this or that done—what I call the housewife's disease: "I must buy this, ring So-and-so, don't forget this, make a note of that"—had to be subdued to the flat, dull state one needs to write in. Sometimes I achieved it by sleeping for a few minutes, praying that the telephone would be silent. Sleep has always been my friend, my restorer, my quick fix, but it was in those days that I learned the value of a few minutes' submersion in . . . where? And you emerge untangled, quiet, dark, ready for work.

As the day went on Lessing would constantly dip in and out of work, taking breaks to putter around the house, washing out a cup, tidying a drawer, or making herself a cup of tea. "I walk and I prowl, my hands busy with this and that," she wrote. "You'd think I was a paragon of concern for house-keeping if you judged by what you saw." But all the time her mind was elsewhere, on the writing project under way—and according to the biographer Carole Klein, these aimless-sounding writing days could be astonishingly productive, with Lessing aiming for at least seven thousand words a day. Throughout her career, the daily wool-gathering proved essential to Lessing's writing process. She considered "the physical as a road into concentration" and compared herself to a painter in this regard. "They wander about the studio, apparently at random," she wrote. "They clean a brush. They throw away another. They prepare a canvas, but you can see their minds are elsewhere. They stare out of the window. They make a cup of coffee. They stand for a long time in front of the canvas, the brush on the alert in their hands. At last, it begins: the work."

Perhaps because she had worked so hard and sacrificed so much to arrange her life in a way that permitted her to write, Lessing was sympathetic to the public's seemingly insatiable appetite for stories about writers' daily routines and work-ing habits. "When we [writers] go about, having temporar-ily become talkers, standing on platforms and holding forth, we are always asked, Do you use a word processor, a pen, a typewriter; do you write every day; what is your routine?" Lessing wrote.

These questions are a fumbling instinct towards this cru-cial point, which is: How do you use your energy? How do you husband it? We all of us have limited amounts of energy, and I am sure the people who are success-ful have learned, either by instinct or consciously, to use their energies well instead of spilling them about.

And this has to be different for every person, writers or otherwise. I know writers who go to parties every night and then, recharged instead of depleted, happily write all day. But if I stay up half the night talking, I don't do so well the next day. Some writers like to start work as soon as they can in the morning, while others like the night or—for me almost impossible—the afternoons. Trial and error, and then when you've found your needs, what feeds you, what is your instinctive rhythm and routine, then cherish it.

ACKNOWLEDGMENTS

Appropriately, this book would not have been possible without the support and insight of several brilliant women. The first was my wife, Rebecca, who read every version of the manuscript, offered crucial encouragement in its early stages, and provided detailed, articulate feedback on later drafts. As an artist who has long had to juggle her creative work with a day job, she was both an inspiration and an ideal reader for this book, and her thoughtful queries and suggestions immeasurably improved it.

Neither this book nor its predecessor would exist without my agent, Meg Thompson, who first recognized that my *Daily Routines* blog had book potential, who found an ideal home for that book at Knopf, and who has skillfully and cheerfully steered me through the publishing business ever since. I would also like to thank her colleague Sandy Hodgman, who has facilitated foreign editions of my work with dedication and aplomb.

At Knopf, Victoria Wilson brought more than forty-five years of publishing experience to bear on this book. Her guidance on the first *Daily Rituals* implicitly shaped the format of this volume, and she suggested many names for me to investigate here, including a number of underrecognized women whose biographies yielded rich material. Her assistant, Marc Jaffee, was an indispensable help throughout, and their colleagues at Knopf were exceptional. I'm especially grateful to the jacket designer, Jason Booher; the text designer, Maggie Hinders; the production editor, Kathleen Fridella; the copy editor, Amy Brosey-Láncošová; and my publicist, Kathryn Zuckerman. At Picador, Sophie Jonathan supplied an additional layer of editorial oversight, providing careful line edits and general encouragement. This book was originally conceived as a Vintage Short, and I owe a debt of gratitude to Maria Goldverg for her early support of the project.

One of my goals with this book was to include more contemporary voices, and I am grateful to the twenty women who took time out of their busy schedules to talk to me (or email with me) about their work habits: Isabel Allende, Charlotte Bray, Renee Cox, Petah Coyne, Hayden Dunham, Nikki Giovanni, Maggi Hambling, Sheila Heti, Joan Jonas, Miranda July, Josephine Meckseper, Julie Mehretu, Marilyn Minter, Meredith Monk, Maggie Nelson, Catherine Opie, Carolee Schneemann, Rachel Whiteread, Julia Wolfe, and Andrea Zittel. For their help arranging these interviews, I would also like to thank Chandra Ramirez, Danielle Wu at Galerie Lelong, Virginia C. Fowler at Virginia Tech, Hugh Monk, Emily Bates at Gavin Brown's Enterprise, Shu Ming Lim and Laura Lupton at Andrea Rosen Gallery, Katie Korns at Meckseper Studio, Sarah Rentz at Julie Mehretu Studio, Genevieve Lowe at Marilyn Minter Studio, Peter Sciscioli and Kirstin Kapustik at the House Foundation for the Arts, Heather Rasmussen at Catherine Opie Studio, Lilah Dougherty, Lisa Varghese at Luhring Augustine, Hazel Willis, Amanda Ameer and Becky Fradkin at First Chair Promotion, and Ben Thornborough at Regen Projects.

Like the first *Daily Rituals,* this book is very much a work of assemblage, with material drawn from published interviews, biographies, magazine profiles, diaries, and letters; I could never have compiled it without the incredible reporting and research of the scholars, journalists, editors, and translators whose work I drew upon. I also could not have done it without the resources of the Los Angeles Public Library, whose staff ferried hundreds of books to and from my local branch library. Additional research was done at the UCLA Library, the Los Angeles County Museum of Art, and the New York Public Library. The majority of this book was written in a former Masonic lodge that has been converted into artists' studios; my gratitude to Nathalie Dierickx and Lisa Raymond for providing an ideal space for creative work. Further gratitude to Anne Thompson for many productive conversations about the book and much else.

For their help tracking down photographs of Edna St. Vincent Millay, special thanks to Holly Peppe, Millay's literary executor; Mark O'Berski at the Edna St. Vincent Millay Society; and Barbara Bair and Bruce Kirby at the Library of Congress. Many others helped with image licensing and text permissions for this book—my sincere thanks to them all. Three books of interviews proved particularly important in my research: Eleanor Munro's *Originals: American Women Artists,* Cindy Nemser's *Art Talk,* and Claudia Tate's *Black Women Writers at Work*. I'm grateful to Georges Borchardt, Inc., Cindy Nemser, Read Hubbard, and Jerome Lindsey for allowing me to publish excerpts from these groundbreaking works.

After the first *Daily Rituals* was published, many people helped bring it to a wider audience. There's not room here for me to mention them all, but I would like to especially thank John Swansburg for inviting me to blog about the book on *Slate,* Tim Ferriss for publishing the audiobook edition, and Brittany Morrongiello, formerly of Knopf's publicity department, for being a tremendous support during the book launch. The late Noah Klersfeld was one of the original book's earliest and most enthusiastic supporters and I'm so sad that he's not here to read the sequel.

When I was twenty-five, Pennell Whitney encouraged me to move from Nashville to New York—and, crucially, provided me with a place to live for the several months it took me to get established there. Although I have since left the city, I now see that move as the decisive pivot of my life; I'm sure neither of these books would have happened without her intervention at that important moment.

Finally, I would like to thank my mother, my father, my stepmother, and my brother for their lifelong love and support; my mother-on-law, Toni, for being the book's unofficial Pacific Northwest ambassador; and the rest of my family and friends for their forbearance, generosity, and goodwill.

NOTES

For each entry in the book, I have provided a list of all my sources—keyed to each subject's name—followed by the exact locations of all quotes. The lists of sources are organized in approximate order of their relevance—that is, those books, interviews, and articles that I relied on most heavily come first. In many cases this is an imprecise ranking, but I made the attempt for utility's sake: Readers wanting to know more about a particular artist's habits would do well to start with the sources at the beginning of each list.

vii **"Habits gradually change"**: *The Diary of Virginia Woolf,* ed. Anne Olivier Bell and Andrew McNeillie, *Volume Three: 1925–1930* (San Diego: Harcourt Brace, 1981), 220. I have taken the liberty of adding the missing apostrophe in the first "one's" here.

xv **"I was never"**: Interview with Smithsonian American Art Museum, "Meet Grace Hartigan," January 16, 2009, https://www.youtube.com/watch?v=e-mzSLQLınk.

xvi **"the Life and the Project"**: Interview with Jonathan Cott, *Susan Sontag: The Complete* Rolling Stone *Interview* (New Haven, CT: Yale University Press, 2013), 109.

xvi ***How the devil:*** Colette, *Earthly Paradise: An Autobiography,* trans. Herman Briffault et al. (New York: Farrar, Straus and Giroux, 1966), 502. Here is the beginning of the passage in question:

> It has taken me a great deal of time to scratch out forty or so books. So many hours that could have been used for travel, for idle strolls, for reading, even for indulging a feminine and

healthy coquetry. How the devil did George Sand manage? Robust laborer of letters that she was, she was able to finish off one novel and begin another within the hour. She never lost either a lover or a puff of her hookah by it, produced a twenty volume *Historie de ma vie* into the bargain, and I am completely staggered when I think of it.

3 **Octavia Butler:** Conseula Francis, ed., *Conversations with Octavia Butler* (Jackson: University Press of Mississippi, 2010); Octavia Butler, " 'Devil Girls from Mars': Why I Write Science Fiction," February 19, 1998, repr. in *Media in Transition,* October 4, 1998, http://web.mit.edu/m-i-t/articles/butler_talk_index.html; Octavia Butler, *Bloodchild and Other Stories,* 2nd ed. (New York: Seven Stories Press, 2005).

3 **"As I was":** "Why I Write."

3 **"horrible little jobs":** *Bloodchild,* 120.

3 **"I felt like":** Interview with Charles Rowell, "An Interview with Octavia E. Butler," *Callaloo,* Winter 1997, in Francis, 74.

3 **"Screw inspiration":** Interview with Randall Kenan, "An Interview with Octavia E. Butler," *Callaloo,* Spring 1991, in Francis, 37.

3 **"look at the lives":** Charles Rowell, 90.

4 **"waking between 5:30":** Quoted in Jane Burkitt, "Nebula Award Nominee Octavia Butler Is Expanding the Universe of Science-Fiction Readers," *Seattle Times,* May 9, 2000, in Francis, 160.

4 **"reading books or sitting":** Interview with Jelani Cobb, "Interview with Octavia Butler," JelaniCobb.com, 1994, in Francis, 57.

4 **"comfortably asocial":** Interview with Mike McGonigal, "Octavia Butler," *Index Magazine,* March 1998, in Francis, 141. The quotation appears in a question from McGonigal: "You've described yourself as being comfortably asocial."

4 **"I enjoy people":** Ibid.

5 **Yayoi Kusama:** Yayoi Kusama, *Infinity Net: The Autobiography of Yayoi Kusama,* trans. Ralph McCarthy (London: Tate Publishing, 2011), Kindle; interview with Birgit Sonna, "Cosmic Play: An Interview with Yayoi Kusama," *Sleek,* Summer 2014, http://www.sleek-mag.com/2014/08/06/yayoi-kusama-interview/.

5 **"I fight pain":** Kusama, loc. 856 of 2458, Kindle.

5 **"Life in the hospital":** Ibid.

5 **"Every day I":** Quoted in Sonna.

6 **Elizabeth Bishop:** George Monteiro, ed., *Conversations with Elizabeth Bishop* (Jackson: University Press of Mississippi, 1996); Gary Fountain and Peter Brazeau, *Remembering Elizabeth Bishop: An*

Oral Biography (Amherst: University of Massachusetts Press, 1994); Thomas Travisano and Saskia Hamilton, eds., *Words in Air: The Complete Correspondence Between Elizabeth Bishop and Robert Lowell* (New York: Farrar, Straus and Giroux, 2008); Robert Boucheron, "Elizabeth Bishop at Harvard," *Talking Writing,* January 21, 2013, http://talkingwriting.com/elizabeth-bishop-at-harvard.

6 **"Some days all":** Interview with Eileen McMahon, "Elizabeth Bishop Speaks About Her Poetry," *The New Paper,* June 1978, in Monteiro, 109.

6 **"she didn't":** Quoted in Fountain and Brazeau, 339.

6 **"To begin with":** Elizabeth Bishop to Robert Lowell, December 5, 1953, in Travisano and Hamilton, 146.

7 **"A poem is":** Quoted in Boucheron.

7 **Pina Bausch:** John O'Mahony, "Dancing in the Dark," *The Guardian,* January 25, 2002, https://www.theguardian.com/books/2002/jan/26/books.guardianreview4; Pina Bausch, "What Moves Me," 2007, Pina Bausch Foundation, http://www.pinabausch.org/en/pina/what-moves-me; interview with Ismene Brown, "theartsdesk Q&A: Meeting Pina Bausch," *theartsdesk,* March 30, 2010, https://theartsdesk.com/dance/theartsdesk-qa-meeting-pina-bausch; Sarah Crompton, "The Mighty Pina Bausch," *Telegraph,* June 11, 2012, https://www.telegraph.co.uk/culture/theatre/dance/9272080/The-mighty-Pina-Bausch.html.

7 **"Pina asks questions":** Quoted in O'Mahony.

7 **"The 'questions' are":** Bausch.

8 **"not something I":** Interview with Brown.

8 **"The anguish that":** Quoted in O'Mahony.

8 **"She works in":** Quoted ibid.

8 **"There is no":** Bausch.

9 **Marisol:** Grace Glueck, "It's Not Pop, It's Not Op—It's Marisol," *The New York Times,* March 7, 1965, https://www.nytimes.com/1965/03/07/archives/its-not-pop-its-not-op-its-marisol-its-not-pop-its-marisol.html; interview with Cindy Nemser, *Art Talk: Conversations with 15 Women Artists,* rev. ed. (New York: Westview Press, 1995); Brian O'Doherty, "Marisol: The Enigma of the Self-Image," *The New York Times,* March 1, 1964, https://www.nytimes.com/1964/03/01/marisol-the-enigma-of-the-selfimage.html; John Gruen, *The Party's Over Now: Reminiscences of the Fifties—New York's Artists, Writers, Musicians, and Their Friends* (New York: Viking, 1967, 1972).

9 **"as a kind of rebellion":** Quoted in Glueck.

9 "The first girl": Quoted ibid.

10 "I don't think": Quoted in O'Doherty.

10 "nails, glue, chair": Glueck.

11 "I do my research": Quoted ibid.

11 "Her discipline is": Quoted ibid.

11 "When Marisol was": Gruen, 200.

12 "A, she's genuinely shy": Quoted in Glueck.

12 "I don't feel": interview with Nemser, 160.

12 "to relax": Ibid., 164.

12 Nina Simone: Nina Simone with Stephen Cleary, *I Put a Spell on You: The Autobiography of Nina Simone* (New York: Pantheon, 1991).

12 "people came to": Ibid., 92.

12 "To cast the spell": Ibid., 93.

14 "would seize up": Ibid.

14 "super-sensitive": Ibid., 94.

14 "Whatever it was": Ibid.

15 Diane Arbus: Arthur Lubow, *Diane Arbus: Portrait of a Photographer* (New York: Ecco, 2016).

15 "is a secret": Quoted ibid., ii.

15 "I can find": Quoted ibid., 4.

15 "a sort of naughty": Quoted ibid., 323.

15 "She would try": Quoted ibid., 327.

16 "It was an endurance process": Quoted ibid.

16 "described going up": Ibid., 494.

16 "I photograph": Quoted ibid., 432.

16 "I do what": Quoted ibid., 170.

19 Louise Nevelson: Louise Nevelson with Diana MacKown, *Dawns + Dusks* (New York: Charles Scribner's Sons, 1976); Laurie Lisle, *Louise Nevelson: A Passionate Life* (New York: Summit Books, 1990); Laurie Wilson, *Louise Nevelson: Light and Shadow* (New York: Thames & Hudson, 2016); interview with Cindy Nemser, *Art Talk: Conversations with 15 Women Artists,* rev. ed. (New York: Westview Press, 1995); Hilton Kramer, "Nevelson," *The New York Times Magazine,* October 30, 1983, https://www.nytimes.com/1983/10/30/magazine/nevelson.html; Andrea K. Scott, "A Life Made Out of Wood, Metal and Determination," *The New York Times,* May 9, 2007, https://www.nytimes.com/2007/05/09/arts/design/09neve.html.

19 "I'm also prolific": Nevelson with MacKown, 121.

19 "I get up": Ibid.

21 "stood up the wood": Quoted in Scott.

21 **"Nothing that one":** Kramer.

22 **"It's a lot":** Nevelson with MacKown, 42.

22 **"I imagine I was kept":** Quoted in Lisle, 281.

22 **"I like to":** Nevelson with MacKown, 115.

23 **Isak Dinesen:** Judith Thurman, *Isak Dinesen: The Life of a Storyteller* (New York: Picador, 1982); Isak Dinesen, *Daguerreotypes and Other Essays* (Chicago: University of Chicago Press, 1979).

23 **"During my last":** Dinesen, 10.

23 **"howling like an animal":** Quoted in Thurman, 257.

23 **"In her late forties":** Thurman, 257.

24 **"would give her":** Ibid.

25 **"I promised the Devil":** Quoted ibid., 258.

25 **Josephine Baker:** Josephine Baker and Jo Bouillon, *Josephine,* trans. Mariana Fitzpatrick (New York: Marlowe, 1988); Lynn Haney, *Naked at the Feast: A Biography of Josephine Baker* (New York: Dodd, Mead, 1981); Stephen Papich, *Remembering Josephine* (Indianapolis: Bobbs-Merrill, 1976); Jean-Claude Baker and Chris Chase, *Josephine: The Hungry Heart* (Holbrook, MA: Adams Publishing, 1993).

25 **"I *had* to":** Baker and Bouillon, 58.

25 **"through a murky Paris":** Ibid., 66.

26 **"Her secret was":** Papich, xv–xvi.

27 **"She was always":** Quoted in Haney, 177.

27 **"Friends often asked":** Baker and Bouillon, 156.

27 **Lillian Hellman:** Jackson R. Bryer, ed., *Conversations with Lillian Hellman* (Jackson: University Press of Mississippi, 1986); Joan Mellen, *Hellman and Hammett: The Legendary Passion of Lillian Hellman and Dashiell Hammett* (New York: HarperCollins, 1996); Margaret Case Harriman, "Miss Lily of New Orleans," *The New Yorker,* November 8, 1941, 22–35; Robert Van Gelder, "Of Lillian Hellman: Being a Conversation with the Author of '*Watch on the Rhine,*'" *The New York Times,* April 20, 1941, https://www.nytimes.com/1941/04/20/archives/of-lillian-hellman-being-a-conversation-with-the-author-of-watch-on.html; Wambly Bald, "It's Just Like Having Another Baby," *New York Post,* November 12, 1946; Deborah Martinson, *Lillian Hellman: A Life with Foxes and Scoundrels* (New York: Counterpoint, 2005); William Wright, *Lillian Hellman: The Image, the Woman* (New York: Simon & Schuster, 1986); Lillian Hellman, *Three: An Unfinished Woman, Pentimento, Scoundrel Time* (Boston: Little, Brown, 1979); Carl Rollyson, *Lillian Hellman: Her Legend and Her Legacy* (New York: St. Martin's Press, 1988).

28 **"My friends come":** Quoted in Van Gelder.

28 **she drank twenty cups:** Bald.

29 **"THIS ROOM IS":** Harriman, 29.

29 **"well over 100,000":** Quoted in Van Gelder.

29 **"elation, depression, hope":** Ibid., 15.

30 **Coco Chanel:** Rhonda K. Garelick, *Mademoiselle: Coco Chanel and the Pulse of History* (New York: Random House, 2014).

30 **"watchful anxiety":** Ibid., 395.

30 **"While much of the staff":** Ibid., 394–95.

31 **"She could remain":** Ibid., 395.

31 **"That word, 'vacation' ":** Quoted ibid., 397.

32 **Elsa Schiaparelli:** Palmer White, *Elsa Schiaparelli* (New York: Rizzoli, 1986); Janet Flanner, "Comet," *The New Yorker,* June 18, 1932, https://www.newyorker.com/magazine/1932/06/18/comet.

32 **"Every morning Elsa":** White, 79.

32 **"Most of her designing":** Ibid., 87.

33 **Martha Graham:** Martha Graham, *Blood Memory* (New York: Doubleday, 1991); Russell Freedman, *Martha Graham: A Dancer's Life* (New York: Clarion Books, 1998); Agnes de Mille, *Martha: The Life and Work of Martha Graham,* 2nd ed. (New York: Random House, 1991); Anna Kisselgoff, "Martha Graham," *The New York Times Magazine,* February 19, 1984, https://www.nytimes.com/1984/02/19/magazine/martha-graham.html; Ernestine Stodelle, *Deep Song: The Dance Story of Martha Graham* (New York: Schirmer Books, 1984); Don McDonagh, *Martha Graham: A Biography* (London: David & Charles, 1973); Martha Graham Dance Company, "Martha Graham Dance Company: History," http://www.marthagraham.org/history/.

34 **"Most of my time":** Graham, 139.

34 **"I chose not":** Ibid., 160.

34 **"permitting life to use you":** Quoted in Martha Graham Dance Company.

34 **"a time of":** Quoted in Freedman, 103.

35 **"Movement in modern dance":** Quoted in Stodelle, 56.

35 **"I owe all":** Quoted in McDonagh, 129.

35 **"I would put":** Quoted in Kisselgoff.

35 **"she was there":** Quoted in de Mille, 138.

35 **"choreographic block":** Graham, 124.

35 **"We used to":** Quoted in de Mille, 146.

35 **"the purge":** Quoted ibid.

35 **A dance critic who profiled:** Kisselgoff.

36 **"Somewhere very long"**: Graham, 14.

37 **Elizabeth Bowen:** May Sarton, *A World of Light: Portraits and Celebrations* (New York: W. W. Norton, 1976); Victoria Glendinning with Judith Robertson, eds., *Love's Civil War: Elizabeth Bowen and Charles Ritchie, Letters and Diaries from the Love Affair of a Lifetime* (Toronto: Emblem, 2009); Victoria Glendinning, *Elizabeth Bowen* (New York: Alfred A. Knopf, 1978); Mary Morrissy, "Closer Than Words," *Irish Times*, January 31, 2009, https://www.irishtimes.com/news/closer-than-words-1.1238445.

37 **"I had never"**: Sarton, 197–98.

38 **"sexless but contented union"**: Morrissy.

38 **"E was discussing"**: Charles Ritchie diary entry, March 3, 1942, in Glendinning with Robertson, 29.

39 **"agitating but makes"**: Elizabeth Bowen to Charles Ritchie, March 6, 1946, in Glendinning with Robertson, 88.

39 **"I discard every"**: Elizabeth Bowen to Charles Ritchie, May 20, 1946, in Glendinning with Robertson, 92.

39 **Frida Kahlo:** Hayden Herrera, *Frida: A Biography of Frida Kahlo* (New York: Perennial, 1983); Catherine Reef, *Frida & Diego: Art, Love, Life* (Boston: Clarion Books, 2014); Martha Zamora, *Frida Kahlo: The Brush of Anguish,* trans. Marilyn Sode Smith (San Francisco: Chronicle Books, 1990); Martha Zamora, ed., *The Letters of Frida Kahlo: Cartas Apasionadas* (San Francisco: Chronicle Books, 1995).

39 **"I have suffered"**: Quoted in Zamora, *Frida Kahlo,* 37.

40 **"When all was well"**: Herrera, 194.

41 **"Frieda [*sic*] has great"**: Quoted ibid., 149.

41 **"I start at"**: Frida Kahlo to Bertram and Ella Wolfe, 1944, in Zamora, *The Letters*, 188.

42 **"I never lost"**: Quoted in Herrera, 390–91.

43 **Agnes de Mille:** Agnes de Mille, *Dance to the Piper* (1951; repr. New York: New York Review Books, 2015), Kindle; Carol Easton, *No Intermissions: The Life of Agnes de Mille* (Boston: Little, Brown, 1996).

43 **"a pot of tea"**: de Mille, loc. 4697 of 5745, Kindle.

43 **"or almost any"**: Ibid., loc. 4702 of 5745, Kindle.

43 **"I start sitting"**: Ibid.

45 **"intelligible only to"**: Ibid., loc. 4722 of 5745, Kindle.

45 **"When a show"**: Easton, 266–67.

46 **"I have yet"**: Quoted ibid., 275.

46 **"with the concentration"**: Quoted ibid., 332.

46 **"fish-out-of-water pose"**: Ibid.

46 **"apt to be short-tempered"**: de Mille, loc. 4722 of 5745, Kindle.

46 **"the tension could"**: Quoted in Easton, 332.

46 **"But when it was right"**: Quoted ibid.

49 **Louisa May Alcott**: John Matteson, *Eden's Outcasts: The Story of Louisa May Alcott and Her Father* (New York: W. W. Norton, 2007); Susan Cheever, *Louisa May Alcott* (New York: Simon & Schuster, 2010); Martha Saxton, *Louisa May: A Modern Biography of Louisa May Alcott* (Boston: Houghton Mifflin, 1977); Louisa May Alcott, *Little Women* (1869; repr. via Oxford Text Archive, http://xroads.virginia.edu/~hyper/alcott/lwtext.html); Nava Atlas, *The Literary Ladies' Guide to the Writing Life* (South Portland, ME: Sellers Publishing, 2011).

49 **"The fit was"**: Quoted in Saxton, 274.

49 **"Every few weeks"**: Alcott, *Little Women.*

51 **"tollgate for conversation"**: Matteson, 334.

51 **"If the pillow"**: Ibid.

52 **"blood & thunder"**: Quoted in Cheever, 108.

52 **"girl's book"**: Saxton, 3. The first volume of *Little Women* was published with the title *Little Women: Meg, Jo, Beth and Amy. The Story of Their Lives. A Girl's Book.*

52 **"I am so full"**: Quoted ibid., 219.

52 **"Though I do not"**: Louisa May Alcott to a reader, December 1878, in Atlas, 165.

53 **"write but two"**: Louisa May Alcott to Frank Carpenter, April 1, 1887, in Atlas, 67.

53 **Radclyffe Hall**: Una Vincenzo, Lady Troubridge, *The Life and Death of Radclyffe Hall* (London: Hammond, Hammond, 1961); Joanne Glasgow, ed., *Your John: The Love Letters of Radclyffe Hall* (New York: New York University Press, 1997); Sally Cline, *Radclyffe Hall: A Woman Called John* (Woodstock, NY: Overlook Press, 1997); Michael Baker, *Our Three Selves: The Life of Radclyffe Hall* (New York: Quill, 1985).

53 **"My daily life"**: Radclyffe Hall to Evgenia Souline, December 17, 1934, in Glasgow, 90.

54 **"launched upon an existence"**: Troubridge, 59.

54 **"inspirational blackout"**: Ibid., 70.

55 **"Whether she felt"**: Ibid.

55 **"neatness complex"**: Quoted in Cline, 149.

55 **"I can never work"**: Quoted ibid., 152.

56 **"I have known"**: Troubridge, 72.

56 **"she never really"**: Ibid., 138.

56 **"I literally wear"**: Radclyffe Hall to Evgenia Souline, December 5, 1934, in Glasgow, 85.

57 **Eileen Gray:** Peter Adam, *Eileen Gray: Architect | Designer: A Biography,* rev. ed. (New York: Harry N. Abrams, 2000).

57 **"Oh, how I abominate"**: Quoted ibid., 215.

57 **"Artists ought not"**: Quoted ibid., 319.

57 **"Only work of some sort"**: Quoted ibid., 320.

57 **Isadora Duncan:** Isadora Duncan, *My Life* (1927; repr. New York: Liveright, 2013); Peter Kurth, *Isadora: A Sensational Life* (Boston: Little, Brown, 2001); Janet Flanner, "Isadora," *The New Yorker,* January 1, 1927, https://www.newyorker.com/magazine /1927/01/01/isadora.

57 **"once gave a house party"**: Flanner.

59 **"So that summer"**: Duncan, 218–19.

60 **"long days and nights"**: Ibid., 60.

60 **"I have met"**: Ibid., 302.

60 **Colette:** Colette, *Earthly Paradise: An Autobiography,* trans. Herman Briffault et al. (New York: Farrar, Straus and Giroux, 1966); Maurice Goudeket, *Close to Colette: An Intimate Portrait of a Woman of Genius* (New York: Farrar, Straus and Cudahy, 1957); Judith Thurman, *Secrets of the Flesh: A Life of Colette* (New York: Alfred A. Knopf, 1999).

61 **"A prison is"**: Colette, 122.

62 **"the opportunity to"**: Quoted in Thurman, 308.

62 **"She was wise"**: Goudeket, 53.

62 **"chiefly between three and six"**: Ibid.

62 **"raft"**: Quoted ibid., 233.

62 **"idle hours curled"**: Colette, 140.

62 **"To write is"**: Ibid.

62 **Lynn Fontanne:** Jared Brown, *The Fabulous Lunts: A Biography of Alfred Lunt and Lynn Fontanne* (New York: Atheneum, 1986); Associated Press, "Lynn Fontanne Is Dead at 95; A Star with Lunt for 37 Years," *The New York Times,* July 31, 1983, https://www .nytimes.com/1983/07/31/obituaries/lynn-fontanne-is-dead-at-95 -a-star-with-lunt-for-37-years.html.

62 **"Miss Fontanne and I"**: "Lynn Fontanne Is Dead at 95."

63 **"They worked out"**: Brown, 179–80.

65 **"Over a period"**: Ibid., 182.

65 **"I think that"**: Quoted ibid., 393.

65 **Edna St. Vincent Millay:** Elizabeth Breuer, "Edna St. Vincent Millay: An Intimate Glimpse of a Famous Poet," *Pictorial Review,* November 1931, 2, 50–57; Nancy Milford, *Savage Beauty: The Life*

of Edna St. Vincent Millay (New York: Random House, 2001); J. D. McClatchy, *American Writers at Home* (New York: Library of America/Vendome Press, 2004).

65 **"When I am"**: Quoted in Breuer, 52.

67 **"Eugen does all"**: Quoted ibid.

67 **"I care an awful lot"**: Quoted ibid.

67 **"When you write"**: Quoted ibid.

67 **"I put it"**: Quoted ibid.

67 **"I can spade"**: Quoted ibid., 54.

68 **Tallulah Bankhead**: Tallulah Bankhead, *Tallulah: My Autobiography* (New York: Harper & Brothers, 1952); Brendan Gill, *Tallulah* (New York: Holt, Rinehart & Winston, 1972).

68 **"I have three phobias"**: Bankhead, 2.

68 **"We're reminiscing about"**: Ibid., 325.

68 **"I've just spent"**: Quoted in Gill, 23.

69 **"sheer drudgery"**: Bankhead, 4.

69 **"The author writes"**: Ibid.

69 **"Above the members"**: Ibid., 3.

69 **"pre-show terror"**: Ibid., 294.

69 **"Ever since *The Squab Farm*"**: Ibid., 207.

70 **Birgit Nilsson**: Winthrop Sargeant, *Divas* (1959; repr. New York: Coward, McCann & Geoghegan, 1973); interview with Bruce Duffie, "Birgit Nilsson—A Celebration," April 20, 1988, http://www.bruceduffie.com/nilsson.html; Bernard Holland, "Birgit Nilsson, Soprano Legend Who Tamed Wagner, Dies at 87," *The New York Times,* January 12, 2006, https://www.nytimes.com/2006/01/12/arts/music/birgit-nilsson-soprano-legend-who-tamed-wagner-dies-at-87.html.

70 **"I do nothing"**: Quoted in Holland.

70 **"Comfortable shoes"**: Quoted ibid.

70 **"A writer or painter"**: Interview with Duffie.

70 **"A singer can"**: Ibid.

71 **"If you rest"**: Quoted in Sargeant, 111.

71 **"I cannot be"**: Quoted ibid., 110.

71 **"I don't like"**: Quoted ibid., 107–8.

71 **"perfectly awful"**: Ibid., 114.

71 **Zora Neale Hurston**: Carla Kaplan, ed., *Zora Neale Hurston: A Life in Letters* (New York: Doubleday, 2002); Valerie Boyd, *Wrapped in Rainbows: The Life of Zora Neale Hurston* (New York: Scribner, 2003); Zora Neale Hurston, *Dust Tracks on a Road: An Autobiography* (1942; repr. New York: HarperPerennial, 1996).

71 **"I have caught fire"**: Zora Neale Hurston to Jean Parker Water-bury, March 18, 1951, in Kaplan, 649–50.

73 **"terrible periods"**: Zora Neale Hurston to Langston Hughes, July 10, 1928, in Kaplan, 121.

73 **"Every now and then"**: Zora Neale Hurston to Carita Doggett Corse, December 3, 1938, in Kaplan, 417–18.

73 **"It was dammed"**: Hurston, 175.

73 **Margaret Bourke-White**: Margaret Bourke-White, *Portrait of Myself* (New York: Simon & Schuster, 1963); Vicki Goldberg, *Margaret Bourke-White: A Biography* (New York: Harper & Row, 1986).

74 **"I wanted to"**: Bourke-White, 300.

74 **"isolated by surrounding"**: Ibid., 301.

74 **"I am a morning writer"**: Ibid.

74 **"a piece of"**: Ibid.

75 **"and by the time"**: Ibid., 302.

75 **"I'm afraid my"**: Ibid.

75 **"The very first time"**: Quoted in Goldberg, 270.

79 **Marie Bashkirtseff**: Marie Bashkirtseff, *The Journal of a Young Artist,* trans. Mary J. Serrano (New York: Cassell & Company, 1889).

79 **"I hate moderation"**: Ibid., 92.

80 **"when I spend"**: Ibid., 210.

80 **"Everything seems petty"**: Ibid., 338.

80 **Germaine de Staël**: J. Christopher Herold, *Mistress to an Age: A Life of Madame de Staël* (Indianapolis: Bobbs-Merrill, 1958).

80 **"One must, in one's life"**: Quoted ibid., 223.

80 **"Madame de Staël worked"**: Quoted ibid., 282.

81 **"Breakfast was between"**: Ibid., 282–83.

82 **"Like all insomniacs"**: Ibid., 283.

82 **"more continuously exacting"**: Quoted ibid., 189.

82 **Marie de Vichy-Chamrond**: Javier Marías, *Written Lives,* trans. Margaret Jull Costa (1999; repr. New York: New Directions, 2006); Benedetta Craveri, *Madame du Deffand and Her World,* trans. Teresa Waugh (Boston: David R. Godine, 1982); *The Unpublished Correspondence of Madame du Deffand . . . ,* trans. Mrs. Meeke (London: A. K. Newman, 1810), Google Books.

82 **"Her life followed"**: Marías, 97.

83 **"one of man's"**: Quoted ibid., 98.

83 **"Exert all your talents"**: Quoted in "Historical Details Respecting Madame du Deffand," in *Unpublished Correspondence,* 17.

83 **"I am left"**: Quoted in Craveri, 106.

83 **Dorothy Parker:** Marion Meade, *Dorothy Parker: What Fresh Hell Is This?* (1987; repr. New York: Penguin Books, 1989); Sam Roberts, "'The Elements of Style' Turns 50," *The New York Times,* April 21, 2009, https://www.nytimes.com/2009/04/22/books/22elem.html.

83 **"If you have":** Quoted in Roberts.

84 **"Almost from the outset":** Meade, 188–89.

85 **"You sit around":** Quoted ibid., 89.

85 **"had a miserable time":** Quoted ibid., 357.

85 **"Everything that isn't writing":** Quoted ibid., 388.

85 **Edna Ferber:** Edna Ferber, *A Kind of Magic* (Garden City, NY: Doubleday, 1963).

85 **"I know of":** Ibid., 44.

86 **"I have written":** Ibid., 43–44

86 **"caramel carpet":** Ibid., 77.

86 **"A room with a View":** Ibid.

86 **Margaret Mitchell:** Darden Asbury Pyron, *Southern Daughter: The Life of Margaret Mitchell* (New York: Oxford University Press, 1991); Anne Edwards, *Road to Tara: The Life of Margaret Mitchell* (New Haven, CT: Ticknor & Fields, 1983); Ellen F. Brown and John Wiley, Jr., *Margaret Mitchell's Gone with the Wind: A Bestseller's Odyssey from Atlanta to Hollywood* (Lanham, MD: Taylor Trade Publishing, 2011).

86 **"I do not":** Quoted in Pyron, 278.

86 **"Writing is a hard job":** Quoted ibid., 233.

87 **"at least twenty":** Quoted ibid., 280.

87 **"something strange":** Quoted in Edwards, 137.

87 **"I not only":** Quoted in Pyron, 223.

87 **"I wouldn't go":** Quoted in Edwards, 223.

88 **Marian Anderson:** Marian Anderson, *My Lord, What a Morning: An Autobiography* (1956; repr. Madison: University of Wisconsin Press, 1992); Raymond Arsenault, *The Sound of Freedom: Marian Anderson, the Lincoln Memorial, and the Concert That Awakened America* (New York: Bloomsbury Press, 2009).

88 **"a voice such":** Arsenault, 58.

88 **"I like to hear":** Anderson, 199.

88 **"Music is an elusive thing":** Ibid., 200.

89 **"Then," she wrote:** Ibid.

89 **Leontyne Price:** Hugh Lee Lyon, *Highlights of a Prima Donna* (New York: Vantage Press, 1973); Winthrop Sargeant, *Divas* (1959; repr. New York: Coward, McCann & Geoghegan, 1973).

90 "On the day": Lyon, 146.

91 "Opera is a": Quoted ibid., 143.

91 Gertrude Lawrence: Sheridan Morley, *Gertrude Lawrence: A Biography* (New York: McGraw-Hill, 1981); Richard Stoddard Aldrich, *Gertrude Lawrence as Mrs. A: An Intimate Biography of the Great Star* (New York: Pickering Press, 1954); Gertrude Lawrence, *A Star Danced* (Garden City, NY: Doubleday, Doran, 1945).

91 "Vitamins should take": Quoted in Aldrich, 164.

91 "My day starts": Quoted in Morley, 136–37.

93 "At such times": Aldrich, 117.

93 "the exquisite, ethereal": Ibid.

93 "put away a meal": Ibid.

93 Edith Head: Edith Head and Paddy Calistro, *Edith Head's Hollywood* (Santa Monica, CA: Angel City Press, 2008); Jay Jorgensen, *Edith Head: The Fifty-Year Career of Hollywood's Greatest Costume Designer* (Philadelphia: Running Press, 2010); David Chierichetti, *Edith Head: The Life and Times of Hollywood's Celebrated Costume Designer* (New York: HarperCollins, 2003).

93 "To be a good designer": Quoted in Jorgensen, 256.

94 "There was no": Head and Calistro, 42.

94 "a better politician": Ibid., 146.

94 "Inside I was": Ibid., 181.

94 "I learned to suppress": Ibid.

94 "I never use": Ibid., 98.

95 "When I'm at the studio": Quoted in Jorgensen, 109.

96 Marlene Dietrich: Marlene Dietrich, *Marlene Dietrich's ABC* (Garden City, NY: Doubleday, 1961); Edith Head and Paddy Calistro, *Edith Head's Hollywood* (Santa Monica, CA: Angel City Press, 2008); Steven Bach, *Marlene Dietrich: Life and Legend* (New York: William Morrow, 1992).

96 "Dietrich was not difficult": Head and Calistro, 37.

96 "would come directly": Quoted in Bach, 370.

96 "It is a sin": Dietrich, 87.

96 "the greatest occupational therapies": Ibid., 47.

96 "The more plentiful": Ibid., 121.

97 Ida Lupino: William Donati, *Ida Lupino: A Biography* (Lexington: University Press of Kentucky, 1996); Ida Lupino with Mary Ann Anderson, *Beyond the Camera* (Albany, GA: BearManor Media, 2011), Kindle; Kevin Crust, "Classic Hollywood: Trailblazer Ida Lupino, a Woman for Her Time—and Ours," *Los Angeles Times,* February 16, 2018, http://www.latimes.com/entertainment/movies

/la-ca-mn-classic-hollywood-lupino-centennial-20180216-story
.html.

97 **"never really liked"**: Quoted in Crust.

97 **"As soon as"**: Quoted in Donati, 229.

97 **"I go out"**: Lupino with Anderson, loc. 730 of 1149, Kindle.

97 **"Ida would sometimes"**: Donati, 163.

98 **"Keeping a feminine approach"**: Lupino with Anderson, loc. 730 of 1149, Kindle.

99 **Betty Comden:** Robert Berkvist, "Comden and Green Throw Another 'Party,'" *The New York Times,* February 6, 1977, https://www.nytimes.com/1977/02/06/archives/comden-and-green-throw-another-party.html; Betty Comden, *Off Stage* (New York: Simon & Schuster, 1995); interview with Michael Riedel and Susan Haskins, *Theater Talk,* CUNY TV, 1997, https://www.youtube.com/watch?v=JjWRzTRG-0c; interview with Tina Daniell and Pat McGilligan, "Betty Comden and Adolph Green: Almost Improvisation," in Pat McGilligan, ed., *Backstory 2: Interviews with Screenwriters of the 1940s and 1950s* (Berkeley: University of California Press, 1991), 73–88.

99 **"We stare at each other"**: Quoted in Berkvist.

99 **"a year of sitting around"**: Interview with Riedel and Haskins.

100 **"at the end"**: Interview with Daniell and McGilligan, 85.

100 **"Confusion still reigns"**: Comden, 124.

100 **"Sheer fear and terror"**: Quoted in Berkvist.

103 **Zoe Akins:** Zoe Akins, "Adventures in Playwrighting," *The New York Times,* September 25, 1921, https://www.nytimes.com/1921/09/25/archives/adventures-in-playwriting.html; Zoe Akins, "Philosophy of an Adaptation," *The New York Times,* January 13, 1935, https://www.nytimes.com/1935/01/13/archives/philosophy-of-an-adaptation-the-philosophy-of-adaptation.html; Alan Kreizenbeck, *Zoe Akins: Broadway Playwright* (Westport, CT: Praeger, 2004).

103 **"to write seven"**: "Philosophy of an Adaptation."

103 **"an indomitable hankering"**: Quoted in Kreizenbeck, 53.

103 **"I write, when"**: "Adventures in Playwrighting."

103 **"I prefer for an act"**: Ibid.

104 **Agnes Martin:** Arne Glimcher, *Agnes Martin: Paintings, Writings, Remembrances* (2012; repr. London: Phaidon, 2016); Donald Woodman, *Agnes Martin and Me* (Brooklyn: Lyon Artbooks, 2015); John Gruen, "Agnes Martin," in *The Artist Observed: 28 Interviews with Contemporary Artists* (Chicago: A Cap-

pella Books, 1991), 77–86; interview with Chuck Smith and Sono Kuwayama, November 1997, https://www.youtube.com /watch?v=_-fJfYjmo5OA; interview with Lyn Blumenthal and Kate Horsfield, "Agnes Martin 1976: An Interview," Video Data Bank, http://www.vdb.org/titles/agnes-martin-1976-interview; Frances Morris and Tiffany Bell, *Agnes Martin* (New York: D.A.P./ Distributed Art Publishing, 2015).

104 **"I have a vacant mind"**: Interview with Smith and Kuwayama.

104 **"Inspiration comes"**: Interview with Blumenthal and Horsfield.

104 **"The most important"**: Agnes Martin, "I Want to Talk to You About My Work . . . ," in Glimcher, 16.

105 **"I don't get up"**: Quoted in Gruen, 85.

105 **"When you're with"**: Quoted ibid., 81.

106 **"For as long"**: Woodman, 98.

106 **"One year"**: Ibid., 101.

107 **"might include eggs"**: Ibid.

107 **"she painted what"**: Ibid., 137.

107 **"You're permanently derailed"**: Quoted in Gruen, 83–85.

107 **Katherine Mansfield**: Katherine Mansfield, *The Katherine Mansfield Notebooks: Complete Edition,* ed. Margaret Scott (Minneapolis: University of Minnesota Press, 2002); Claire Tomalin, *Katherine Mansfield: A Secret Life* (New York: Alfred A. Knopf, 1988).

108 **"Well I must"**: Mansfield, July 13, 1921, in *Notebooks*, volume 2, 280.

108 **"What happens as a rule"**: Ibid., 280–81.

109 **Katherine Anne Porter**: Joan Givner, ed., *Katherine Anne Porter: Conversations* (Jackson: University Press of Mississippi, 1987); interview with Barbara Thompson Davis, "Katherine Anne Porter, The Art of Fiction No. 29," *The Paris Review,* Winter–Spring 1963, https://www.theparisreview.org/interviews/4569/katherine -anne-porter-the-art-of-fiction-no-29-katherine-anne-porter; Joan Givner, *Katherine Anne Porter: A Life* (New York: Simon & Schuster, 1982); Hilton Als, "Enameled Lady," *The New Yorker,* April 20, 2009, https://www.newyorker.com/magazine/2009/04/20 /enameled-lady.

109 **"little dull jobs"**: Interview with Davis.

109 **"It just simply"**: Ibid.

109 **"I think I've"**: Ibid.

110 **"prestige depended upon"**: Truman Capote, *Answered Prayers* (New York: Vintage, 1987), 14.

111 **"never did resist"**: *A Life*, 165.

111 **"It doesn't actually"**: Quoted in John Dorsey, "Katherine Anne Porter On:," *Sun Magazine*, October 26, 1969, in *Conversations*, 142.

111 **"I went up"**: Interview with Davis.

112 **"Any such alienation"**: Quoted in James Ruoff, "Katherine Anne Porter Comes to Kansas," *Midwest Quarterly*, June 1963, in *Conversations*, 65.

112 **Bridget Riley**: Robert Kudielka, *The Eye's Mind: Bridget Riley, Collected Writings, 1965–2009* (London: Ridinghouse, 2009).

112 **"An artist feels"**: Interview with Isabel Carlisle, 1998, in Kudielka, 160.

112 **"In a daydream"**: Interview with Mel Gooding, 1988, in Kudielka, 147.

113 **"takes and needs"**: Bridget Riley, "Painting Now," 1996, in Kudielka, 302.

114 **"Boredom is"**: Interview with Nikki Henriques, 1988, in Kudielka, 27.

114 **"It's not right"**: Ibid.

114 **"I am not"**: Interview with Isabel Carlisle, 1998, in Kudielka, 161.

114 **Julie Mehretu**: Telephone interview with the author, October 11, 2016.

117 **Rachel Whiteread**: Telephone interview with the author, October 4, 2016.

117 **Alice Walker**: Alice Walker, *In Search of Our Mothers' Gardens: Womanist Prose* (1967; repr. San Diego: Harcourt Brace Jovanovich, 1983); Rudolph P. Byrd, *The World Has Changed: Conversations with Alice Walker* (New York: The New Press, 2010); Meredith May, "A Rigorous Look at Writer Alice Walker's Life," *SFGate*, February 4, 2014, https://www.sfgate.com/tv/article/A-rigorous-look-at-writer-Alice-Walker-s-life-5203987.php.

118 **"just clear the horizon"**: Interview with Amy Goodman, "I Am a Renegade, an Outlaw, a Pagan—Author, Poet and Activist Alice Walker in Her Own Words," *Democracy Now!*, February 13, 2006, in Byrd, 273.

118 **"What is all"**: Alice Walker, "Writing *The Color Purple*," in Walker, 356.

118 **"We would sit"**: Ibid., 359.

119 **"just quieted down"**: Ibid.

119 **"adored" her daughter**: Ibid.

119 **"So, just when"**: Ibid.

119 **"I don't know"**: Quoted in May.

119 **Carole King:** Interview with Paul Zollo, "Carole King," in Paul Zollo, *Songwriters on Songwriting,* 2nd ed. (Cambridge, MA: Da Capo Press, 2003), 141–47; Carole King, *A Natural Woman: A Memoir* (New York: Grand Central Publishing, 2012).

119 **"I'm one of those"**: King, 253.

120 **"I have found"**: Interview with Zollo, 143.

120 **"When the ego"**: King, 364.

120 **"when the thing"**: Ibid., 364–65.

121 **Andrea Zittel:** Email interview with the author, August 2017.

122 **Meredith Monk:** Telephone interview with the author, July 17, 2017.

125 **Grace Paley:** Interview with Jonathan Dee, Barbara Jones, and Larissa MacFarquhar, "Grace Paley, The Art of Fiction No. 131," *The Paris Review,* Fall 1992, https://www.theparisreview.org /interviews/2028/grace-paley-the-art-of-fiction-no-131-grace -paley; interview with Gail Pool and Shirley Roses, "An Interview with Grace Paley," *Boston Review,* Fall 1976, https://bostonreview .net/grace-paley-interview-gail-pool-shirley-roses.

125 **"I remember somebody"**: Interview with Pool and Roses.

125 **"absolutely resonant"**: Interview with Dee, Jones, and MacFarquhar.

125 **"I'm almost invariably stuck"**: Ibid.

126 **"Art comes from"**: Ibid.

129 **Susan Sontag:** Leland Poague, ed., *Conversations with Susan Sontag* (Jackson: University Press of Mississippi, 1995); Sigrid Nunez, *Sempre Susan: A Memoir of Susan Sontag* (New York: Atlas, 2011); Daniel Schreiber, *Susan Sontag: A Biography,* trans. David Dollenmayer (2007; repr. Evanston, IL: Northwestern University Press, 2014); Jonathan Cott, *Susan Sontag: The Complete* Rolling Stone *Interview* (New Haven, CT: Yale University Press, 2013); Susan Sontag, *Reborn: Journals and Notebooks, 1947–1963,* ed. David Rieff (New York: Farrar, Straus and Giroux, 2008); Susan Sontag, *As Consciousness Is Harnessed to Flesh: Journals and Notebooks, 1964–1980,* ed. David Rieff (New York: Farrar, Straus and Giroux, 2012); David Rieff, *Swimming in a Sea of Death: A Son's Memoir* (New York: Simon & Schuster, 2008); Joan Acocella, "The Hunger Artist," *The New Yorker,* March 6, 2000, https://www.new yorker.com/magazine/2000/03/06/the-hunger-artist; interview with Victor Bockris, "Susan Sontag: The Dark Lady of Pop Philosophy," *High Times,* March 28, 1973, repr. in Victor Bockris, *Beat*

Punks: New York's Underground Culture from the Beat Generation to the Punk Explosion (1998; repr. New York: Open Road Media, 2016), Kindle; Ellen Hopkins, "Susan Sontag Lightens Up," *Los Angeles Times,* August 16, 1992, http://articles.latimes .com/1992-08-16/magazine/tm-6833_1_susan-sontag; Susan Sontag, "Pilgrimage," *The New Yorker,* December 21, 1987, https://www .newyorker.com/magazine/1987/12/21/pilgrimage-susan-sontag; interview with Edward Hirsch, "The Art of Fiction No. 143: Susan Sontag," *The Paris Review,* Winter 1995, https://www.theparis review.org/interviews/1505/susan-sontag-the-art-of-fiction-no-143 -susan-sontag; Michael D'Antonio, "Little David, Happy at Last," *Esquire,* March 1990, 128–35; Suzy Hansen, "Rieff Encounter," *The Observer,* May 2, 2005, http://observer.com/2005/05/rieff -encounter/.

129 "Somewhere along the line": Quoted in Cott, 109.

129 "that long prison": Sontag, "Pilgrimage."

129 "It never occurred": Quoted in Hopkins.

130 "watched twenty Japanese films": Richard Howard, quoted in Schreiber, 96.

130 "aiming for a": Nunez, 84–85.

130 "If I had to choose": Rieff, 15.

130 "More than ever": Sontag, *As Consciousness Is Harnessed to Flesh,* 299.

130 "What I want": Ibid., 300.

130 "very long, intense": Quoted in Cott, 80.

130 "I am not": Interview with Charles Ruas, "Susan Sontag: Me, Etcetera . . . ," *The Soho News,* November 12–18, 1980, in Poague, 179.

131 "Kafka had a fantasy": Interview with Marithelma Costa and Adelaida López, "Susan Sontag: The Passion for Words," *Revista de Occidente,* December 1987, in Poague, 229.

131 "I didn't cook": Quoted in D'Antonio, 132.

132 "grew up on coats": Quoted in Acocella.

132 "When I was writing": Quoted in Nunez, 104.

132 "While she was": Ibid.

133 "though in diminishing doses": David Rieff, editor's note in Sontag, *As Consciousness Is Harnessed to Flesh,* 11.

133 "I use speed": Interview with Bockris.

133 "To write is": Sontag, *Reborn,* 218.

133 "thrilling": Interview with Amy Lippman, "A Conversation with Susan Sontag," *Harvard Advocate,* Fall 1983, in Poague, 204.

133 "Work is more fun": Ibid.
133 Joan Mitchell: Patricia Albers, *Joan Mitchell: Lady Painter* (New York: Alfred A. Knopf, 2011); Eleanor Munro, *Originals: American Women Artists,* new ed. (New York: Da Capo Press, 2000); Deborah Solomon, "In Monet's Light," *The New York Times Magazine,* November 24, 1991, http://www.nytimes.com/1991/11/24/magazine/in-monet-s-light.html.
134 "You have a feeling": Quoted in Solomon.
134 "more available": Quoted in Albers, xx.
134 "was in her": Quoted ibid., 193.
134 "at least once": Ibid., 226.
134 "if she did not drink": Quoted ibid., 320.
134 "The idea of": Quoted in Solomon.
135 "How goes your": Munro, 237.
135 "Not always": Quoted ibid., 237.
136 "everything looks the same": Quoted ibid.
136 "her survival bag": Albers, 380.
137 "like a place": Quoted ibid., 377.
137 "No one can": Quoted ibid., 14.
137 "one has to be": Ibid.
137 Marguerite Duras: Laure Adler, *Marguerite Duras: A Life,* trans. Anne-Marie Glasheen (Chicago: University of Chicago Press, 1998); Leslie Garis, "The Life and Loves of Marguerite Duras," *The New York Times Magazine,* October 20, 1991, https://www.nytimes.com/1991/10/20/magazine/the-life-and-loves-of-marguerite-duras.html; Marguerite Duras with Jérôme Beaujour, *Practicalities,* trans. Barbara Bray (New York: Grove Weidenfeld, 1990); Marguerite Duras, *Writing,* trans. Mark Polizzotti (Cambridge, MA: Lumen Editions, 1998).
137 "It's like a crisis": Quoted in Adler, 282.
138 "working at her desk": Adler, 257.
138 "I'm a real writer": Quoted in Garis.
138 Penelope Fitzgerald: Hermione Lee, *Penelope Fitzgerald: A Life* (New York: Alfred A. Knopf, 2014); Penelope Fitzgerald, *The Afterlife,* ed. Terence Dooley (New York: Counterpoint, 2003); Joan Acocella, "Assassination on a Small Scale," *The New Yorker,* February 7, 2000, 80–88.
138 "I hope you'll": Quoted in Lee, 324.
139 "I've come to see art": Quoted ibid., 186.
139 "Faced by piles": Quoted ibid., 191.
140 "during my free periods": Quoted ibid., 207.

140 **"I'm very annoyed"**: Quoted ibid., 215.

140 **"I have remained"**: Penelope Fitzgerald, "Curriculum Vitae," 1989, in *The Afterlife,* 347.

141 **Barbara Hepworth**: Sophie Bowness, ed., *Barbara Hepworth: Writings and Conversations* (London: Tate Publishing, 2015); interview with Cindy Nemser, *Art Talk: Conversations with 15 Women Artists,* rev. ed. (New York: Westview Press, 1995).

141 **"I am basically"**: Barbara Hepworth, "The Sculptor Speaks," recorded talk for the British Council, December 8, 1961, in Bowness, 153.

141 **"I think one"**: Interview with Peggy Archer for *Woman's Hour,* BBC Home Service, July 28, 1967, in Bowness, 207.

141 **"I have always thought"**: Barbara Hepworth in *Women and Men's Daughters: Portrait Studies by Zsuzsi Roboz,* ed. William Wordsworth (London 1970) in Bowness, 225.

141 **"emotionally exhausting"**: Quoted in John Carpenter diary entry, October 2, 1952, in Bowness, 264.

141 **"You have to work"**: Quoted in Mervyn Levy, "Impulse and Rhythm: The Artist at Work—9," *The Studio,* September 1962, in Bowness, 271.

141 **"I had to have"**: Interview with Tom Greenwell, "Talking Freely: Barbara Hepworth Gives Her Views to Tom Greenwell," *Yorkshire Post,* November 14, 1962, in Bowness, 278–79.

143 **"We lived a life"**: Quoted in Nemser, 14.

143 **"Light and space"**: Interview with Edouard Roditi, "Barbara Hepworth," *Dialogues on Art* (London: 1960), in Bowness, 134.

143 **"I don't actually"**: Quoted in Atticus, "Graven Image," *Sunday Times,* March 17, 1968, in Bowness, 283.

143 **Stella Bowen**: Stella Bowen, *Drawn from Life* (1941; repr. London: Virago Press, 1984); Drusilla Modjeska, *Stravinsky's Lunch* (New York: Farrar, Straus and Giroux, 1999).

144 **"had a genius"**: Bowen, 162.

144 **"shock absorber"**: Ibid., 78.

144 **"Ford never understood"**: Ibid., 82–83.

145 **"If you are"**: Ibid., 141.

146 **Kate Chopin**: Per Seyersted, ed., *The Complete Works of Kate Chopin* (Baton Rouge: Louisiana State University Press, 1969); Emily Toth, *Unveiling Kate Chopin* (Jackson: University Press of Mississippi, 1999); Per Seyersted, *Kate Chopin: A Critical Biography* (1969; repr. Baton Rouge: Louisiana State University Press, 1979).

146 **"swarming about her"**: Quoted in Toth, 109.

146 **"How do I write?":** Kate Chopin, "On Certain Brisk, Bright Days," *St. Louis Post-Dispatch,* November 26, 1899, in Seyersted, *Complete Works,* 721–22.

147 **"spent only an average":** Seyersted, *Critical Biography,* 62.

147 **"There are stories":** Kate Chopin, "On Certain Brisk, Bright Days," *St. Louis Post-Dispatch,* November 26, 1899, in Seyersted, *Complete Works,* 722.

147 **"the short story":** Quoted in Seyersted, *Critical Biography,* 116.

147 **"I am completely":** Quoted ibid., 117.

148 **Harriet Jacobs:** Jean Fagan Yellin, *Harriet Jacobs: A Life* (New York: Basic Civitas Books, 2004); Harriet Jacobs, *Incidents in the Life of a Slave Girl* (1861; repr. via Academic Affairs Library, University of North Carolina at Chapel Hill, http://docsouth .unc.edu /fpn/jacobs/jacobs.html).

148 **"useful in some way":** Quoted in Yellin, 120.

148 **"I have not":** Quoted ibid., 129.

149 **"could steal away":** Ibid.

149 **"The poor Book":** Ibid.

149 **"at irregular intervals":** Jacobs, *Incidents,* preface.

149 **"been interrupted":** Quoted in Yellin, 135.

149 **Marie Curie:** Eve Curie, *Madame Curie,* trans. Vincent Sheean (1937; repr. New York: Da Capo Press, 2001); Susan Quinn, *Marie Curie: A Life* (New York: Simon & Schuster, 1995); Barbara Goldsmith, *Obsessive Genius: The Inner World of Marie Curie* (New York: Atlas, 2005); Marie Curie, *Pierre Curie, with Autobiographical Notes by Marie Curie,* trans. Charlotte Kellogg and Vernon Kellogg (1923; repr. Mineola, NY: Dover, 2012).

150 **"I would have":** Quoted in Quinn, 154.

150 **"One can discern":** Quoted ibid.

151 **"It looked like a stable":** Quoted in Goldsmith, 91.

151 **"I had to work":** Quoted in Quinn, 155.

151 **"I would be":** Marie Curie, 92.

151 **"the heroic period":** Marie Curie to Louis Vauthier, in Eve Curie, 169.

151 **"In spite of":** Quoted in Eve Curie, 170–71.

152 **"Our life is":** Marie Curie to Bronisława Dłuska, 1899, in Eve Curie, 172.

152 **"You hardly eat":** Quoted in Goldsmith, 97.

153 **"We refuse with":** Quoted in Quinn, 197.

157 **George Eliot:** Kathryn Hughes, *George Eliot: The Last Victorian* (New York: Farrar, Straus and Giroux, 1999); Gordon S. Haight, *George Eliot: A Biography* (New York: Oxford University Press,

1968); *The Journals of George Eliot,* ed. Margaret Harris and Judith Johnston (Cambridge, UK: Cambridge University Press, 1998).

157 **"could never write":** Quoted in Hughes, 293.

157 **"I had hardly a day":** Quoted ibid., 311.

158 **"We have so much happiness":** Quoted ibid., 251.

158 **Edith Wharton:** Hermione Lee, *Edith Wharton* (New York: Alfred A. Knopf, 2007); Edith Wharton, *A Backward Glance* (1933; repr. New York: Touchstone, 1998); Percy Lubbock, *Portrait of Edith Wharton* (1947; repr. New York: Kraus Reprint, 1969); Maureen Adams, *Shaggy Muses: The Dogs Who Inspired Virginia Woolf, Emily Dickinson, Elizabeth Barrett Browning, Edith Wharton, and Emily Brontë* (New York: Ballantine Books, 2007); J. D. McClatchy, *American Writers at Home* (New York: Library of America/Vendome Press, 2004); Philip Kennicott, "Character Study," *The Washington Post,* August 31, 2008, http://www.washingtonpost.com/wp-dyn/content/article/2008/08/29/AR2008082900761.html.

158 **"equally real yet":** Wharton, 205.

158 **"flanked by night tables":** Quoted in Lee, 670.

159 **"a thin silk sacque":** Quoted ibid., 670–71.

160 the **"ruling passions":** Quoted in Kennicott.

160 **"very little allusion":** Lubbock, 22.

160 **"The slightest interruption":** Quoted in Adams, 169.

160 **Anna Pavlova:** Margot Fonteyn, *Pavlova: Portrait of a Dancer* (New York: Viking, 1984); Victor Dandré, *Anna Pavlova in Art & Life* (1932; repr. New York: Benjamin Blom, 1972).

160 **"On the day":** Anna Pavlova, "A Dancer's Day," in Fonteyn, 30–31.

161 **"the whole of":** Dandré, 123.

161 **"She was always":** Ibid.

162 **"People imagine we":** Anna Pavlova, "First Tour," in Fonteyn, 33.

162 **Elizabeth Barrett Browning:** Margaret Forster, *Elizabeth Barrett Browning: A Biography* (New York: Doubleday, 1989); Julia Markus, *Dared and Done: The Marriage of Elizabeth Barrett and Robert Browning* (New York: Alfred A. Knopf, 1995); "Elizabeth Barrett Browning," Britannica Online Encyclopedia, https://www.britannica.com/biography/Elizabeth-Barrett-Browning.

162 **"I love your verses":** Quoted in "Elizabeth Barrett Browning."

162 **"the happy winter":** Quoted in Forster, 278.

162 **"She and Robert":** Quoted ibid.

163 **"favored a poet's":** Markus, 161.

164 **"irritable" to "steady"**: Quoted in Forster, 156.

164 **"My opium comes"**: Quoted in Markus, 40–41.

164 It was **"perfectly true"**: Quoted ibid., 278.

164 **Virginia Woolf**: Hermione Lee, *Virginia Woolf* (1996; repr. New York: Vintage, 1999); *The Diary of Virginia Woolf, Volume Two: 1920–1924,* ed. Anne Olivier Bell and Andrew McNeillie (San Diego: Harcourt Brace, 1978); *The Diary of Virginia Woolf, Volume Three: 1925–1930,* ed. Anne Olivier Bell and Andrew McNeillie (San Diego: Harcourt Brace, 1981); *The Diary of Virginia Woolf, Volume Four: 1931–1935,* ed. Anne Olivier Bell and Andrew McNeillie (San Diego: Harcourt Brace, 1982); *The Diary of Virginia Woolf, Volume Five: 1936–1941,* ed. Anne Olivier Bell and Andrew McNeillie (San Diego: Harcourt Brace, 1984); *The Letters of Virginia Woolf, Volume Three: 1923–1928,* ed. Nigel Nicolson and Joanne Trautmann (San Diego: Harcourt Brace, 1977); *The Letters of Virginia Woolf, Volume Four: 1929–1931,* ed. Nigel Nicolson and Joanne Trautmann (San Diego: Harcourt Brace, 1978); Virginia Woolf, *The Death of the Moth and Other Essays,* 2nd ed. (London: Hogarth Press, 1942); Julia Briggs, *Virginia Woolf: An Inner Life* (Orlando: Harcourt, 2005).

164 **"eking out"**: Woolf, "George Moore," *Vogue,* June 1925, in *Death of the Moth,* 103.

164 **"A good day"**: Virginia Woolf, June 23, 1936, in *Diary, Volume Five,* 25.

164 **"Few people can"**: Ibid.

164 **"She structured her working life"**: Lee, 405.

165 **"How great writers"**: Virginia Woolf, March 17, 1923, in *Diary, Volume Two,* 240.

166 **"L. thinks my writing"**: Virginia Woolf to Violet Dickinson, June 4, 1912, in *Letters, Volume One,* 500.

166 **"Neither of us"**: Quoted in Lee, 332.

166 **"I hope I"**: Woolf, "Professions for Women," 1933, in *Death of the Moth,* 152.

167 **"street haunting"**: Woolf, "Street Haunting: A London Adventure," 1930, in *Death of the Moth,* 29.

167 **"extremely happy walking"**: Virginia Woolf, September 5, 1926, in *Diary, Volume Three,* 107.

167 **"nosing along, making up phrases"**: Virginia Woolf to Vita Sackville-West, February 17, 1926, in *Letters, Volume Three,* 241.

167 **"slip[ped] easily from writing"**: Virginia Woolf, June 11, 1922, in *Diary, Volume Two,* 176.

167 **"On and on"**: Quoted in Lee, 419.

167 **"The truth is"**: Virginia Woolf, September 23, 1933, in *Diary, Volume Four,* 179.

167 **"I was irritated"**: Quoted in Lee, 427.

167 **"I wake filled"**: Virginia Woolf to Ethel Smyth, September 21 or 22, 1930, in *Letters, Volume Four,* 218.

168 **Vanessa Bell**: Frances Spalding, *Vanessa Bell* (New Haven, CT: Ticknor & Fields, 1983); Quentin Bell and Virginia Nicholson, *Charleston: A Bloomsbury House and Garden* (New York: Henry Holt, 1997); Lisa Tickner, "The 'Left-Handed Marriage': Vanessa Bell & Duncan Grant," in *Significant Others: Creativity & Intimate Partnership,* ed. Whitney Chadwick and Isabelle de Courtivron (New York: Thames and Hudson, 1993), 65–81; *The Letters of Virginia Woolf, Volume Three: 1923–1928,* ed. Nigel Nicolson and Joanne Trautmann (San Diego: Harcourt Brace, 1977); *The Diary of Virginia Woolf, Volume Three: 1925–1930,* ed. Anne Olivier Bell and Andrew McNeillie (San Diego: Harcourt Brace, 1981).

168 **"marvelous practical power"**: Quoted in Spalding, 165.

168 **"the unwobbling pivot"**: Quoted in Tickner, 65.

168 **"Charleston in its heyday"**: Quoted in Bell and Nicholson, 123.

170 **"like two sturdy"**: Quoted ibid., 70.

170 **"I never saw"**: Virginia Woolf to Roger Fry, September 16, 1925, in *Letters, Volume Three,* 209.

170 **"pour out pure gaiety"**: Virginia Woolf to Vita Sackville-West, January 31, 1926, in *Letters, Volume Three,* 237.

171 **"I have spilt"**: Virginia Woolf, August 19, 1929, in *Diary, Volume Three,* 243.

171 **Maggi Hambling**: Correspondence with the author, January–September 2017; "Maggi Hambling on 'Brilliant Ideas,'" Bloomberg TV, December 19, 2016, https://www.bloomberg.com/news/videos/2016-12-19/maggi-hambling-on-brilliant-ideas.

171 **"Work can make"**: Correspondence with the author.

171 **"full of optimism"**: Ibid.

171 **"As with Hamlet"**: Ibid.

171 **"be at the ready"**: Ibid.

171 **"Perhaps it is"**: Ibid.

172 **"My first experience"**: Ibid.

172 **"a disgustingly healthy muesli"**: Ibid.

172 **"and I am often"**: Ibid.

172 **"the whiskey beckons"**: Ibid.

172 **"have a chat"**: Ibid.

172 **"I can even be pleased"**: Ibid.

173 **"Resignation and relief"**: Ibid.

173 **"Everything has to be"**: "Maggi Hambling on 'Brilliant Ideas.' "

173 **Carolee Schneemann:** Telephone interview with the author, March 29, 2017.

173 **Marilyn Minter:** Telephone interview with the author, February 15, 2017.

176 **Josephine Meckseper:** Email interview with the author, January–February 2017.

178 **Jessye Norman:** Jessye Norman, *Stand Up Straight and Sing!* (Boston: Houghton Mifflin Harcourt, 2014).

178 **"I do not"**: Ibid., 212–13.

178 **"Hydration; that is all"**: Ibid., 213.

179 **Maggie Nelson:** Telephone interview with the author, August 24, 2016.

180 **Nikki Giovanni:** Telephone interview with the author, April 25, 2017.

185 **Anne Bradstreet:** Charlotte Gordon, *Mistress Bradstreet: The Untold Life of America's First Poet* (New York: Little, Brown, 2005).

185 **"more than almost any other"**: Ibid., 195.

185 **"for most of this time"**: Ibid.

185 **"The silent night's"**: Quoted ibid., 177.

186 **Emily Dickinson:** Richard B. Sewall, *The Life of Emily Dickinson,* 2nd ed. (Cambridge, MA: Harvard University Press, 1980); Vivian R. Pollak, ed., *A Historical Guide to Emily Dickinson* (New York: Oxford University Press, 2004); Thomas H. Johnson, ed., *Emily Dickinson: Selected Letters* (Cambridge, MA: Belknap Press, 1971); Alfred Habegger, *My Wars Are Laid Away in Books: The Life of Emily Dickinson* (New York: Modern Library, 2002); Thomas Wentworth Higginson, "Emily Dickinson's Letters," *The Atlantic Monthly,* October 1891, https://www.theatlantic.com /magazine/archive/1891/10/emily-dickinsons-letters/306524/; J. D. McClatchy, *American Writers at Home* (New York: Library of America/Vendome Press, 2004).

186 **"I will tell"**: Emily Dickinson to Abiah Root, November 21, 1847, in Sewall, 365.

188 **"foreign to my thought"**: Emily Dickinson to Thomas Wentworth Higginson, June 7, 1862, in Higginson.

188 **"Our mother had"**: Quoted in Habegger, 342.

189 **"The impression undoubtedly"**: Higginson.

189 **"I never was"**: Quoted in Pollak, 15.

189 **"I had no Monarch":** Emily Dickinson to Thomas Wentworth Higginson, August 1862, in Johnson, 178.

190 **Harriet Hosmer:** Cornelia Carr, *Harriet Hosmer: Letters and Memories* (1912; repr. London: Forgotten Books, 2015).

190 **"I am as busy":** Harriet Hosmer to Wayman Crow, February 1870, ibid., 280.

190 **"She was never idle":** Ibid., xiii.

190 **"I am the only faithful worshipper":** Harriet Hosmer to Wayman Crow, August 1854, ibid., 35.

190 **Fanny Trollope:** Anthony Trollope, *An Autobiography and Other Writings* (New York: Oxford University Press, 2014), Kindle; Teresa Ransom, *Fanny Trollope: A Remarkable Life* (New York: St. Martin's Press, 1995); Lucy Poate Stebbins and Richard Poate Stebbins, *The Trollopes: The Chronicle of a Writing Family* (New York: Columbia University Press, 1945).

191 **"Of the mixture":** Trollope, loc. 849 of 6906, Kindle.

192 **"She had much":** Ibid., loc. 859 of 6906, Kindle.

192 **Harriet Martineau:** Harriet Martineau, *Autobiography,* ed. Maria Weston Chapman (Boston: James R. Osgood, 1877), Internet Archive.

192 **"From the age":** Ibid., 142.

192 **"had no power":** Ibid.

192 **"I have not":** Ibid., 143.

193 **"I can speak":** Ibid., 144.

194 **"those embarrassments and depressions":** Ibid.

194 **"I never pass":** Ibid., 145.

194 **"Fresh air and cold water":** Ibid., 146.

195 **Fannie Hurst:** Fannie Hurst, *Anatomy of Me: A Wonderer in Search of Herself* (Garden City, NY: Doubleday, 1958); Brooke Kroeger, *Fannie: The Talent for Success of Writer Fannie Hurst* (New York: Times Books, 1999); Walter Bagehot, *The Works of Walter Bagehot, with Memoirs by R. H. Hutton,* vol. 1, ed. Forrest Morgan (Hartford, CT: Travelers Insurance Company, 1889), Google Books.

195 **"Writers, like teeth":** Bagehot, 34.

195 **"that stubborn hiatus":** Hurst, 148.

195 **"That monkey on my back":** Ibid., 148–49

195 **"My own workaday":** Ibid., 316,

195 **Emily Post:** Edwin Post, *Truly Emily Post* (New York: Funk & Wagnalls, 1961); Laura Claridge, *Emily Post: Daughter of the Gilded Age, Mistress of American Manners* (New York: Random House, 2008).

196 **"We used to"**: Post, 208.

196 **"She had improvised"**: Ibid., 221.

197 **"If I were"**: Quoted in Claridge, 432.

197 **Janet Scudder**: Janet Scudder, *Modeling My Life* (New York: Harcourt, Brace, 1925).

197 **"These long hot days"**: Ibid., 121–23.

200 **"I can never"**: Ibid., 21.

200 **Sarah Bernhardt**: Edmond Rostand, preface to Jules Huret, *Sarah Bernhardt*, trans. George A. Raper (London: Chapman & Hall, 1899), vii–xii; Cornelia Otis Skinner, *Madame Sarah* (Boston: Houghton Mifflin, 1967); Robert Gottlieb, *Sarah: The Life of Sarah Bernhardt* (New Haven, CT: Yale University Press, 2010); Louis Verneuil, *The Fabulous Life of Sarah Bernhardt*, trans. Ernest Boyd (New York: Harper & Brothers, 1942); Arthur Gold and Robert Fizdale, *The Divine Sarah: A Life of Sarah Bernhardt* (New York: Vintage, 1992); Suze Rueff, *I Knew Sarah Bernhardt* (London: Frederick Muller, 1951); "Face of Great Actress Subtle Even in Death," *Los Angeles Times,* March 28, 1923, http://www.latimes.com/local/obituaries/archives/la-me-sarah-bernhardt-19230328-story.html

201 **"Bernhardt last night"**: Quoted in Gold and Fizdale, 133.

202 **"No person"**: Quoted in "Face of Great Actress."

202 **"A brougham stops"**: Rostand, x–xi.

203 **"a state of temporary insanity"**: Ibid., xii.

203 **"returns to her room"**: Ibid., xii–xiii.

203 **"This is the Sarah"**: Ibid., xiii.

203 **"Life engenders life"**: Quoted in Skinner, xvi.

204 **Mrs. Patrick Campbell**: Margot Peters, *Mrs. Pat: The Life of Mrs. Patrick Campbell* (New York: Alfred A. Knopf, 1984); Alan Dent, *Mrs. Patrick Campbell* (London: Museum Press, 1961); Mrs. Patrick Campbell, *My Life and Some Letters* (New York: Dodd, Mead, 1922).

204 **"The life of the stage"**: Campbell, 285.

204 **"the exacting perfectionism"**: Peters, 190.

204 **"Her neatness amazed me"**: Quoted in Dent, 230–31.

207 **Niki de Saint Phalle**: Niki de Saint Phalle, *Traces: An Autobiography Remembering 1930–1949* (Lausanne: Acatos, 1999); Niki de Saint Phalle, *Harry and Me: The Family Years, 1950–1960* (Zürich: Benteli, 2006); Christiane Weidemann, *Niki de Saint Phalle* (Munich: Prestel, 2014); Ariel Levy, "Beautiful Monsters," *The New Yorker,* April 28, 2016, https://www.newyorker.com/magazine/2016/04/18/niki-de-saint-phalles-tarot-garden.

207 **"So you're one"**: Saint Phalle, *Harry and Me*, 115.

207 **"hurt me to the quick"**: Ibid.

207 **"live her artistic adventure"**: Quoted in Weidemann, 75.

208 **"My secret jealous lover"**: Quoted ibid., 36.

209 **"I enjoyed living"**: Quoted ibid., 78.

209 **"Enthusiasm is a virus"**: Saint Phalle, *Traces*, 121.

209 **"People are very important"**: Ibid.

210 **Ruth Asawa**: Daniell Cornell et al., *The Sculpture of Ruth Asawa: Contours in the Air* (Berkeley: University of California Press, 2006).

210 **"My materials were simple"**: Quoted ibid., 19.

210 **Lila Katzen**: Interview with Cindy Nemser, *Art Talk: Conversations with 15 Women Artists*, rev. ed. (New York: Westview Press, 1995); Eleanor Munro, *Originals: American Women Artists*, new ed. (New York: Da Capo Press, 2000).

211 **"I was going"**: Interview with Nemser, 202.

211 **"adamant about my not working"**: Ibid., 204.

211 **"I worked from eight"**: Ibid., 206–7.

212 **"Here are some crayons"**: Ibid., 206.

212 **Helen Frankenthaler**: Interview with Julia Brown, "A Conversation: Helen Frankenthaler and Julia Brown," Spring–Fall 1997, in *After Mountains and Sea: Frankenthaler, 1956–1959* (New York: Guggenheim Museum, 1998); Barbara Rose, *Frankenthaler* (New York: Harry N. Abrams, 1970); Carl Belz, "Helen Frankenthaler and the 1950s," 1981, in *Painted on 21st Street: Helen Frankenthaler from 1950 to 1959*, ed. John Elderfield (New York: Gagosian Gallery/Abrams, 2013); Madeleine Conway and Nancy Kirk, *The Museum of Modern Art Artists' Cookbook* (New York: Museum of Modern Art, 1977).

212 **"A really good picture"**: Quoted in Rose, 85.

212 **"One prepares"**: Interview with Cindy Nemser, "Interview with Helen Frankenthaler," *Arts Magazine*, November 1961, quoted in Belz, 154.

212 **"I tend to focus"**: Interview with Brown, 42.

213 **"I will often"**: Ibid.

213 **"catharsis"**: Quoted in Conway and Kirk, 53.

213 **"My usual regime"**: Quoted Ibid.

214 **Eileen Farrell**: Eileen Farrell and Brian Kellow, *Can't Help Singing: The Life of Eileen Farrell* (Boston: Northeastern University Press, 1999).

214 **"Some people think"**: Ibid., 174.

214 **"There was a little restaurant":** Ibid., 174–75.

215 **"Those weren't discreet":** Quoted ibid., 175.

215 **Eleanor Antin:** Howard N. Fox, *Eleanor Antin* (Los Angeles: Los Angeles County Museum of Art, 1999); Eleanor Munro, *Originals: American Women Artists,* new ed. (New York: Da Capo Press, 2000); Grace Glueck, "In a Roguish Gallery: One Aging Black Ballerina," *The New York Times,* May 12, 1989, https://www.nytimes.com/1989/05/12/movies/in-a-roguish-gallery-one-aging-black-ballerina.html.

216 **"get out of my own skin":** Quoted in Glueck.

216 **"Because the one thing":** Quoted in Fox, 211.

216 **"It seems to me":** Quoted in Munro, 424.

217 **Julia Wolfe:** Telephone interview with the author, February 15, 2017.

218 **Charlotte Bray:** Telephone interview with the author, January 26, 2017.

219 **Hayden Dunham:** Interview with the author, May 5, 2017.

222 **Isabel Allende:** Telephone interview with the author, August 23, 2016.

224 **Zadie Smith:** Interview with Michele Norris, "In Essays, Author Zadie Smith Reveals Her Process," November 11, 2009, *NPR Books,* https://www.npr.org/templates/story/story.php?storyId=120320510; interview with Isaac Chotiner, "Zadie Smith on Male Critics, Appropriation, and What Interests Her Novelistically About Trump," *Slate,* November 16, 2016, http://www.slate.com/articles/arts/books/2016/11/a_conversation_with_zadie_smith_about_cultural_appropriation_male_critics.html; Yevgeniya Traps, "Zadie Smith on 'Little Sparks of Something Like Actual Life' and Her Latest, 'NW,'" *Politico,* October 2, 2012, https://www.politico.com/states/new-york/albany/story/2012/10/zadie-smith-on-little-sparks-of-something-like-actual-life-and-her-latest-nw-067223; Zadie Smith, *NW* (New York: Penguin Books, 2012), Kindle.

224 **"I think you":** Interview with Norris.

224 **"very slowly":** Quoted in Traps.

224 **"creating the time":** Smith, loc. 4532 of 4566, Kindle.

224 **"I still have":** Interview with Chotiner.

225 **Hilary Mantel:** Hilary Mantel, "My Writing Day," *The Guardian,* April 16, 2016, https://www.theguardian.com/books/2016/apr/16/hilary-mantel-my-writing-day; Sophie Elmhirst, "The Unquiet Mind of Hilary Mantel," *New Statesman,* October 3, 2012, https:

//www.newstatesman.com/culture/culture/2012/10/unquiet-mind
-hilary-mantel; Hilary Mantel, "Hilary Mantel's Rules for Writers," *The Guardian,* February 22, 2010, https://www.theguardian
.com/books/2010/feb/22/hilary-mantel-rules-for-writers; Larissa
MacFarquhar, "The Dead Are Real," *The New Yorker,* October 15,
2012, https://www.newyorker.com/magazine/2012/10/15/the-dead
-are-real; interview with Mona Simpson, "Hilary Mantel, The Art
of Fiction No. 226," *The Paris Review,* Spring 2015, https://www
.theparisreview.org/interviews/6360/hilary-mantel-art-of-fiction
-no-226-hilary-mantel; interview with Anna Metcalfe, "Small
Talk: Hilary Mantel," *Financial Times,* May 8, 2009, https://www
.ft.com/content/bf2db6a6-3b5e-11de-ba91-00144feabdco.

225 **"Some writers claim":** Mantel, "My Writing Day."

226 **"days of easy flow":** Ibid.

226 **"a long thinker":** Ibid.

226 **"tense up till my body locks":** Ibid.

226 **"Take a walk":** Mantel, "Rules for Writers."

226 **"Sometimes people ask":** Quoted in Elmhirst.

227 **Catherine Opie:** Interview with the author, November 2, 2016.

229 **Joan Jonas:** Telephone interview with the author, May 15, 2017.

233 **Marie-Thérèse Rodet Geoffrin:** Dena Goodman, *The Republic of
Letters* (Ithaca, NY: Cornell University Press, 1994).

233 **"First, she made":** Goodman, 91.

233 **"Our Fridays are":** Quoted in Goodman, 89.

234 **"I live here":** Madame Geoffrine to Marie-Thérèse, marquise de
La Ferté-Imbault, July 8, 1766, in Goodman, 78–79.

235 **Elizabeth Carter:** Montagu Pennington, *Memoirs of the Life of
Mrs. Elizabeth Carter with a New Edition of Her Poems,* [. . .]
(London: F. C. and J. Rivington, 1807), Google Books.

235 **"Very early in life":** Ibid., 5–6.

236 **"As you desire":** Quoted ibid., 90–91.

236 **"several lessons":** Quoted ibid., 91.

237 **"My first care":** Quoted ibid., 92–93.

237 **"hardly ever read":** Ibid., 95.

237 **"Besides the taking snuff":** Ibid., 15.

238 **Mary Wollstonecraft:** Claire Tomalin, *The Life and Death of Mary
Wollstonecraft* (New York: Harcourt Brace Jovanovich, 1974);
William Godwin, *Memoirs of the Author of a Vindication of the
Rights of Woman* (1798; repr. Project Gutenberg, https://www
.gutenberg.org/files/16199/16199-h/16199-h.htm).

238 **"undoubtedly a very":** Godwin.

238 **"Life is but a labour"**: Quoted in Tomalin, 168.

238 **Mary Shelley:** Charlotte Gordon, *Romantic Outlaws: The Extraordinary Lives of Mary Wollstonecraft and Her Daughter Mary Shelley* (New York: Random House, 2015); Anne K. Mellor, *Mary Shelley: Her Life, Her Fiction, Her Monsters* (New York: Methuen, 1988); Mary Shelley, author's introduction to *Frankenstein; or, The Modern Prometheus* (1818; repr. Ware, Hertfordshire: Wordsworth Classics, 1999), 1–5.

239 **"speak of many"**: Shelley, 5.

239 **"not once did he offer"**: Gordon, 243.

239 **"And now, once"**: Shelley, 5.

239 **Clara Schumann:** Nancy B. Reich, *Clara Schumann: The Artist and the Woman* (Ithaca, NY: Cornell University Press, 1985); John N. Burk, *Clara Schumann: A Romantic Biography* (New York: Random House, 1940).

240 **"My piano playing"**: Clara Schumann, June 2, 1841, in Reich, 110.

240 **"took his customary beer"**: Reich, 130.

240 **"Clara realizes that"**: Quoted in Burk, 217.

240 **"Nothing surpasses creative activity"**: Quoted in Reich, 228.

241 **Charlotte Brontë:** Elizabeth Gaskell, *The Life of Charlotte Brontë* (1857; repr. New York: Penguin, 1997); *The Letters of Charlotte Brontë, Volume One: 1829–1847,* ed. Margaret Smith (Oxford: Clarendon Press, 1995).

241 **"I see now"**: Charlotte Brontë to Emily Brontë, June 8, 1839, in *Letters,* 191.

241 **"Sometimes weeks or even months"**: Gaskell, 233.

242 **"Charlotte told me"**: Ibid., 235.

243 **Christina Rossetti:** Jan Marsh, *Christina Rossetti: A Writer's Life* (New York: Viking, 1995).

243 **"entirely of the casual"**: Quoted ibid., 69.

243 **"I never had"**: Quoted ibid., 548.

243 **"Write to order"**: Quoted ibid., 294.

243 **Julia Ward Howe:** Maud Howe, *The Eleventh Hour in the Life of Julia Ward Howe* (Boston: Little, Brown, 1911), Google Books; Elaine Showalter, *The Civil Wars of Julia Ward Howe* (New York: Simon & Schuster, 2016).

244 **"First, and last"**: Maud Howe, 37.

245 **"came down in the morning"**: Ibid., 50.

245 **"for her spirits"**: Ibid., 49–50.

245 **"Then came the morning walk"**: Ibid., 54.

245 **"tone up her mind"**: Quoted ibid., 59.

245 **"put the iron"**: Quoted ibid.

245 **"It was said"**: Ibid., 48.

245 **"talk, whist, music"**: Ibid., 61.

246 **"in a state"**: Quoted in Showalter, 83.

246 **"like blindness, like death"**: Quoted ibid.

246 **"for a statement"**: Maud Howe, 74.

246 **"To Learn, To Teach"**: Quoted ibid.

246 **Harriet Beecher Stowe**: Joan D. Hedrick, *Harriet Beecher Stowe: A Life* (New York: Oxford University Press, 1994); Annie Fields, ed., *Life and Letters of Harriet Beecher Stowe* (Boston: Houghton, Mifflin, 1898).

246 **"If I am to write"**: Quoted in Fields, 104.

247 **"Since I began"**: Quoted in Hedrick, 195.

247 **"The nursery & the kitchen"**: Quoted ibid., 239.

247 **"already besieged with applications"**: Quoted ibid., 246.

248 **"we shall do"**: Quoted ibid., 260.

248 **Rosa Bonheur**: Anna Klumpke, *Rosa Bonheur: The Artist's (Auto)biography,* trans. Gretchen van Slyke, 2nd ed. (Ann Arbor: University of Michigan Press, 2001); Dore Ashton with Denise Browne Hare, *Rosa Bonheur: A Life and a Legend* (New York: Viking Press, 1981).

248 **"I strongly disapprove"**: Quoted in Gretchen van Slyke, "Introduction to the English Edition," in Klumpke, xxxii.

250 **"I always go"**: Quoted in Klumpke, 33.

250 **"Now I tend"**: Quoted ibid., 39.

250 **"of all kinds"**: Ibid., 201.

250 **"Not at all"**: Quoted ibid., 202.

250 **"dogs, horses, donkeys"**: Ibid., 203.

250 **"In the evening"**: Quoted in Ashton with Hare, 171.

251 **"a kind of cabin"**: Quoted ibid., 163.

251 **"I am an old rat"**: Quoted ibid., 159.

251 **Eleanor Roosevelt**: Eleanor Roosevelt, *You Learn by Living: Eleven Keys for a More Fulfilling Life* (New York: Harper Perennial, 1960); David Emblidge, ed., *My Day: The Best of Eleanor Roosevelt's Acclaimed Newspaper Columns, 1936–1962* (New York: Da Capo Press, 2001); *The Autobiography of Eleanor Roosevelt* (1961; repr. New York: Da Capo Press, 1992); Blanche Wiesen Cook, *Eleanor Roosevelt: Volume One, 1884–1933* (New York: Penguin, 1992); Bernard Asbell, ed., *Mother & Daughter: The Letters of Eleanor and Anna Roosevelt* (New York: Coward, McCann & Geoghegan, 1982).

252 **"There are three ways"**: Roosevelt, *You Learn by Living*, 45.

252 **"I don't normally"**: Roosevelt, *Autobiography*, 290.

252 **"She gets along"**: Quoted in Cook, 466.

253 **"I used to just cringe"**: Quoted in Asbell, 298.

253 **Dorothy Thompson**: Peter Kurth, *American Cassandra: The Life of Dorothy Thompson* (Boston: Little, Brown, 1990).

253 **"by hand, in bed"**: Ibid., 263.

254 **"I am living"**: Quoted ibid., 264.

257 **Janet Frame**: Janet Frame, *An Angel at My Table: An Autobiography: Volume Two* (New York: George Braziller, 1984); Janet Frame, *The Envoy from Mirror City: An Autobiography: Volume Three* (New York: George Braziller, 1985); Michael King, *Wrestling with the Angel: A Life of Janet Frame* (Washington, DC: Counterpoint, 2000); Jane Campion, "In Search of Janet Frame," *The Guardian*, January 19, 2008, https://www.theguardian.com /books/2008/jan/19/fiction5.

257 **"I had an army hut"**: Frame, *An Angel*, 142.

258 **"He did not get up"**: Ibid., 143–44.

259 **"averting his gaze"**: Ibid., 150.

259 **"and discuss the writing"**: Ibid.

259 **"I did not"**: Frame, *The Envoy*, 119.

260 **"Frame was not like anyone"**: Campion.

260 **"bear any sound"**: Ibid.

260 **"I think it's all that matters"**: Quoted in King, 421.

261 **Jane Campion**: Virginia Wright Wexman, *Jane Campion: Interviews* (Jackson: University Press of Mississippi, 1999).

261 **"It starts with a feeling"**: Quoted in Jay Carr, "Jane Campion, the Classical Romantic," *The Boston Globe,* November 14, 1993, in Wexman, 168.

261 **"I have to spend"**: Quoted in Sue Williams, "A Light on the Dark Secrets of Depression," *Australian,* May 2, 1995, in Wexman, 176.

261 **"Sometimes I'm having"**: Quoted in Kennedy Fraser, "Portrait of a Director," *Vogue,* January 1997, in Wexman, 197.

261 **Agnès Varda**: T. Jefferson Kline, *Agnès Varda: Interviews* (Jackson: University Press of Mississippi, 2014).

262 **"But I drew"**: Quoted in Gordon Gow, "The Underground River," *Films and Filming,* March 1970, in Kline, 43.

262 **"an underground river"**: Quoted ibid., 44.

262 **"not because I"**: Interview with Jacqueline Levitin, "Mother of the New Wave: An Interview with Agnès Varda," *Women and Film,* nos. 5–6, 1974, in Kline, 55.

262 **"There are two problems"**: Ibid., 60.

262 **"there is only one solution"**: Ibid.

263 **"I told myself"**: Interview with Mireille Amiel, "Agnès Varda Talks About the Cinema," *Cinéma,* December 1975, trans. T. Jefferson Kline, in Kline, 65.

263 **"to film as"**: Interview with Françoise Aude and Jeane-Pierre Jeancolas, "Interview with Agnès Varda," *Positif,* April 1982, trans. T. Jefferson Kline, in Kline, 111.

263 **"You know artists"**: Interview with Françoise Wera, "Interview with Agnès Varda," *Ciné-Bulles,* no. 3, 1985, trans. T. Jefferson Kline, in Kline, 124–25.

264 **"the privilege of having"**: Quoted in Jean Decock, "Interview with Varda on *The Vagabond,*" *French Review,* February 1988, in Kline, 149.

264 **"I tend to wear out"**: Ibid.

264 **Françoise Sagan**: Interview with Jean-Jacques Pauvert, *Night Bird: Conversations with Françoise Sagan,* trans. David Macey (New York: Clarkson N. Potter, 1980); interview with Blair Fuller and Robert B. Silvers, "Françoise Sagan, The Art of Fiction No. 15," *The Paris Review,* Autumn 1956, https://www.theparis review.org/interviews/4912/francoise-sagan-the-art-of-fiction-no -15-francoise-sagan; Richard Williams, "Françoise Sagan: 'She Did What She Wanted,'" *The Guardian,* February 28, 2014, https://www.theguardian.com/books/2014/feb/28/francoise-sagan -bonjour-tristesse.

264 **"two or three months"**: Interview with Fuller and Silvers.

264 **"I simply started"**: Ibid.

264 **"wanted passionately to"**: Ibid.

265 **"an 18-year-old"**: Quoted in Williams.

265 **"I don't like"**: Interview with Pauvert, 53.

266 **"Sometimes I write"**: Ibid., 62.

266 **"There's never any plan"**: Ibid., 61.

266 **"There mustn't be"**: Ibid.

266 **"humiliating," she said**: Ibid., 62–63.

266 **Gloria Naylor**: Maxine Lavon Montgomery, ed., *Conversations with Gloria Naylor* (Jackson: University Press of Mississippi, 2004); interview with Donna Perry, "Gloria Naylor," in Donna Perry, *Backtalk: Women Writers Speak Out* (New Brunswick, NJ: Rutgers University Press, 1993), 217–44.

267 **"I didn't realize"**: Interview with Kay Bonetti, "An Interview with Gloria Naylor," American Audio Prose Library, 1988, in Montgomery, 52.

267 "I was working": Ibid.

267 "not an overly disciplined person": Ibid., 53.

267 "My needs are simple": Interview with Perry, 241.

267 "a transcriber of stories": Interview with Sharon Felton and Michelle C. Loris, "The Human Spirit Is a Kick-Ass Thing," *The Critical Response to Gloria Naylor,* 1997, in Montgomery, 141.

267 "The process starts": Interview with Perry, 225.

268 Alice Neel: Phoebe Hoban, *Alice Neel: The Art of Not Sitting Pretty* (New York: St. Martin's Press, 2010); interview with Cindy Nemser, *Art Talk: Conversations with 15 Women Artists,* rev. ed. (New York: Westview Press, 1995).

268 "If you decide": Interview with Nemser, 109.

269 "I felt women represented": Quoted in Hoban, 266.

269 Shirley Jackson: Ruth Franklin, *Shirley Jackson: A Rather Haunted Life* (New York: Liveright Publishing, 2016); Harvey Breit, "Talk with Miss Jackson," *The New York Times Book Review,* June 26, 1949, https://www.nytimes.com/1949/06/26/archives/talk-with-miss-jackson.html.

269 "You were encouraged": Quoted in Franklin, 11.

270 "50 per cent": Quoted in Breit.

270 "seems to have derived": Franklin, 172.

270 "Writing in the interstices": Ibid.

271 "My husband fights": Quoted in Breit.

271 Alma Thomas: Merry A. Foresta, *A Life in Art: Alma Thomas, 1891–1978* (Washington, DC: Smithsonian Institution Press, 1981); Eleanor Munro, *Originals: American Women Artists,* new ed. (New York: Da Capo Press, 2000).

271 "for educated young": Quoted in Adolphus Ealey, "Remembering Alma," in Foresta, 11.

271 "I never lost": Quoted ibid.

272 "a woman simply": Quoted ibid., 12.

273 "I don't know": Quoted in Munro, 195–96.

273 "Do you have any idea": Quoted in Adolphus Ealey, "Remembering Alma," in Foresta, 12.

273 Lee Krasner: Gail Levin, *Lee Krasner: A Biography* (New York: William Morrow, 2011); B. H. Friedman, *Jackson Pollock: Energy Made Visible* (1972; repr. Cambridge, MA: Da Capo Press, 1995); Eleanor Munro, *Originals: American Women Artists,* new ed. (New York: Da Capo Press, 2000); Charlotte Streifer Rubinstein, *American Women Artists: From Early Indian Times to the Present* (Boston: Avon, 1982).

273 "I sacrificed nothing": Quoted in Levin, 2.

274 "very supportive": Quoted ibid., 220.

274 "Since Pollock was a turbulent man": Quoted ibid.

274 "He always slept": Quoted in Friedman, 87.

275 "marvelous bread and pies": Quoted ibid.

275 "pasty crusts of grey": Rubinstein, 272.

275 "a very neurotic rhythm": Quoted in Levin, 403.

276 "I believe in listening": Quoted in Munro, 119.

276 Grace Hartigan: William T. La Moy and Joseph P. McCaffrey, eds., *The Journals of Grace Hartigan* (Syracuse: Syracuse University Press, 2009), Kindle.

276 "Now my days": Ibid., June 30, 1955, loc. 2083 of 2260, Kindle.

278 "I am in": Ibid., January 18, 1955, loc. 1859 of 2260, Kindle.

278 "Art cannot be seized": Ibid., May 25, 1955, loc. 1998 of 2260, Kindle.

278 "One must be fierce": Ibid., June 23, 1955, loc. 2057 of 2260, Kindle.

278 Toni Cade Bambara: Interview with Claudia Tate, *Black Women Writers at Work* (New York: Continuum, 1983), 12–38; Toni Cade Bambara, "What It Is I Think I'm Doing Anyhow," in *The Writer on Her Work,* ed. Janet Sternburg, rev. ed. (New York: W. W. Norton, 2000), 153–68.

279 "There's no particular routine": Interview with Tate, 30–33.

280 "I'd never fully appreciated": Bambara, 166.

280 Margaret Walker: Margaret Walker, *How I Wrote* Jubilee *and Other Essays on Life and Literature,* ed. Maryemma Graham (New York: Feminist Press, 1990); Margaret Walker, "On Being Female, Black, and Free," in *The Writer on Her Work,* ed. Janet Sternburg, rev. ed. (New York: W. W. Norton, 2000), 95–106; interview with Claudia Tate, "Margaret Walker," in *Black Women Writers at Work* (New York: Continuum, 1983), 188–204.

280 "To choose the life": Walker, "On Being," 100.

281 "People ask me": Walker, *How I Wrote,* 61.

282 "worked from seven": Ibid.

282 "went back to the typewriter": Ibid.

282 "You just become": Interview with Tate, 191–192.

285 Tamara de Lempicka: Laura Claridge, *Tamara de Lempicka: A Life of Deco and Decadence* (New York: Clarkson Potter, 1999); Judith Mackrell, *Flappers: Six Women of a Dangerous Generation* (New York: Sarah Crichton Books, 2013); Baroness Kizette de Lempicka-Foxhall with Charles Phillips, *Passion by Design: The Art and Times of Tamara de Lempicka* (New York: Abbeville Press, 1987).

285 **"The poor baby"**: Quoted in Mackrell, 78.

285 **"By the fall"**: Claridge, 91.

287 **"It is an artist's duty"**: Quoted in Mackrell, 108.

287 **"There are no miracles"**: Quoted in Lempicka-Foxhall, 77.

287 **Romaine Brooks**: Diana Souhami, *Wild Girls: Paris, Sappho, and Art: The Lives and Loves of Natalie Barney and Romaine Brooks* (New York: St. Martin's Griffin, 2007); Meryle Secrest, *Between Me and Life: A Biography of Romaine Brooks* (Garden City, NY: Doubleday, 1974); Susan Stamberg, "Painter Romaine Brooks Challenged Conventions in Shades of Gray," NPR Morning Edition, August 17, 2016, https://www.npr.org/2016/08/17/489757481 /painter-romaine-brooks-challenged-conventions-in-shades-of -gray.

288 **"She had an English chauffeur"**: Souhami, 119.

288 **"really painted as"**: Quoted in Stamberg.

289 **"ladies with high collars"**: Quoted in Souhami, 2.

289 **"I shut myself up"**: Quoted in Secrest, 284.

289 **"For me, to live alone"**: Quoted ibid., 332.

290 **"I suppose an artist"**: Quoted in Souhami, 138.

290 **Eudora Welty**: Interview with Linda Kuehl, "Eudora Welty, The Art of Fiction No. 47," *The Paris Review*, Fall 1972, https: //www.theparisreview.org/interviews/4013/eudora-welty-the-art -of-fiction-no-47-eudora-welty; Peggy Whitman Prenshaw, ed., *Conversations with Eudora Welty* (Jackson: University Press of Mississippi, 1984); Peggy Whitman Prenshaw, ed., *More Conversations with Eudora Welty* (Jackson: University Press of Mississippi, 1996); Suzanne Marrs, *Eudora Welty: A Biography* (Orlando: Harvest, 2006).

290 **"I've found it possible"**: Interview with Kuehl.

290 **"because it's much more convenient"**: Ibid.

290 **"so that in the end"**: Ibid.

290 **"It gives me"**: Ibid.

291 **"Oh, boy,"**: Interview with Dannye Romine Powell, "Eudora Welty," *Parting the Curtains: Interviews with Southern Women Writers,* 1994, in Prenshaw, *More Conversations,* 172.

292 **"It's the act"**: Ibid., 174.

293 **Elena Ferrante**: Elena Ferrante, *Frantumaglia: A Writer's Journey,* trans. Ann Goldstein (New York: Europa Editions, 2016).

293 **"I don't have"**: Interview with Karen Valby, "Elena Ferrante: The Writer Without a Face," trans. Michael Reynolds, *Entertainment Weekly,* September 5, 2014, in Ferrante, 238.

293 **"I write continuously":** Interview with Rachel Donadio, "Writing Has Always Been a Great Struggle for Me," *The New York Times,* December 9, 2014, in Ferrante, 254.

293 **"a little corner":** Interview with Elissa Schappell, "Elena Ferrante Explains Why, for the Last Time, You Don't Need to Know Her Name," trans. Michael Reynolds, *Vanity Fair,* August 28, 2015, in Ferrante, 337.

293 **"a very small space":** Ibid.

293 **"If I don't feel":** Interview with Maurício Meirles, "Elena Ferrante, que esconde sua identidade há mais de 20 anos, tem livro lançado no Brasil," *O Globo,* May 28, 2015, in Ferrante, 303.

293 **Joan Didion:** Interview with Linda Kuehl, "Joan Didion, The Art of Fiction, No. 71," *The Paris Review,* Fall–Winter 1978, https://www.theparisreview.org/interviews/3439/joan-didion -the-art-of-fiction-no-71-joan-didion; Emma Brockes, "Interview: Joan Didion," *The Guardian,* December 16, 2005, https://www .theguardian.com/film/2005/dec/16/biography.features; interview with Sheila Heti, "Joan Didion," *The Believer,* 2012, https://www .believermag.com/exclusives/?read=interview_didion.

293 **"The most important":** Interview with Kuehl.

294 **"most of the day":** Quoted in Brockes.

294 **"Writing," she said:** Interview with Heti.

295 **"It feels very different":** Ibid.

295 **Sheila Heti:** Email correspondence with the author, September 2016.

297 **Miranda July:** Telephone interview with the author, September 20, 2016.

299 **Patti Smith:** Kristina Rodulfo, "Patti Smith: New York Is No Longer Welcoming to Artists and Dreamers," *Elle,* October 6, 2015, https://www.elle.com/culture/books/news/a31004/new-york-city -then-and-now-according-to-patti-smith/; Patti Smith, *M Train* (New York: Alfred A. Knopf, 2015).

299 **"I get up":** Quoted in Rodulfo.

299 **"I have a fine desk":** Smith, 27.

300 **"Yesterday's poets":** Ibid., 32.

300 **Ntozake Shange:** Interview with Claudia Tate, *Black Women Writers at Work* (New York: Continuum, 1983), 149–74; interview with Serena Anderlini, "Drama or Performance Art? An Interview with Ntozake Shange," *Journal of Dramatic Theory and Criticism,* Fall 1991, 85–97.

300 **"I write whenever":** Interview with Tate, 168.

300 **"I do feel"**: Interview with Anderlini, 95.

301 **Cindy Sherman:** Interview with Kenneth Baker, "Cindy Sherman: Interview with a Chameleon," *San Francisco Chronicle,* July 8, 2012, repr. Walker Art Center, November 1, 2012, https://walkerart .org/magazine/cindy-sherman-walker-art-center; interview with Betsy Berne, "Studio: Cindy Sherman," *Tate Arts and Culture,* May/June 2003, http://www.tate.org.uk/context-comment/articles /studio-cindy-sherman; interview with Betsy Sussler, "Cindy Sherman by Betsy Sussler," *Bomb,* Spring 1985, https://bombmagazine .org/articles/cindy-sherman/; interview with Molly Ringwald, "I Had a Little Pegboard," *Women in Clothes,* eds. Sheila Heti, Heidi Julavits, and Leanne Shapton (New York: Blue Rider Press, 2014), 281–284; Tim Adams, "Cindy Sherman: 'Why Am I in These Photos?,'" *The Guardian,* July 3, 2016, https://www.theguardian.com /artanddesign/2016/jul/03/cindy-sherman-interview-retrospective -motivation.

301 **"Even having an assistant"**: Interview with Baker.

301 **"thinking this was"**: Interview with Berne.

301 **"The levels I try to get"**: Ibid.

302 **"of *becoming* a different person"**: Interview with Sussler.

302 **"I'm not a nine-to-five"**: Quoted in Adams.

302 **"I guess it's a crapshoot"**: Interview with Ringwald.

302 **"There is usually"**: Interview with Baker.

303 **Renee Cox:** Telephone interview with the author, June 17, 2017.

304 **Petah Coyne:** Telephone interview with the author, February 22, 2017.

309 **Djuna Barnes:** Phillip Herring, *Djuna: The Life and Work of Djuna Barnes* (New York: Viking, 1995).

311 **"to write in bed"**: Ibid., 198.

311 **"the moors of Hayford Hall"**: Quoted ibid., 192.

311 **"It's getting the awful rust"**: Quoted ibid., 235.

312 **Käthe Kollwitz:** Martha Kearns, *Käthe Kollwitz: Woman and Artist* (Old Westbury, NY: Feminist Press, 1976); Hans Kollwitz, ed., *The Diary and Letters of Kaethe Kollwitz,* trans. Richard Winston and Clara Winston (Evanston, IL: Northwestern University Press, 1988).

312 **"There were grave"**: Käthe Kollwitz to Karl Kollwitz, June 13, 1916, in Hans Kollwitz, 70.

312 **"She followed"**: Kearns, 63.

313 **"She constantly swung"**: Hans Kollwitz, 7.

313 **"At no other time"**: Quoted in Kearns, 192.

314 **Lorraine Hansberry:** Lorraine Hansberry, *To Be Young, Gifted and Black,* adapted by Robert Nemiroff (New York: Signet, 1970); Patricia C. McKissack and Frederick L. McKissack, *Young, Black, and Determined: A Biography of Lorraine Hansberry* (New York: Holiday House, 1998).

314 **"The days pass":** Hansberry, 143.

314 **"Blobby-globby days":** Ibid.

314 **"work or perish":** Ibid., 177.

314 **"They say that":** Ibid., 182.

315 **"I have rearranged":** Ibid., 185.

316 **"The magic has come":** Ibid., 197.

316 **Natalia Ginzburg:** Natalia Ginzburg, *It's Hard to Talk About Yourself,* eds. Cesare Garboli and Lisa Ginzburg, trans. Louise Quirke (Chicago: University of Chicago Press, 2003); Natalia Ginzburg, *The Little Virtues,* trans. Dick Davis (New York: Arcade, 1985).

316 **"There was a silence":** Lisa Ginzburg, preface to Natalia Ginzburg, *It's Hard to Talk About Yourself,* ix.

317 **"I could not":** Natalia Ginzburg, *Little Virtues,* 62.

317 **"control" the feeling:** Ibid.

317 **"greedily and joyfully":** Ibid., 63.

317 **"profound melancholy":** Interview with Marino Sinibaldi, "The Job of the Writer," Chapter Three, Natalia Ginzburg, *It's Hard to Talk About Yourself,* 84.

318 **"secrets and shadows":** Natalia Ginzburg, *Little Virtues,* 65.

318 **"You cannot deceive":** Ibid., 66.

318 **"I have to say":** Interview with Marino Sinibaldi, "The Job of the Writer," Chapter Three, Natalia Ginzburg, *It's Hard to Talk About Yourself,* 84.

318 **Gwendolyn Brooks:** Gloria Wade Gayles, ed., *Conversations with Gwendolyn Brooks* (Jackson: University Press of Mississippi, 2003).

318 **"This should encourage":** Quoted in Roy Newquist, *Conversations* (Chicago: Rand McNally, 1967) in Gayles, 27.

319 **"primarily a housewife":** Ibid.

319 **"scarcely put pen":** Interview with Ida Lewis, "My People Are Black People," *Essence,* April 1971, in Gayles, 62.

319 **"managed to keep at it":** Ibid.

319 **"A poem rarely comes":** Interview with Hoyt Fuller, Eugenia Collier, George Kent, and Dudley Randall, "Interview with Gwendolyn Brooks," *In the Memory and Spirit of Frances, Zora, and Lorraine: Essays and Interviews on Black Women and Writing,*

ed. Juliette Bowles (Washington, DC: Institute for the Arts and the Humanities/Howard University, 1979), in Gayles, 67.

319 **"It is hard"**: Interview with Paul Angle, "An Interview with Gwendolyn Brooks," *Report from Part One* (Detroit: Broadside Press, 1968), in Gayles, 14.

320 **Jean Rhys**: Carole Angier, *Jean Rhys: Life and Work* (Boston: Little, Brown, 1990); Francis Wyndham and Diana Melly, eds., *The Letters of Jean Rhys* (New York: Elisabeth Sifton Books, 1984); Jean Rhys, *My Day* (New York: Frank Hallman, 1975); Diana Athill, *Stet: A Memoir* (New York: Grove Press, 2000); Lilian Pizzichini, *The Blue Hour: A Life of Jean Rhys* (New York: W. W. Norton, 2009).

320 **"Her inability to cope"**: Athill, 153.

321 **"I've brought trouble"**: Quoted in Angier, 484.

321 **"This place, which I imagined"**: Jean Rhys to Selma Vaz Dias, January 9, 1961, in Wyndham and Melly, 200.

321 **"moo at me"**: Jean Rhys to Maryvonne Moerman, October 6, 1960, in Wyndham and Melly, 195.

322 **"She needs endless supplies"**: Quoted in Angier, 491.

322 **"I've some wonderful pep pills"**: Jean Rhys to Francis Wyndham, 1961, in Wyndham and Melly, 207.

322 **"I feel I have been here"**: Jean Rhys to Maryvonne Moerman, March 4, 1962, in Wyndham and Melly, 211.

322 **"I do feel that"**: Jean Rhys to Diana Athill, May 23, 1963, in Wyndham and Melly, 221.

322 **"When I remember"**: Jean Rhys to Diana Athill, September 2, 1964, in Wyndham and Melly, 286.

323 **"Such a funny existence"**: Jean Rhys to Maryvonne Moerman, November 9, 1965, in Wyndham and Melly, 293.

323 **"the one place"**: Rhys, 5.

323 **"Isn't the sadness"**: Ibid., 6.

324 **Isabel Bishop**: Helen Yglesias, *Isabel Bishop* (New York: Rizzoli, 1988); interview with Barbaralee Diamonstein-Spielvogel, "Inside New York's Art World: Isabel Bishop," https://www.youtube.com/watch?v=moOzXiAG3TE; Eleanor Munro, *Originals: American Women Artists,* new ed. (New York: Da Capo Press, 2000); Henry James, "The Middle Years," in *Tales of Henry James,* ed. Christof Wegelin and Henry B. Wonham, 2nd ed. (New York: W. W. Norton, 2003), 211–28.

324 **"Then something happened"**: Interview with Diamonstein-Spielvogel.

324 **"a rather shabby business region"**: Quoted in Yglesias, 66.

324 **"romantic realist"**: Interview with Diamonstein-Spielvogel.

324 **"I was trying"**: Quoted in Yglesias, 24.

325 **"I do use"**: Quoted ibid., 18.

325 **"verify what I was doing"**: Quoted ibid., 16.

325 **"Is it so?"**: Interview with Diamonstein-Spielvogel.

326 **"It was like eating"**: Quoted in Yglesias, 16.

326 **"It was very important"**: Quoted ibid., 17.

326 **"It was helpful"**: Quoted ibid.

326 **"We work in the dark"**: James, 227.

327 **"I've thought about"**: Quoted in Munro, 146.

327 **Doris Lessing:** Doris Lessing, *Walking in the Shade: Volume Two of My Autobiography, 1949–1962* (New York: HarperPerennial, 1998); Doris Lessing, *Under My Skin: Volume One of My Autobiography, to 1949* (New York: HarperCollins, 1994); Carole Klein, *Doris Lessing: A Biography* (New York: Carroll & Graf, 2000); interview with Dwight Garner, "A Notorious Life," *Salon*, November 11, 1997, https://www.salon.com/1997/11/11/lessing/; Sameer Rahim, "Doris Lessing: In Her Own Words," *Telegraph*, November 17, 2013, https://www.telegraph.co.uk/culture/books/booknews/10455645/Doris-Lessing-in-her-own-words.html.

328 **"This was a terrible thing"**: Interview with Garner.

328 **"No one can write"**: Quoted in Rahim.

329 **"There was a constellation"**: Lessing, *Under My Skin*, 410.

329 **"I woke at five"**: Lessing, *Walking in the Shade*, 102.

329 **"I walk and I prowl"**: Ibid., 103.

330 **seven thousand words**: Klein, 134.

330 **"the physical as a road"**: Lessing, *Walking in the Shade*, 103.

330 **"They wander about"**: Ibid.

330 **"When we [writers]"**: Ibid., 136–37.

INDEX

Page numbers in *italics* refer to illustrations.

ILLUSTRATION CREDITS